Border Abolition Now

"This outstanding collection provides a rich, hopeful, and indispensable guide to border abolition. Written by and for thinkers, dreamers, and organizers, this book shows us how the world could be otherwise: borderless, flourishing, free."
—Luke de Noronha, co-author, *Against Borders: The Case For Abolition*

"This groundbreaking collection shows us, analytically and in practice, how no borders and prison and police abolition are shared political projects. It is learning at its most powerful, reframing thinking and activism with the aim of building justice. A must read."
—Bridget Anderson, Professor of Migration, Mobilities and Citizenship, University of Bristol

Border Abolition Now

Edited by Sara Riva, Simon Campbell,
Brian Whitener, and Kathryn Medien

First published 2024 by Pluto Press
New Wing, Somerset House, Strand, London WC2R 1LA
and Pluto Press, Inc.
1930 Village Center Circle, 3-834, Las Vegas, NV 89134

www.plutobooks.com

British Library Cataloguing in Publication Data
A catalogue record for this book is available from the British Library

ISBN 978 0 7453 4898 8 Paperback
ISBN 978 0 7453 4900 8 PDF
ISBN 978 0 7453 4899 5 EPUB

This book is printed on paper suitable for recycling and made from fully managed and sustained forest sources. Logging, pulping and manufacturing processes are expected to conform to the environmental standards of the country of origin.

Typeset by Stanford DTP Services, Northampton, England

Simultaneously printed in the United Kingdom and United States of America

Contents

Introduction   1
Sara Riva, Simon Campbell, Brian Whitener,
and Kathryn Medien

1. *Women in Exile*'s story   11
Elizabeth Ngari and Doris Dede

CONSTELLATION I: ABOLITIONIST THEORIES IN
BORDER CONTEXTS

2. Unfolding and flourishing: strategies of border abolition
feminism   19
Leah Cowan, Francesca Esposito, Sarah Hopwood, Aminata
Kalokoh, Vânia Martins, and Elahe Zivardar

3. Surplus people of the world unite! On borders, policing,
and abolition   36
Vanessa E. Thompson

4. #AbolishICE, #AbolishFrontex, abolish borders:
toward an abolitionist border study and struggle   54
Josue David Cisneros

5. *Interview with Black Alliance for Just Immigration (BAJI)*   69

CONSTELLATION II: ABOLITIONISMS AGAINST THE
BORDER COMPLEX

6. The place of asylum and empire in contemporary abolition   79
Jenna M. Loyd

7. Abolition, not relocation: moving from humanitarian
containment toward camp abolition   98
Simon Campbell

8. "Alternatives to detention" and the carceral state in
the UK   115
Lauren Cape-Davenhill

9. *Golden Gulag* in Italy? For the abolition of the reception-
industrial complex   130
Francesco Marchi

10. *Abolish Frontex* and end the EU Border regime   147
Mark Akkerman

CONSTELLATION III: POLITICAL HORIZONS OF
BORDER ABOLITIONISM

11. "Shut them down": non-reformist reforms in
anti-detention organizing   157
Helen Brewer, Tom Kemp, Bobby Phe Amis, and Joel White

12. Abolitionist potential and ambivalences in daily
struggles against the border regime   174
Watch the Med – Alarm Phone

13. Capitalism, mobility, and racialization: abolitionisms
at the border   193
Brian Whitener

14. Rising waters from New York City to Pakistan:
abolitionist organizing at the intersection of immigration
justice and the climate crisis   210
Vignesh Ramachandran and Akash Singh

15. *Interview with Contra Viento y Marea, El Comedor
Comunitario*   230

Afterword   241
Gracie Mae Bradley

Notes on Contributors   246

Index   253

Introduction

Borders must be abolished. That is the simple thesis of this book. Why? Because borders are more than just lines on a map; they are social constructions and material infrastructures that produce death and devastation.[1] Borders create divisions, enable domination, and, rather than making us secure, secure the conditions necessary for the reproduction of racism, capitalism, and patriarchy. While border abolition might be a recent coinage, it forms a part of much longer and living traditions of anti-carceral, anti-state and no-border organizing. We understand abolition to mean, in conversation with these traditions, not just tearing down, but building anew. As Ruth Wilson Gilmore says: "Abolition is a fleshly and material presence of social life lived differently." Or as Fred Moten and Stefano Harney put it: abolition must be the abolition of police, prisons, and courts, but also the "founding of new society."[2] *Border Abolition Now* builds on the work of those who have come before us and who have argued that borders, the police, and prisons, are not "natural" institutions. Walking alongside them, we hope to show how border abolition, grounded in movements and people organizing from below, is a critical, and dynamic, political project of the present.

Our demand, *Border Abolition Now*, is not a call to end border controls while keeping broader societal infrastructures intact. Rather, it seeks the abolition of borders in all their guises and disguises and, in so doing, demands the radical remaking of social relations, socio-economic systems, and political structures. As such, the book you hold in your hands is a collection of essays, interviews, activist and academic knowledges about how to abolish borders and a snapshot of recent theorizations, histories, and practices of border abolition as a political project. The chapters, starting from a variety of political and geographical locations, document the extensive and changing reach of border regimes, theorize and historicize border abolition as theory and practice, and detail political organizing that aims to minimize the violence of borders for those on the move and work toward a world in which borders are obsolete.[3]

The pieces collected in this volume emerge from the "Border Abolition 2021" conference that took place online on June 18th and 19th, 2021. This first-of-its-kind conference brought together people and groups opposing the border in all its forms, "from immigration detention, prison, and militarized border sites," and enacting "solidarity practices that resist expanding systems of everyday bordering... envisioning the creation of systems of care, safety and support that many of our communities lack." Over the course of two days, more than 700 people joined talks and workshops, sharing experiences from different struggles and making connections with researchers and activists from across the world. This book acknowledges the importance of this meeting point, is indebted to all of the conference organizers and speakers, and is informed by the discussions and resonances of abolitionist praxis across different spaces, times and struggles against the imperialism of borders. We hope with this collection you can feel what we felt during those days: though struggle is hard, we are not alone!

These pages bring together critical border studies scholars and activists, abolitionist organizers, and migrants to engage more deeply with the abolitionist tradition. We argue that what abolition brings to border studies is a means for understanding the spread of carceral and policing apparatuses across a long historical arc; a vision that undoing police and carceral regimes requires the fundamental transformation of all existing social institutions; and a political commitment to building new worlds beyond police and prisons as well as a political emphasis on the *active* dismantling of carceral and border regimes. In bringing abolition into conversation with border regimes, this volume also centers important commonalities and points of contact between these analytics and asks the question of what can border, prison and police abolitionists learn from each other. Thinking border regimes and abolition together allows for focusing on long-standing struggles for self-determination, the right to move or to remain in place and the connections between present and past mobility struggles; the changing regimes of colonial and imperial racialization and the constitution of enemies and "others;" and the historical agency of enslaved, oppressed, and bonded peoples who have always fought for their self-preservation and liberation and whose many victories form the basis for the political horizon of contemporary border abolitionism.

From the beginning of colonial enterprises and the transatlantic slave trade, imperial formations have used racialized border, carceral, and surveillance technologies to control, prevent, or incite mobility. This continues to be true, but the last two decades have seen an unprecedented expansion of carceral, police, and encampment regimes connected to global borders combined with a rising tide of fascist and extreme nationalist movements aimed at "securing" homelands and "cleansing" nations of "foreigners" and others. We see border abolition as a site for understanding historically how the Westphalian system of nation-states was imposed on a globe that asked for nothing of the sort.[4] And we propose border abolition as a necessary analytic for grasping the conjoined acceleration of carceral border regimes and extreme nationalism, and for imagining a politics which would halt their spread.

As editors, five concerns were central as we started to put this collection together. First, we wanted to make visible the state-sanctioned violence that borders cause. In order to denaturalize how borders work, it is imperative to make visible the violence they produce and reproduce, which is also an important step in demythologizing borders as "protective."

Second, in order to understand how borders are connected to carceral and policing regimes, we need to make visible how border abolition is a feminist praxis. An intersectional transnational lens acknowledges the ways in which different struggles are related by connecting histories of oppression and recognizing how different dimensions of identity impact our experience and understanding of the world. A transnational feminist framework is necessary for the exploration of border abolition as theory and as political praxis or as "a practice that is collective and feminist."[5]

Third, we wondered what new horizons might exist for border abolition as an analytic. By bringing border abolition into conversation with a vast array of university disciplines and centering the possibilities for new alliances among different social actors, organizers and sites of resistance, we wanted to uncover new ways of doing abolitionism across geographical locations.

Fourth, we wanted to develop further the scholar–activist nexus which has generated many central contributions to the critical border studies literature.[6] Working in solidarity with people on the move and those targeted by border control is a dynamic site of knowledge production and theory-making about the nature and evolution of border institutions and practical know-how about navigating these spaces, forming relationships, and building communities of care and resistance.[7] We wanted our contributors to draw from different locations, disciplines, and struggles to bring a much-needed bottom-up and global perspective to border abolitionist praxis.

Finally, we sought to plumb the complexities of border abolition on the ground and the myriad ways in which different groups resist. Border abolition is not a linear process, but a messy one enmeshed with conflict and (theoretical and on-the-ground) contradictions. We hoped to center and learn from the messy contradictions of a practice that is often easier to theorize about than to carry out, without collapsing the power dynamics which make it so pressing as a struggle.

We were also moved by a sense of historical urgency and the necessity of abolishing border regimes. In the last decade, openly fascist and nationalist movements have swept into the halls of power across the globe. The rising tide of fascism rides on renewed nationalisms, defenses of the homeland against immoral "globalists," and the expulsion and cleansing of the nation of others. Each of these aspects requires and is underpinned by an increasingly sophisticated carceral border complex which comprises infrastructures for the policing of migrants and refugees. If once in the moment of anti-globalization movements, critical border studies scholars and activists made the demand of "no borders," our demand today, as a stay against creeping global fascism, must be "border abolition now" which means both an end to borders and also to the infrastructures of deprivation, surveillance, and death attached to the border complex.

The present volume argues that the seeds for overcoming the xenophobia of the far-right and liberal democratic regimes lies in the border abolitionist vision of a just world for all. This demand is not made in isolation, rather it recognizes that border controls are embedded within the quotidian functioning of nation-states and are central to the modern workings of imperialism and racialized capitalism. Such an understanding builds on the important work of scholar-activists, including Ruth Wilson Gilmore[8] and Harsha Walia,[9] whose scholarship has differently demonstrated how carceral and border violence is entangled within wider infrastructures, such as policing, housing, and capitalism's expanding frontiers, and enmeshed within the racializing logics of imperialism, dispossession and appropriation.

We believe that the call for border abolition intersects with police and prison abolition work to produce a unique analysis of some of the most pressing societal issues of our time. For decades, prison and police abolitionists have argued policing brings neither safety, nor security, nor order. In a similar way, critical migration and border studies scholars have noted that borders, instead of providing safety, security, or stability, are violent spaces that produce vulnerability, migrant illegality, inequality, and threats to life. A border abolition perspective allows us to see the profound continuities between the carceral regimes that structure contemporary societies premised on exclusion and forcible confinement[10] and to imagine new solidarities between movements against police and prisons and borders. In making visible how the prison industrial complex collides with regimes of border militarization and surveillance, detention, and deportation, the present volume reveals how this confluence updates and interacts with legacies of state oppression, colonialism, imperialism and racism.[11] In charting the historical genealogies of technocratic models of rule through borders and policing regimes, *Border Abolition Now* also traces the blueprints of contemporary global racial ordering.

As much as the last decade has witnessed the rise of extreme nationalist movements, it has also seen the spread of abolitionist and border abolitionist organizing to all parts of the world. Abolitionist, anti-racist, and anti-policing demands and abolitionist alternatives for restructuring the safety of communities and individuals (e.g., transformative justice and defunding the police) are now common currency of the most cutting-edge political formations including border and migrant organizing. *Border Abolition Now* concretizes the analytic of border abolition and aims to spur the development of social movements which could confront the xenophobia and carceral border regimes on which the new far-right depends.

Of course, we also acknowledge that this book represents a politics that is a work-in-progress. Much radical and transformative work is being carried out in locations that are not in this volume, by activists that do not feature here. We also recognize the privileged positionality of many contributors to this volume, and that abolitionist struggles against the border are being pushed foremost by migrant-activist communities themselves. Therefore this book doesn't aim to define border abolition merely from an academic position, but seeks to tap into and learn from existing organizing.

We designed this volume to offer entry points for readers from a variety of backgrounds and at different stages of the journey into border abolitionist politics. We have organized the chapters in this book into three constellations to spotlight key aspects of contemporary border abolitionism: the first draws out how abolitionist theory is being thought and advanced in border contexts; the second explores border abolition in practice and in relation to specific components of the border complex; and the third shows how political theories and political horizons of border abolition are developing through challenges arising from border regimes. In between each constellation is a collection of dispatches from a range of different migrant-led groups and solidarity organizations. These punctuate the volume, acting as interlocutors between the essays and foregrounding the voices of those engaged in everyday practices of abolition. These dispatches provide points of passage through the book and articulations of abolition from particular places, times, and positionalities.

Our first dispatch, from *Women in Exile* (Chapter 1), examines practices and challenges of border abolition from the perspective of migrant feminist organizing. The opening constellation (Chapters 2–4) explores how abolitionist theory is being engaged in border contexts. Together, these chapters enumerate how emergent trajectories and new abolitionist horizons are being envisioned through feminist and anticolonial praxis, as well as through attention to lived experiences of borders and organizing against them. Leah Cowan et al.'s piece (Chapter 2) considers how border controls enact gendered violence through, for example, family visa stipulations and family reunification policies which reproduce the gender binary and privilege the heteronormative family. Vanessa E. Thompson (Chapter 3) argues that capitalism and "carceral racism" are central to the functioning of border regimes and key to understanding abolitionist resistance to them. Rounding out the constellation, Josue David Cisneros's intervention (Chapter 4) outlines an abolitionist approach to border studies and an abolitionist praxis for no-borders organizing.

Our next dispatch, an interview with the *Black Alliance for Just Immigration* (BAJI), centers on the connections between border abolition and Black liberation. The infrastructures that undergird the border complex and their relationship to race, empire, and capital are taken up by this second constellation (Chapters 6–9), which examines how abolition is thought through specific contexts and components of the border (specifically, asylum, camps, alternatives to detention and reception). Jenna M. Loyd's piece attends to the complicated terrain navigated by abolitionists in the face of asylum regimes and their connection to imperialism (Chapter 6). Tracing geographies of encampment in the European border complex, Simon Campbell (Chapter 7) positions humanitarian relocation within histories of regional white supremacy and explores abolitionist resistance to them. Lauren Cape-Davenhill (Chapter 8) examines alternatives to detention and brings much-needed attention to modulations in carcerality outside the prison. Finally, in Francesco Marchi's analysis of expansions in the Italian border complex (Chapter 9), we see how carceral fixes are rendered through humanitarian reception.

The dispatch from Mark Akkerman on the *Abolish Frontex* campaign (Chapter 10) addresses the intersection of struggles against borders, colonialism, policing and the weapons industry. In this final constellation (Chapters 11–14), political theories of abolition are advanced and challenged by theoretical concerns emerging from border contexts and specific conditions of border organizing. Opening this collection of chapters, Helen Brewer et al.'s contribution to anti-detention organizing in the UK (Chapter 11) explores the links between border violence and the prison system, charting the potential of non-reformist reforms to disrupt the reproduction of incarceration. The dialogue between activists from *Watch the Med – Alarm Phone* (Chapter 12) traces how migrant solidarities are criminalized and how activists negotiate abolitionist politics in real time. Brian Whitener (Chapter 13) argues for incitement and fixity of labor as central to capitalism and as a key site where processes of racialization are grounded, while Vignesh Ramachandran and Akash Singh (Chapter 14) highlight critical intersections between climate change and transnational abolitionist organizing. One final dispatch, a rousing conversation with *Contra Viento y Marea* on the complexities of abolitionist organizing on the US–Mexico border, closes out this constellation. The volume concludes with Gracie Mae Bradley's incisive afterword, which highlights some of the principal interventions into current abolitionist and liberatory debates and conversations of the pieces gathered here.

We want to end this introduction by centering a key through line in this book – one which is essential for any border abolitionist practice – namely care, mutual aid and love as antidotes to the violence of carceral structures. The interview with *Contra Viento y Marea* underscores the importance of organizing on "the basis of friendship" and how the provision of community space, shelter, and resources can enact resistance and materially create the "new vision of what we want to see happen in our society." For their part, *Alarm Phone* remind us that "abolition does not mean to only abolish something, but also to create an environment where people can leave and travel, and live where they want to live as well as where they are able to." *Alarm Phone*'s telephone line is an attempt at creating a new network and community, one that facilitates movement and acts as a much-needed infrastructure of care for those on the move. These are only two of the many examples of care, mutual aid and love that echo across this volume. It is our belief that the connections found in new social relations are our reminder that in the deathly spaces created by borders there are spaces of resistance made possible through our commitment to one another. As editors, we hope these threads of hope, love and care accompany each of you as you find your way through this book and stay with you as you journey back out in the world, wherever that may find you.

NOTES

1. Bridget Anderson, Nandita Sharma, and Cynthia Wright, "Editorial: Why No Borders?" *Refuge* 26, September 1, 2009. doi: 10.25071/1920-7336.32074
2. Clément Petitjean, "Prisons and Class Warfare: An Interview with Ruth Wilson Gilmore," *Verso* (blog), August 2, 2018. www.versobooks.com/blogs/news/3954-prisons-and-class-warfare-an-interview-with-ruth-wilson-gilmore; Fred Moten and Stefano Harney, *The Undercommons*. New York: Minor Compositions, 2013, p. 42.
3. Angela Y. Davis, *Are Prisons Obsolete?* New York: Seven Stories Press, 2011.
4. We acknowledge the often fraught nature of some conversations between Indigenous and critical border studies, while at the same time we hold out the possibility for a series of more capacious and creative imaginings of how to think beyond the historical inheritance of capitalist states – and alongside and with traditions and histories which have held open other possibilities for collective forms of social reproduction and care.
5. Angela Y. Davis, Gina Dent, Erica R. Meiners, Beth E. Richie, *Abolition. Feminism. Now.* New York: Penguin, 2022, p.16. It is important to note, especially for those in a European context, that this is the volume's framing of feminist abolition, as opposed to that of the abolition of sex work which has a political currency in countries like France and Spain.
6. Harsha Walia, *Undoing Border Imperialism*. Anarchist Intervention Series 06. Oakland; Edinburgh: Washington, DC: AK Press; Institute for Anarchist Studies, 2013; Natasha King, *No Borders: The Politics of Immigration Control and Resistance*. London: Zed Books, 2016.
7. Aziz Choudry, *Learning Activism: The Intellectual Life of Contemporary Social Movements*. Toronto: University of Toronto Press, 2015. Laurence Cox, "Scholarship and activism: A Social Movements Perspective." *Studies in Social Justice* 9(1), 2015: 34-53. David Featherstone, *Solidarity: Hidden Histories and Geographies of Internationalism*. London: Bloomsbury Publishing, 2012.
8. Ruth Wilson Gilmore, *Golden Gulag: Prisons, Surplus, Crisis, and Opposition in Globalizing California*. Berkeley: University of California Press, 2007; Ruth Wilson Gilmore, *Abolition Geography: Essays Towards Liberation*. New York: Verso, 2022.
9. Harsha Walia, *Undoing Border Imperialism*. Anarchist Intervention Series 06. Oakland; Edinburgh: Washington, DC: AK Press; Institute for Anarchist Studies, 2013; Harsha Walia, *Border and Rule: Global Migra-*

tion, Capitalism, and the Rise of Racist Nationalism. Chicago: Haymarket Books, 2021.

10. Jenna Loyd, Matt Mitchelson and Andrew Burridge (Eds.), *Beyond Walls and Cages: Prisons, Borders, and Global Crisis.* University of Georgia Press, 2012.

11. M. Alexander, *The New Jim Crow: Mass Incarceration in the Age of Colorblindness.* New York: The New Press, 2012; A. Davis, *Are Prisons Obsolete?* New York: Seven Stories Press, 2003; Nadine El-Enany, *Bordering Britain: Law, Race and Empire.* Manchester: Manchester University Press, 2020; A. Vitale, *The End of Policing.* London: Verso, 2017.

1

Women in Exile's story
Loud and clear against isolation and building intersectional bridges

Elizabeth Ngari and Doris Dede

Self-description of the organization

Women in Exile is an initiative of refugee women founded in Brandenburg in 2002 by refugee women* to fight for their rights.[1] We decided to organize as a refugee women*'s group because we have experienced that refugee women are doubly discriminated against, not only by racist laws and discriminative refugee laws in general, but also as women*.

In 2011 *Women in Exile & Friends* was formed where activists in solidarity without refugee backgrounds joined the fight. Together we fight for the abolition of all laws discriminatory to asylum seekers and migrants and against the interconnections of racism and sexism. We perceive ourselves as a feminist organization and we're one of the few links between the women's movement and the refugees' movement.[2]

"No *Lager* for Women and Children! Abolish all *Lagers!*"

The call to close all camps is a central demand for *Women in Exile*. As a group of refugee women, we have been visiting other refugee women in Brandenburg and other federal states for more than 20 years. Through several conversations, workshops and discussions, we know what the situation of the women* in the *Lagers* (the German word used for camps) is like, especially in the rural regions. The women* have traumatic escape stories and very often feel threatened by the staff and male fellow residents in the camps. They are often insulted, forced to do cheap labor (1 euro/hour job), and sexually and physically harassed. They have no privacy and do not know how to protect themselves. In addition, there is the legal-formal asylum apparatus whose procedures they do not understand and which poses a very concrete threat to them. In our combined fights, we demand:

- No *Lager* for Women and Children! Abolish all *Lagers*! Europewide!
- Stop pushing us into inappropriate hygienic and traumatizing conditions!
- Stop our forced mass accommodation in camps!
- Right to come, right to go and right to stay for all!
- Freedom of movement!

Refugee women getting loud

Women in Exile consider ourselves as a bridge between the women's movement and the political struggle of refugees in Germany. We advocate for a feminist approach where there are no men, because in mixed groups – where refugee women* and men do politics together – there is often no space for specific issues concerning women*. In 2011, we opened our organization with the addition *& Friends* to support activists without refugee backgrounds, because we found out that: "the fights are the same, but with different approaches." Our key focus is on empowering activism and campaigns to improve the situation of refugee women* since the reality of refugee women* in this society is made invisible by only seeing us as victims without a voice. At demonstrations, rallies, creative actions, bus tours, conferences or events like the "Building Bridges Festival," we raise our voices and get loud.

A key example of raising our voices was during *Women in Exile's* 20th-anniversary celebrations, which we marked with an international conference "Breaking Borders to Build Bridges" in 2023, where we also launched our collectively written book of the same title.[3] At this event many topics were tackled, such as the climate crisis and political, ecological, cultural and economic reasons for displacement and forced resettlement, difficulties and violence that LGBTIQ migrants and refugees experience, war and how women* suffer as victims of military aggressions etc. Working on the connections of these different oppressions is important to our abolitionist vision, and connects to the group's main goal: "the utopia of a just society without exclusion and discrimination, with equal rights for all people, no matter where they come from or where they go."[4]

From personal problems to political activism: this is how we do our empowerment

However, as long as this utopia has not yet been achieved, there is a need for protected spaces, so-called "safe spaces," in which refugee women* can speak freely about their specific experiences of discrimination. The creation of such spaces is therefore fundamental to our work. In this way, we can support each other in dealing with the problems confronting us every day. The solidarity of refugee women* with each other in a peer-to-peer approach – through equal participation – is the basis for learning and growing together in a family atmosphere. This creates a feeling of solidarity, and it becomes clear: no woman* is alone with her experiences. This is how we execute our empowerment work.

Through discussions in the safe spaces, the women* become aware of their shared experiences of discrimination and political options for action. Through individual healing, strengthening, and self-empowerment, they create the basis for their political activism. In addition, through *Women in Exile's* work they receive further training in workshops about their rights and possibilities, so that they can carry their concerns into society in an informed and self-determined way. Apart from the political aspect, the empowerment of the refugee women* also contributes to strengthening everyone to improve their individual situation.

Working together to make the fight stronger

Cooperation with other political groups also plays an important role in the empowerment work. *Women in Exile* are aware of the limits of their own capabilities, for example, in legal matters or when filing applications. Refugee women* often lack knowledge of the German system, which is further complicated by language barriers and limited financial resources. To overcome these limitations, we make specific use of already existing solidarity structures, especially those from feminist activism. Under the idea of "working together to make the fight stronger" we cooperate with supporters and networks on our own terms. It is important for us to use the support of other groups and networks, as well as individual supporters, in such a way that we can organize ourselves in the long run.

The *Friends* use their privileges to support *Women in Exile* in our political work by making certain resources available. They relieve the activists of *Women in Exile*, for example, in carrying out childcare, translation, or in the organization of financing and transport. They can also contribute language and legal knowledge as well as personal talents, such as filming the group's actions. The cooperation is often based on a friendly relationship, so sometimes the *Friends* simply stand by as friends. The *Friends* support the work of *Women in Exile* by creating and offering spaces. They also participate in the elaboration of political strategies with the refugee women*.

All in all, it can be seen that empowerment in *Women in Exile* is thought together with solidarity. The empowerment of individual refugee women* begins with the exchange and recognition of their shared experiences. The resulting sense of community and family atmosphere strengthens the self-empowerment of the women*. This is an empowerment that is increased by the practice of solidarity not only among the refugee women*, but also with activists without a refugee background and networks that share their privileges with the refugee women*. Empowerment is neither possible purely from within oneself nor purely through others but requires cooperation in solidarity.

Nevertheless, the use of solidarity outside the core group of refugee women* does not lead to a weakening or decline in the self-determination of *Women in Exile*. Despite all the support, "it is central to the cooperation with *Women in Exile & Friends* that the refugee women* ... have their say"[5] to counteract possible dominance structures within the organization. With the opening of the organization for non-refugee women* in 2011, this was directly addressed in workshops as a preventive measure. Accordingly, the cooperation between the refugee women* and the *Friends* can be seen as a best practice example in anti-racism work, breaking with hierarchies and talking to each other on an equal footing, hence equal participation. Besides raising awareness across multiple platforms about the necropolitical *Lager* system and border regime – such as in demonstrations, rallies, panel discussions, workshops, interviews, and social media – *Women in Exile* mobilizes refugee women* on the ground by going from camp to camp, sharing and exchanging information about their rights and fighting isolation. Furthermore, *Women in Exile* organizes bus tours almost yearly, traveling throughout Germany to mobilize refugee women* in camps to build and strengthen feminist abolitionist solidarity.

As *Women in Exile & Friends*, one of our interconnected activities is caring for those threatened by deportations and facing racist injustices. For example, the case of our late sister Rita Awuor Ojunge, a Black refugee woman who was murdered near the *Lager* in Hohenleipisch, where she was forced to stay and struggled for a decent life for her and her children. Her body was only found three months after her disappearance, located just 200 meters from the *Lager*.[6]

Women in Exile practices abolition as an emancipatory commitment that is not reducible to *Lagers* or prisons but rather encircles all fields of social and ecological life, ranging from interconnected forms of violence and exploitation, to access to health care and reproductive justice, housing, emancipatory education, and the freedom to move as well as to stay. *Women in Exile* also highlights the role of neocolonial power structures and the colonial continuity of border regimes, *Lagers*, and deportation, linking struggles internationally, especially within Europe, to what is happening at the outer borders, the Black Mediterranean and detention centers elsewhere, while focusing on the most vulnerable.

We don't want to be that dependent on others
Conceptually, white saviorism also exists in the context of migration, though many may not see it as such. Therefore, it is always very important that help from "outside" is only accepted when strictly necessary. We know exactly what we want and what we need, and are aware of societal power and relations of dominance. Thus, we choose only those co-operations that help our own political goals. This requires a continuous and active examination of the difficulty of external support. For the women* at *Women in Exile & Friends*, another central element of our activism is not only self-determination, but also a constant reflection of our own prejudices and of our work.

People should make their fight other people's fight
However, political circumstances prevent the necessary changes to achieve social justice for refugee women*. Activists conduct their

political struggle in a societal atmosphere in which the situation for refugees is increasingly deteriorating. Even though *Women in Exile & Friends* are successfully empowering themselves, major societal changes have failed to materialize for the time being due to the current political framework. It is necessary that each person becomes aware of their privileges and opportunities and, like *Women in Exile & Friends*, uses them to create spaces for a more just society. In the light of increasing right-wing tendencies, the organization therefore justifiably demands more solidarity: "People should make their fight other people's fight and let's leave no one behind!"

Notes

1. The asterisk is used here to include all persons who identify themselves as women.
2. More about us on our website: www.women-in-exile.net
3. Women in Exile, *Breaking Borders to Build Bridges*, Münster: Edition Assemblage, 2022.
4. Über Uns, "Women in Exile & Friends." Accessed October 17, 2023. www.women-in-exile.net/en/ueber-uns/
5. "Women in Exile & Friends." Accessed October 17, 2023. www.women-in-exile.net/
6. "Hohenleipisch Report 'Women in Exile & Friends.'" Accessed October 17, 2023. www.women-in-exile.net/en/bericht-ueber-hohenleipisch/

CONSTELLATION I

Abolitionist Theories
in Border Contexts

2

Unfolding and flourishing

Strategies of border abolition feminism

Leah Cowan, Francesca Esposito, Sarah Hopwood,
Aminata Kalokoh, Vânia Martins, and Elahe Zivardar[1]

As abolitionist calls continue to proliferate globally and abolition becomes a more influential political goal, Angela Y. Davis,
Gina Dent, Erica R. Meiners, and Beth E. Richie have noted that
these struggles' "collective feminist lineages are increasingly less
visible, even during moments made possible precisely because
of feminist organising, especially that of young queer people of
colour whose pivotal labour and analysis is so often erased."[2] We
agree on the urgent need to acknowledge and reinvigorate these
feminist lineages, because "abolition is most effectively advanced
by naming and elevating an analysis and practice that is collective and feminist."[3] Overall, our aim is that this collective work can
become part of the burgeoning ecosystem of abolition feminism
being created and practiced around the world. We are feminist
border abolitionists.

This shared contribution emerges from a panel on "Feminist
Strategies and Practices of Border Abolition" which was part of
the online 2021 Border Abolition Conference (see Introduction
in the volume).[4] In our discussion we sought to connect theoretical discussions on border violence and abolition with our daily
experiences and struggles by weaving together lived experience,
activism, and scholarship. In doing so, we wished to acknowledge
the feminist ancestry of struggles against borders, in all their forms,
and to share knowledge, visions, and praxes for resistance. Our
guiding questions included: What are the intersecting (gendered,
sexualized, racialized, class-based) mechanisms of power and
harm at play in the border-industrial complex, and how can we

better understand and challenge them? And what microcosms of violence and oppression do these mechanism (re)produce, and how can intersectional feminisms and queer politics inspire our struggles for abolishing borders, both inside and outside the spaces of violent border control?

In order to create this contribution we built on our critical reflections, considering what border abolition feminism means to us; the importance of a feminist lens in our struggles for abolishing borders, and ways of envisioning a feminist borderless future. It is through these lines of inquiry and our process of collective reflection that this piece is articulated.

WHY BORDER ABOLITION

Border abolition is not a new analytical framework, nor an emerging critical approach to migration governmentality. Border abolition is a vision of the world we want to live in, which goes beyond the violences of borders. Abolition is a collective, radical imagining of a different way of being together based on social justice, not criminal punishment. It is premised upon growing a political community where structures of inequality are dismantled and everyone can have a meaningful and dignified life with unconditional access to fundamental goods, such as housing, education, health and well-being care, and nourishing food. On this basis, this project is a crucial part of contemporary struggles for the commons.[5] Yet border abolition is also a political method and practice; one which is critical to how we connect as human beings and center solidarity and mutuality in our relationships and everyday interactions. As stressed by Critical Resistance organizers, the essence of abolitionism is "living this vision in our daily lives."[6]

Importantly, the abolition of borders is a key part of a broader project pursued against the backdrop of racial capitalism; an idea outlined by Cedric Robinson[7] and later Jodi Melamed[8] that capitalism is accumulated by moving through relationships of inequality between groups of people. This project includes abolishing the police, prisons, and all carceral and punitive systems that uphold inequality, including the gender binary, the nuclear family,[9] and all fixed categories and limitations that keep us in places of danger and slow-walking death.

Thinking about capitalism and its foundations, we can note how easily wealth and goods are able to cross borders, whereas people, particularly working-class and racialized communities, are not. As Bridget Anderson, Nandita Sharma, and Cynthia Wright argue, "The simultaneous process of granting more freedom to capital and less to migrants is far from a contradiction and is in fact a crucial underpinning of global capitalism and the equally global system of national states."[10] Border controls are benign and trivial for rich people, they simply do not exist in the same way for the extremely wealthy as they do for the international working class. Imperial formations have historically used racialized and classed border controls as a means to advance their project of wealth extraction and accumulation. Evidencing the colonial legacies of contemporary border regimes, the wealth produced in colonized and formerly colonized territories commonly "migrates" to European metropolises, whereas the communities affected by this massive expropriation and exploitation are unable to move across borders in the same way.[11] In these analyses, it is crucial to acknowledge the intersectionality of race, class, gender, and sexuality, the complex matrix of oppressions they produce, and to connect this to the coloniality of power. For instance, decolonial feminist scholars, such as Maria Lugones,[12] have shown how modern gender structures, including separate roles for women and men, emerged through colonial rule.

Against these genealogies of violence and exploitation, border abolition is a radical political project of centering life and working for everyone's freedom. The freedom to move, the freedom to stay, and the freedom to leave are core claims in this project. As we write these pages, the central Mediterranean Sea has been the scene of yet another tragedy where, once again, many people have lost their lives at the hands of the violent European border regime.[13] This tragedy and the embodied struggles of those who challenge borders, in the central Mediterranean Sea as elsewhere, highlights the importance of border abolition as a life-affirming project. And yet the analytic and the political imagination it enables are not – and should not be – limited to nation-state borders and their contestation. As mentioned above, a border abolition project must address all relations of power and violence, as well as all liminal spaces produced in-between by bordering processes.[14]

Returning to the inherent coloniality of borders, border regimes have been used to create and maintain the artificial divides between citizens, racialized citizens (for whom citizenship is eternally precarious), and non-citizens. These divides, which ultimately determine who does or does not belong to our political and imagined communities, are enforced through exclusionary citizenship regimes. Yet the world was not created with bordered nation-states, and this harmful border-making project, premised upon the pursuit of power, control, capital and possession can be undone. The border abolition project is fundamentally about an interwoven and beautiful exercise of moving, imagining, and building something different and better together.

A FEMINIST LENS ON BORDER ABOLITION

As international feminist organizers we have campaigned to end immigration detention, to stop charter flights and deportations, to abolish prisons and push for demilitarization, alongside working toward the collective goal of ending gender violence. We understand that borders and their violence are inherently gendered. Borders reproduce binaried understandings of gender, they produce sites of harm for workers engaged in gendered forms of labor, such as sex work and domestic work, and enforce limiting, harmful, heteronormative, and ultimately colonial, concepts of families and relationships.[15] In this view, and as Enrica Rigo and Francesca De Masi point out reflecting on the experience of the Italian feminist movement *Non Una di Meno* (Not One Less) and the ways they organized for a "common battle against violence across borders," the struggle for freedom of movement "is a struggle against dispossession and violence and to this extent it is also our struggle: it is a *feminist* struggle [emphasis added]."[16]

THE WEAPONIZATION OF WOMEN'S BODIES
FOR BORDER REINFORCEMENT

A feminist perspective on border violence also includes opposing the mainstream representation of migrant women as "vulnerable subjects" who are the victims of cruel smugglers and traffickers. This rhetoric of passive victimhood is used by governments to justify their impetus to fortify borders, to stop new arrivals, and to pass unjust and repressive legislation. The discourse that border security is needed to stop vulnerable women and children from being trafficked has become a major tactic for the normalization of racist border violence. Legislation on trafficking also serves this purpose, demonstrated by the rhetoric used by the UK government in the Modern Slavery Act 2015 and the Nationality and Borders Act 2022. These Acts take up the mission of the "fight against traffickers' business model" to legitimize further border violence against undocumented migrants and to implement deadly policies that make migration routes across the British Channel more risky and treacherous.

Similarly, the feminist abolition movement has consistently highlighted that the increased criminalization of domestic and sexual abuse (through the creation of new laws, increased police powers, and harsher prison sentences among other strategies) does not prevent gender violence, and that criminalization does not keep us safe.[17] Moreover, the carceral system enables further violence against communities marginalized by structures of oppression. Women's protection from violence is often used as a justification for the increased punishment and repression of people who challenge borders, specifically racialized and working-class men.

Within a British context, the government and right-wing press routinely use women's "protection" as a justification for increased focus on deportations, particularly of people who are criminalized due to acts or allegations of sexual violence.[18] Similar to the way Davis theorized that "Prisons do not disappear social problems, they disappear human beings";[19] deportations are used to "disappear" people but do not address the root causes of gender violence. Instead, the border-industrial complex further perpetuates systems of gendered and racialized harm. Additionally, the deportation regime undermines the prison system's own so-called "rehabilitation logic," for if prison "worked" to "cure" people of their abusive tendencies toward women there would be no need to deport them after a period of incarceration for "women's protection." Moreover, by this logic, those who have harmed, and allegedly "cannot change," will continue to pose a risk to women in whichever country they are being taken to. The illogics of the system point to the flimsiness of the facade that border controls are a viable tool for ending gender violence.

In another example, in February 2023, a small group of people organized a violent racist and fascist "protest" outside a hotel being used to house people navigating the asylum system in Liverpool, UK.[20] The fascist protesters claimed that this riot was in response to one of the asylum-seeking men living in this hotel sexually harassing a young white woman. The alleged violence against a woman was used as the impetus or justification for the rioting and extreme racist violence. We have seen fascists and racists manufacturing similar narratives elsewhere too, for example in Cologne, Germany, and the US. Around the globe, racists and right-wing governments perpetuate this same idea, ignoring the fact that the vast majority of interpersonal violence is perpetrated by men that women/girls know, primarily within their own homes. Akin to the prison-industrial complex, borders fundamentally don't protect us, instead they perpetuate and further cycles of intersectional harm and abuse.

EVERYDAY BORDER CONTROLS AND THE PRODUCTION OF GENDERED VIOLENCE

In the UK context, the border regime's most recent iteration is the hostile environment, which is a web of policies and laws that make it punishing for migrant communities to stay in the country, as well as targeting racialized communities in general.[21] In step with this, the practice of integrating immigration checks into multiple facets of ordinary life has extended the British border from its geographical territorial perimeter into an expansive, internalized border enacted in the everyday.[22] The hostile environment is profoundly gendered and deeply impacts working-class and racialized women in particular. The No Recourse to Public Funds (NRPF) condition that blocks access to welfare benefits for people who have insecure immigration status is illustrative of these gendered impacts. The lives of women, who are more likely to be sole carers of their children, are made untenable by the NRPF condition, which pushes them into poverty, homelessness, and situations of exploitation.

In particular, it is extremely difficult to leave a domestic violence situation if a survivor cannot access benefits or social housing due to having NRPF. Furthermore, Multi-Agency Risk Assessment Conferences (MARACs), which, in the UK, oversee domestic abuse cases that are deemed high risk, tend to happen around survivors, often without their presence or direct involvement. This again invokes the "vulnerable subject" rhetoric as survivors are excluded from discussions supposedly about "her own safety" (that are really focused on managing neoliberal conceptions of "risk") and for some migrant women include suggestions that returning to her country of origin will resolve the domestic abuse. The idea that the deportation of a survivor, or of someone who has perpetrated harm against them, is a solution to gender violence, illustrates the way that some forms of feminism or anti-violence work have become complicit in the carceral state and the border regime. Besides demonstrating the interweaving of criminal and immigration controls under the banner of preventing violence against women and girls, the example of MARACs (which are attended by domestic violence support workers) making immigration enforcement recommendations further evidences how everyday bordering practices have been incorporated into the NGO and anti-violence sector. In part this has happened within the "women's sector" in the UK (and the US) in step with the rise of neoliberalism since the 1980s, due to the way that funding has been systematically gutted from feminist organizations since that decade. In reaction to a reduced funding landscape, feminist organizations have had to form allegiances with the state in order to "keep doing their work."[23] Neoliberal ideology has seeped into feminist movements and domestic abuse provision, to the detriment of women who are at the sharp end of state-based oppression.[24]

Using a border abolition feminism lens we can identify the creep of carceral feminism in anti-violence work and ask: Is this a segment of our movement that needs to be rebuilt from the ground up? Or to what extent is mainstream feminism, in the UK as elsewhere, inherently carceral and professionalized, meaning that the alternative places where abolitionist feminist work is happening –

in grassroots and informal spaces – are where we can find radical inspiration to imagine new and creative ways to move forward? In many ways, marginalized communities often already practice abolitionist solidarity among each other, though potentially this work is not framed in the language of "abolition." Community groups may not postulate their resistance in theoretical concepts or academic language; they are practicing Border Abolitionist feminism in the everyday. We can be led and inspired by these groups and grassroots movements, flourishing and resisting around the world, to think more creatively about strategies and actions to address gender violence, without the need for state or private funding.

THE IMMIGRATION-DETENTION-INDUSTRIAL COMPLEX

Similarly to NRPF, the detention of women for immigration purposes often replicates gendered violence itself, both mirroring the control and violence of abusive interpersonal relationships and gendered power dynamics.[25] Many women held in detention centers are already survivors of gendered forms of abuse, including domestic and sexual violence, but instead of receiving "protection," as state authorities claim to provide, women are harmed and retraumatized by the state and their corporate allies.[26] Women in detention often cannot sleep at night because the jingling of keys by guards is reminiscent of being locked up in a room or imprisoned in their own homes by abusive ex-partners. Additionally, if the abusive ex-partner is a policeman or person in authority the re-traumatization and mirroring of structural harm can be magnified. This returns us to the importance of, through a border abolition feminism perspective, examining the links between intimate, interpersonal, institutional, and state violence, and how these various forms of violence are interconnected and mutually reinforcing of each other.[27]

Resistance from women inside the immigration detention-industrial complex comes in various forms. As a survivor of immigration detention herself, Aminata highlights how, "in times of resistance, the whole idea is to fight the system, to go against the system, and this happens on a daily basis." Elahe, also a survivor of an Australian refugee offshore detention center on Nauru island, highlights that:

> Women were the main voices of protest inside the camps, and the main organizers of resistance to our detention, whereas most of the men detained with us had already sunk into depression and apathy. I felt it my duty to try to tell the outside world about the terrible conditions and the horror of this policy in general. The strength of refugee women in the face of the injustice, cruelty, discrimination, and the hate that they suffered at the hands of those whom they had thought would help them, the Australian authorities. They suffered a lot as girls, as women, as wives, as sisters, as mothers, but when they became weak and close to breaking down, they still kept moving gracefully, as if dancing. While they appeared to dance, they kept giving birth to their love and power to everything and everyone. They are goddesses of love and strength.[28]

People locked up inside detention centers practice resistance and solidarity on an everyday basis. Daily acts of resistance and solidarity are one of the most potent strategies for dismantling this harmful system. Every time a detention center is closed, it is due to the resistance of people detained inside. Through their protests and acts of resistance, detained people have been able to damage facilities and undermine the smooth operation of the immigration detention-industrial complex. Below, Elahe provides a powerful account of women's creative and embodied struggles against this harmful carceral system – an illustration of border abolition feminism in action.

> *My name is Elahe Zivardar, known as Ellie Shakiba, an architect, artist, and journalist from Iran. In 2013 I fled my country, got into a boat from Indonesia, heading to Christmas Island of Australia. I sought asylum from Australia. There, I thought, is one of the best places for women. It is a first-world country that respects human rights, especially women's rights. Well, I admit now that I was very wrong.[29] I was detained on Christmas Island for more than five months. Then one morning in January 2014 I was transferred to*

the Australian refugee offshore detention center on the Island of Nauru. I was exiled and imprisoned in Nauru for six years until 2019 when I was welcomed to the United States of America as a "genuine" refugee.

I did a lot of filming and photography inside and outside the detention center in Nauru, and now I am making a documentary film about this.[30] But the way that art helped me more directly while in detention was through my paintings.[31] Painting was like therapy for me and many other detainees in the camp. However, I continued to paint after I left Nauru as the trauma and the feelings I had stored inside me that had built up over 6 years of detention still needed an outlet. I have since created a series of paintings which I call the border-industrial complex, and all of which depict a different aspect of our unjust detention in Nauru.

My work (https://shakibaproductions.com) embodies the situation of women who have fled from oppression, including myself, only to be subjected to other forms of oppression again.[32]

THE BODY AS BORDER

Borders seek to uphold normative gender categories, including in the way that, for example, in the UK, spousal or finance visas are given out to people who are married or in state-sanctioned relationships. These relationships revolve around nuclear family units, and operate as productive units under our racialized and gendered capitalist system. The government uses these policies to continue to build this ideal of what is a "family" and what is the role of women within the nuclear family. Spousal visas, in particular, reproduce the cis-heternormative idea of a nuclear family. This reinforcement of the nuclear family through visa rules poses barriers to border-crossing for queer people living in countries formerly colonized by European states that imposed anti-gay laws, making it extremely difficult for them to "evidence" their relationships in ways that fit the state's cis-heternormative vision for what a relationship should be. Furthermore, as long established by feminist activists and thinkers, women's and children's economic dependency on partners who hold privilege and power along lines of gender and class, and more, can have extremely dangerous consequences, especially when this is enforced by the state.

Border abolition feminism enables us to also think of the body as a border in itself. This concept of the "body as a border" is fed by Latin American feminisms and the idea of the connection between humans and between humans and the earth as one place (*pachamama*).[33] Due to this bond between bodies and the land, particularly in Indigenous communities, displacement becomes a strategy of border governmentality. When we think of the body as a border we can also see how the project of nation-state building utilizes women's bodies to mark boundaries, either of modesty or modernity. Palestinian women, for example, found ways of reclaiming the borders of those territories through "implicit and explicit resistance," to resist their bodies being used to reinstate state borders by Israeli and Palestinian factions.[34]

It is also not possible to talk about border abolition feminism without talking about labor justice and workers rights, and particularly the way that gendered labor and unpaid care work is penalized by the border regime. The border regime enables the exploitation of cheap migrant labor; of situations where people are pushed to accept low pay and poor working and living conditions, as seen, for example, in the intensive greenhouse fruit production across the Iberian Peninsula, the seasonal fruit pickers in the UK, or the agricultural work in Italy or the US (just to mention a few examples). The same logic was reproduced recently with Ukrainian displaced people, with countries such as Portugal offering to receive refugees in order to suppress work needs in the tourism industry. Border regimes not only allow the exploitation of people's labor, but also control social reproduction, that is, people's bodies and activities to preserve and reproduce life. The border is a site of harm for all people doing work that is criminalized, including sex workers, and mainstream feminism has a long and a problematic history of failing to recognize sex work as work and not supporting and fighting for justice for sex workers.

Migrant women are often structurally at the sharpest end of interconnected state-sanctioned and interpersonal violence and oppression. A feminism which proposes and fights for everyone's freedom must embrace the centering of migrant women's experiences and their struggles for life. This is why we speak of and call for a Feminist Border Abolition movement.

ENVISIONING BORDERLESS FEMINIST FUTURES

Currently, it may seem the world we want to live in is increasingly distant and unreachable, somehow fading away. The constant commodification of essential aspects of everyday life such as housing, health and food security is deeply linked to a deterioration of working and living conditions. Present-day capitalism can restrict our capacity for imagining different futures and enacting resistance. Against this backdrop, NGO-ized forms of feminism have oftentimes become (or been forced to become) more focused on maintaining the current system than producing any form of transformative change.[35] Yet we believe that a border abolition feminism vision is about hope. To find this hope, and nurture our radical creativity, we focus on the localized, often small-scale experiences that are happening right now, which center their organizing capacity in day-to-day activities. Material and economic limitations, while grinding and often deadly, also pose opportunities for building solidarity and fight-back.

As discussed above, resistance is largely led by grassroots communities targeted by border enforcement laws designed to impoverish, control, and surveil them. Resistance is often organized around material everyday needs and not always conceptualized as political or abolitionist; although we would argue it is border abolition feminism in action. There are also politically organized groups resisting the border regime and its violent ramifications. *Action Against Detention and Deportations*,[36] for instance, is a UK-based coalition of groups and individuals committed to ending detention, deportations, and the wider "hostile environment" against people racialized as migrants and non-citizens. It is a grassroots network which centers on mutual care and provides a platform for people of color, queer people, and migrant activists to lead the struggle.

Resistance is local and international at the same time. We celebrate and learn from experiences and communities of resistance around the world. As Elahe recounts, in Nauru, both inside and outside of detention, women worked together and campaigned for all the illegally incarcerated refugees (women, men, gender non-conforming people, unaccompanied minors and families) to be released.[37] Women led, organized, and succeeded in this campaign against border governmentality. Despite very limited support from a small number of organizations, detained women succeeded in securing freedom for some families in Nauru. The government of Australia became aware of the power of feminism in action and feared the increased media attention on this site of border violence; as a result, many were released – in particular women and children. By removing women's voices from the discourse about protests from Nauru, the state and media once again muted resistance, but as border abolition feminists we will not allow this state violence to be forgotten. We need to put an end to this form of incarceration, once and for all.

Imagining different feminist borderless futures means embracing the struggles led by those at the sharp end of violent border regimes and state-sanctioned intersectional oppression. This involves embracing Indigenous, decolonial, Black and trans-feminist struggles and absorbing inspiration from the ways that intersectional and abolitionist feminisms and queer politics produce transformative changes. For example, Jineology, a radical analytical feminist framework utilized in the Kurdish political project, was inspired by Black and anti-colonial feminisms that aimed to politicize grassroots women.[38] Kurdish women have been at the forefront of creating infrastructures and organizing communities, working toward building schools, libraries, academies, and cooperatives, and promoting principles of feminist economy. They have also been promoting a new justice system aiming to abolish punishment and working toward abolishing the police. In Latin America, inspired by the Indigenous peoples of the region, the *buen vivir* movement advocates for a way of living based on communal practices and care, respect for all human beings and harmony with Mother Earth, without borders.[39] The movement struggles for diversity, life, and the equality of redistribution and has been an important impetus for resistance within the anti-extractivist movements in South America. In South Africa, the Xhosa philosophy of Ubuntu stresses the importance of the collective, the wellbeing of one human being is deeply rooted in the wellbeing of another human being and the wellbeing of the community.[40] These examples offer different routes into the border abolition feminism project, for as Ruth Gilmore argues, this task is to build "the future from the present, in all ways we can."[41]

Small groups and communities that self-organize themselves and little by little build alternative worldviews, are the central sites where the political project of border abolition feminism is unfolding and flourishing. By coming together we imagine, and at the same time enact, a borderless feminist future, a future where we can all live free from violence and incarceration, a future where we can all thrive. It is in these organizing processes, sometimes messy, almost always joyful, that we believe the revolutionary potential of our movement lies.

NOTES

1. Authors' names are reported in alphabetical order.
2. A. Davis, G. Dent, E. Meiners, and B. Richie, *Abolition. Feminism. Now. Abolition*. Chicago: Haymarket Books, 2022, p. ix.
3. Ibid.
4. The panellists comprised Francesca and Sarah, who are scholars and activists engaged in both feminist movements and no-border/anti-detention struggles in the UK, Italy, and Portugal; Vânia who has a long history of involvement in the internationalist feminist movement and works as a community advocate supporting migrant women surviving gendered violence in the UK; Aminata, who brings expertise from organizing, public speaking, and sharing visions on the violence of the detention and deportation regime informed by her experience inside Yarl's Wood detention centre in Bedford (UK); Leah who writes on state violence and works at an advice centre that supports migrant families with No Recourse to Public Funds (NRPF) in England; Elahe who shared her powerful artwork which, building on her experience of detention by the Australian government, explores some of the creative, joyful, and everyday ways that women in Nauru immigration detention centre resist their oppression; and, finally, Myrto and Anna, who are co-directors of the The Feminist Autonomous Centre for research, a community-based research centre in Athens which organizes an annual Feminist No Borders Summer School and is a key space of transnational feminist autonomous knowledge production.

5. B. Anderson, N. Sharma, and C. Wright, "Editorial: Why No Borders?" *Refuge*, 26(2), 2009: 5.

6. Critical Resistance. "What is Abolition?" http://criticalresistance.org/about/not-so-common-language/ (no date)

7. C. Robinson, *Black Marxism: The Making of the Black Radical Tradition*. London: Zed Press, 1983.

8. J. Melamed, *Represent and Destroy: Rationalizing Violence in the New Racial Capitalism* (New ed.). University of Minnesota Press, 2011. doi: 10.5749/j.ctttsrj6

9. S. Lewis, *Abolish the Family: A Manifesto for Care and Liberation*. London: Verso, 2022.

10. Anderson, Sharma, and Wright, "Editorial: Why No Borders?", 5 .

11. N. El-Enany, *Bordering Britain: Law, Race and Empire,* 1st edition. Manchester: Manchester University Press, 2020.

12. M. Lugones, "The Coloniality of Gender." *Worlds and Knowledges Otherwise* 2, 2008: 1–17.

13. www.theguardian.com/world/2023/feb/27/italy-shipwreck-more-bodies-pulled-from-sea-calabria

14. A. Lindberg, *Deportation Limbo. State Violence and Contestations in the Nordics.* Manchester: Manchester University Press, 2022.

15. L. de Noronha, "Deportation, Racism and Multi-Status Britain: Immigration Control and the Production of Race in the Present." *Ethnic and Racial Studies* 42(14), 2019: 2413–2430; M. Smith and J. Mac, *Revolting Prostitutes: The Fight for Sex Workers' Rights*. London: Verso, 2018; N. Yuval-Davis, G. Wemyss, and K. Cassidy, "Everyday Bordering, Belonging and the Reorientation of British Immigration Legislation," *Sociology*, 52(2), 2018: 228–244.

16. E. Rigo, & F. De Masi, "Fighting Violence across Borders: From Victimhood to Feminist Struggles." *South Atlantic Quarterly*, 118(3), 2019: 670–677; see also Non Una di Meno. Abbiamo un piano. Piano femminista contro la violenza maschile sulle donne e la violenza di genere (We Have a Plan: Feminist Plan to Combat Male Violence Against Women and Gender-Based Violence), 2017.

17. INCITE, *Color of Violence, The INCITE! Anthology*. Durham; London: Duke University Press, 2006.

18. www.standard.co.uk/news/uk/jamaica-deportation-rape-crime-murder-home-office-immigration-b138825.html

19. A. Davis, *Are Prisons Obsolete?* New York: Seven Stories Press, 2003.

20. www.bbc.co.uk/news/uk-england-merseyside-64689140

21. Goodfellow, M. *Hostile Environment: How Immigrants Became Scapegoats*. London: Verso, 2019.

22. Ibid., 14.

23. G. R. Mehrotra, E. Kimball, and S. Wahab, "The Braid That Binds Us: The Impact of Neoliberalism, Criminalization, and Professionalization

on Domestic Violence Work." *Affilia*: 31(2), 2016, pp. 153–163; INCITE! Women of Color Against Violence (Ed.), *The Revolution Will Not Be Funded: Beyond the Non-Profit Industrial Complex*. Durham; London: Duke University Press, 2007.

24. Ibid., 22.
25. Esposito, F. *International Women's Day 2021: The Gendered Harms of Detention: Celebrating the IWD by Supporting Anti-Detention Struggles*, 2021. https://blogs.law.ox.ac.uk/centres-institutes/centre-criminology/blog/2021/03/international-womens-day-2021-gendered-harms; Canning, V. *Gendered Harm and Structural Violence in the British Asylum System*. London: Routledge, 2017.
26. Ibid., 24.
27. Ibid., 2 and 16.
28. E. Zivardar, "I Have Experienced Australia's Detention Policy First-Hand – It's Time To End It." *The Guardian*, 2022; E. Zivardar and M. Ghadiri, "Journalism, Borders and Oppression: The Nauru Context." In B. Behrouz (author), O. Tofighian, and M. Mansoubi (Eds and Trans.), *Freedom, Only Freedom: The Writings of Behrouz Boochani*. London: Bloomsbury Academic, 2023; E. Zivardar (with M. Ghadiri), "Nauru Imprisoned Exiles Collective." In: R. Braidotti, G. Klumbyte, and E. Jones (Eds), *More Posthuman Glossary*. London: Bloomsbury, 2023, pp. 83–85; O. Tofighian, B. Boochani, Mira, and E. Zivardar, "Narratives of Resistance from Indefinite Detention: Manus Prison Theory and Nauru Imprisoned Exiles Collective." In: J. Bennett (Ed.), *The Big Anxiety: Taking Care of Mental Health in Times of Crisis*. London: Bloomsbury Academic, 2023.
29. www.theguardian.com/commentisfree/2023/jun/30/i-know-firsthand-the-torture-of-offshore-detention-how-can-labor-maintain-such-a-racist-system
30. E. Zivardar and O. Tofighian, "The Torture of Australia's Offshore Immigration Detention System." *OpenDemocracy*, March 16, 2021. www.opendemocracy.net/en/beyond-trafficking-and-slavery/the-torture-of-australias-offshore-immigration-detention-system/; E. Shakiba and O. Tofighian, "'Searching for Aramsayesh Gah' – A Film about Borders, Violence and Imagining an Abode for Serenity." *Border Criminologies Blog*, March 11, 2021. www.law.ox.ac.uk/research-subject-groups/centre-criminology/centreborder-criminologies/blog/2021/03/searching
31. Shakiba/Zivardar. "19th July." Southerly Writing Through Fences: Archipelago of Letters: 182; "Nameless." Southerly Writing Through Fences: Archipelago of Letters: 2021: 231–232.
32. E. Zivardar, "I Have Experienced Australia's Detention Policy First-Hand – It's Time To End It."

33. https://capiremov.org/en/experience/feministschool-state-and-democ-racy-are-battlegrounds-of-feminist-struggle/
34. S. Abusalama, "Women Revolt: Between Media Resistance and the Rein-forcement of Oppressive Gender Structures." *A Journal for Body and Gender Research*, 2, 2016.
35. Ibid., 22.
36. https://sites.google.com/view/no-deportations
37. E. Zivardar, "I Have Experienced Australia's Detention Policy First-Hand – It's Time To End It."
38. D. Dirik, *The Kurdish Women's Movement History, Theory, Practice.* London: Pluto Press, 2022.
39. K. Artaraz, M. Calestani, and M. L. Trueba, "Introduction: Vivir bien/ Buen vivir and Post-Neoliberal Development Paths in Latin America: Scope, Strategies, and the Realities of Implementation." *Latin American Perspectives*, 48(3), 2021: 4–16.
40. T. Metz, "Ubuntu as a Moral Theory and Human Rights in South Africa." *African Human Rights Law Journal* 11(2), 2011: 532–559.
41. M. Smith, *Abolitionist Assemblage: Compiling Fragmented Freedoms and Imagining the World Anew*, 2021. Abolition-is.com

3

Surplus people of the world unite!

On borders, policing, and abolition

Vanessa E. Thompson

Movements against borders and policing have entered into a new phase in and beyond Europe in the last decades. Various self-organized refugee, migrant, and anti-racist collectives, such as *Women in Exile* or the newly founded network *Abolish Frontex*, have formed transnational coalitions and networks that engage in border and police abolition as well as abolitionist worldmaking. In this chapter, I argue that these movements put surplus resistance as part of class struggle on the map: the resistance of precarious, wageless people and people rendered disposable, who are especially targeted by police and border violence as methods of racial capitalism. Engaging with the practices of some of these collectives, I argue that border and police abolition is crucial to the resistance against racial capital. These practices, as I demonstrate, also point to the international dimension of abolitionist resistance.

In the first part of this chapter, I lay out the function of borders and policing as methods to control people who are rendered surplus in this conjuncture of racial capital. The second section engages with the modalities of abolitionist resistances. Finally, I argue that these formations are part of an abolitionist transnational multitude that is central to the abolition of racial capitalism.

INTRODUCTION

Last June 24 was the one-year anniversary of the Melilla Massacre, in which 37 African migrants were killed by Moroccan security forces and the Spanish Guardia Civil and hundreds were injured. As many migrants who survived the massacre argue, it was a bloodbath,[1] a total neglect and abjection of human life. EU politicians, however, such as Spain's president, described the massacre as "an attack against the territorial integrity" of Spain,[2] thereby re-actualizing the figure of migration as one of the major threats to European integrity and sovereignty.[3] The recent drowning of about 600 people near the Southern Greek town of Pylos on June 14, 2023, is part of this logic of death, in which the Hellenic Coast Guard was actively involved.[4]

It is important to name these incidents of mass violence and murder not as an accident or mere shipwreck, but as actively produced premature death. These massacres, as well as the mainstream silence around these incidents of mass violence and border killings, are foundational to the current political crisis instead of an exception.[5] Abolitionist theories and politics are crucial to understand as well as to challenge this normalization, as they allow for a conjunctural analysis[6] of policing, border regimes, and racism, on the one hand, and on the other allow for the analysis of resistances and their transnational potential for building different worlds.

In the following, I discuss the function of borders and policing in this current phase of racial capitalism[7] and their relation to the control and management of people who are increasingly rendered as surplus, or redundant to the needs of racial capital and therefore disposable. Although the creation of a relative surplus population is inherent to racial capital, fulfilling the function of a reserve army that forces down the wage rate, it is no longer needed in the same way in this phase of neoliberal racial capitalism with its modes of automation and financial extraction. As a result, "the geographies of surplus and of disposable life are growing everywhere."[8] The former reserve army has migrated to disposability, to people who are no longer useful to racial capital. A majority of humanity is therefore rendered surplus. Police and borders are the methods to control, contain, concentrate and manage these populations, including through lethal measures. As I will show in this article, the production of so-called surplus populations (surplusification) operates through a specific form of racism, carceral racism. After this exploration, I turn to the modalities of abolitionist resistance against policing and borders in and beyond Europe by drawing on the work of the *Black Vests* in France, *Refugees in Libya*, and

Women in Exile. The practices put forward by these and related collectives present forms of surplus resistance that need to be conceptualized as multiple and beyond more classical notions of class struggle. The final part discusses these struggles as part of an abolitionist transnational multitude that is central to the abolition of racial capitalism.[9]

ON BORDERS, POLICING, AND THE ROLE OF CARCERAL RACISM

Policing as well as borders are not natural to human societies. They have not always been there but emerge in a specific time and place and have specific functions. Historically, they occurred to activate, protect, and ensure the sovereignty of (imperial) state authority through violence and coercive force. They furthermore played a crucial role in the creation and fabrication of racial capitalist relations and the control and management of the mobility of labor power.[10] Policing was first exercised in the form of laws and police science during the withering of feudalism in continental Europe. Through these and related violent measures the masses were separated from the means of production and then criminalized for their practices of survival to also recruit them into the capitalist wage relation as well as relations of less free and unfree labor – often structured through the technology of racism. Policing was thus crucial for the fabrication of the racial capitalist order of exploitation and dispossession.[11] Borders, as a shifting and flexible "regime of practices, institutions and discourses"[12] that organize im/mobility, labor and the hierarchization of exploitation of mobile labor forces, were similarly essential to the reproduction of capitalism as borders and their technologies such as passports controlled the movement of labor forces. In fact, the control and governance of mobile labor forces is crucial for all projects of domination and exploitation: Ranging from feudal lords restraining serfs to their land to work the land, European projects of (internal and external) enslavement and mass deportation to exploit forced and unfree labor to various forms of colonialism and the control of land and colonized populations,[13] or the management of temporary labor migration (often from the colonies or peripheries) after the Second World War.[14] Policing and bordering practices shaped these forms of exploitation through regulating who can move (or will be moved) and who needs to stay within colonial geographies. In early modern Europe, for instance, so-called vagabondage was criminalized to not only force people into wage labor but also to make them stay put. This affected especially Roma people who have been criminalized and brutalized in Europe for centuries.[15] Critical genealogies of (often explicitly racist) passport technologies such as the *Zigeungerkartei* ("gypsy" register) or *The Book of Negroes* provide earlier records of attempts to circumscribe Black and Brown people's mobility as part of the projects of dehumanization and exploitation.[16] Differential forms of labor exploitation and dehumanization throughout the history of racial capitalism were thus also operationalized through police and border power. "Police, prisons and borders operate through a shared logic of immobilization"[17] that is crucial for the workings of racial capitalism.

The specific articulations of policing and borders are contingent on time and space, especially in relation to racial capitalist dynamics that also change through collectivized struggles waged against them.[18] However, police and bordering processes continue to play an indispensable, albeit differentializing[19] role in the reproduction of the racial capitalist order and the management of labor power. As abolitionist scholars have long argued, carceral regimes must be analyzed in relation to societal conjunctures through attending to related but distinct social, political, economic and ideological contradictions that shape a specific period instead of viewing history simply as a series of repeated events.[20]

The contemporary conjuncture of borders and policing is embedded in the dynamics and crisis-driven relations since the 1970s, though technologies and practices of containment and violence that have, of course, much longer histories.[21] We are witnessing a complex convergence in which racist nationalism, migration regimes, and carcerality are reconstructed and expand against the background of the poly-crisis of capitalism that encompasses overaccumulation and labor, climate catastrophe, neo-imperialism and warfare, a crisis of mass displacement, care, and social reproduction.[22] As the abolitionist and Marxist geographer Ruth Wilson Gilmore argues in her analysis of the massive expansion of the prison system in the US, the mass expansion of the prison system is a congealing and logical (but not inevitable) result of and "response" to the idlefication and surpluses of labor, land, finance capital and state capacity.[23] She shows that major shifts in political economy during the 1970s related to de-industrialization, capital mobility, and "natural" disasters, produced a variety of surplus (people, land, finance capital, and state capacity) that were dealt with in certain ways. The crisis of Fordism in industrialized economies in the 1970s also enhanced various articulations of carceral/ security "fixes" in Europe.[24] This crisis and its neoliberal response of austerity, privatization and outsourcing can't be understood without attending to the adjustments of securitization and militarization, as Stuart Hall also argued in his profound UK-based analysis of the moral panic around mugging and the criminalization of Black under-employed and jobless youth as an articulation of the "policing of the crisis."[25]

Thus, the poly-crisis of racial capitalism has not only produced mass unemployment, precarity and increasing poverty but also strategies of a carceral and militarized management of the crisis on local and global scales.[26] Racial capitalism hinges on border and policing regimes to regulate its crisis and contradictions. These political as well as ideological methods are also put forward as a way of controlling and managing "surplus populations," those that migrated from the reserve army of labor to no longer having value for capital[27] and who are driven out of the production process.[28]

Against the background of surplusification and with regard to policing in Europe, we can observe an expansion of urban policing (and of the moral panics that accompany the carceral expansion), especially in impoverished, often racialized working class and working poor districts: from Berlin's Kreuzberg to the *banlieues* of Paris or Marseille, from London's Tottenham to the Bijlmer in Amsterdam, to Molenbeek and Schaerbeek in Brussels, and various other postcolonial European urban areas. This expansion unfolds as a state "response" to the crisis produced by racial capitalism as well as to the resistances of the late 1960s and 1970s, wherein migrant workers organized mass resistance to state racism, regimes of super-exploitation, colonialism and imperialism. The cycles of urban rebellions that are often a response to police killings of (post-)migrant working class and working poor youth like after the murder of Mark Duggan in Tottenham or recently after the murder of Nahel Merzouk in Paris, illuminate how the policing of the crisis is articulated in various urban European contexts. The function of policing in this conjuncture, besides protecting and ensuring the racial capitalist order and property relations, is the management and control of the under- and unemployed sections of the working class, often migrant, so-called refugee, and under-employed, and the criminalization of their means of survival, including breaking rules or trying to make ends meet in informal and criminalized economies.

However, as myself and others have argued elsewhere, the expansion of policing and securitization as part of a punitive turn to manage the urban poor and "dangerous underclasses," disproportionally racialized (including their potential for rebellions and survival tactics), can't be disconnected from the carceral and neo-imperial governance of migration and the neo-imperial externalization of borders.[29] In fact, domestic securitization and external militarization are two sides of the same coin and are often interwoven. As William Robinson argues, the repressive management of migration can't be separated from the formation of a global police state.[30]

Since the late 1970s in various European countries (among other countries in the Global North), we have seen an expansion of border fortification, deportation and detention regimes, the increasing tightening of asylum laws and neo-imperial border externalization policies and practices.[31] These developments unfold through complex arrangements of various (often conflicting) actors, ranging from political parties to transnational state apparatuses, geopolitical formations, NGOs, progressive movements, as well as pre-fascist and nationalist forces. Such developments are differential and more easily detectable through a focus on the hierarchization of the visa system or the borderless movement of capital and militaries; while the movement of the masses of poor and displaced people is restricted and/or controlled. Global border and migration management unfold alongside productive as well as repressive means. The inherent connections between the production and manufacturing of poverty, migration, control of mobility and criminalization are of course not new. What characterizes the current context, however, is the massive production of surplus lives and the over-determination as well as radicalization of carceral and necropolitical "responses" to surplus crisis.

In the current phase of racial capitalism, which hinges on carcerality and repressive transformation or what Jackie Wang calls carceral capitalism,[32] we need to also conceptualize the current dominant form of racism as carceral racism, that is, as I have argued elsewhere, a racism that operates through the processes of surplusification (instead of just operating through markers of biologistic conceptions of race or racialized markers of culture).[33] As critical scholars of race and racism have long argued, racism is neither simply an ideology nor simply a color phenomenon nor a phenomenon bound solely to the projects of European external enslavement and colonization. Rather, racism is a societal relation of hierarchization of (produced and naturalized) difference that is embedded in as well as co-constitutes the mode of value production and its means of domination and exploitation. As such, forms of (proto-)racism already operated as a material force in feudal Europe.[34] This neither implies that racism always operates in the same way or through the same markers (skin color, etc.), rather, it is historically contingent and context-specific. Nor does this imply that racism is a more important contradiction than capitalism. Quite the contrary, it actually helps to understand how racism and capitalism, racial capitalism, are co-constitutive and how racism shapes the nature of value production and capital accumulation. As Gilmore argues, "capitalism requires inequality, racism enshrines it."

Carceral racism is one of the current dominant forms of racism and operates not solely through the means of exploitation, but especially through the manufacturing and management of surplus, beyond skin color or the naturalization of culture. It is a racism that materializes and naturalizes those groups that are manufactured as disposable through the processes of neoliberal racial capitalism and its production as well as responses to crisis, such as mass impoverishment, surplusification, wagelessness, and precarization, and rationalizes the control, surveillance, and punishment of these groups. At the brunt end of carceral racism are the Black and Brown unemployed youth in the favelas, the *banlieues*, and ghettos, the illegalized migrant, the global and multi-racial house-less and homeless, the incarcerated and detained, the users of criminalized drugs, those who are accused of social fraud – groups that are produced as disposable through the logics of racial capitalism. It is the racism that kills, to echo A. Sivanandan. The racism that produces and deals with "the fastest-growing and most novel social class on the planet"[35] through modes of immobilization like warehousing and detention, through letting die and active killing. Carceral racism co-produces and structures modes of life and death within the current phase of racial capitalism in which an ever-increasing part of the working class becomes redundant.[36]

The increasing surplusification of humanity, the exclusion of billions of people from the socio-economic order, a result of the shifting modes of wealth extraction,[37] the mass displacement caused through war, neo-imperialism, climate catastrophe, and extractivism, and the carceral responses that accompany these processes, poses crucial questions to our understandings of resistance. In this conjuncture of surplusification, we cannot solely consider the mobilization of labor as the dominant form of class struggle based on the key role of the proletariat in the process of production. There are at least two reasons for this. The first is one of necessity when considering the growing population of surplus. The second is based on the crucial role of the marginalized sectors of the proletariat as well as the paupers, which many anti-colonial theorists have also emphasized. Also in this current phase, there are constant challenges to the racial capitalist order and its methods of policing and bordering, that is also why bordering and policing practices are not simply fortresses[38] and groups rendered surplus and criminalized are not simply victims. Paying attention to surplus resistances can help us to imagine the broadness and multiplicity of struggles against racial capitalism, its methods, and toward a new and different world.

SURPLUS RESISTANCE

People will always try to subvert (or resist) the violent conditions they find themselves in, and this includes the mass rebellions in urban areas globally, the struggles against extractivism and land theft, the flight and migration from war zones (in many senses of the word) and the movement toward other localities and futures. Since the Black rebellions in 2020, we have seen radical abolitionist organizing growing globally. In Europe, this organizing has its own specific and transatlantic historical legacy, ranging from struggles and rebellions against the plantation economy in European colonies such as Haiti and abolitionist solidarity in the colonial metropoles such as sugar strikes and the free-produce movement in France (which boycotted goods from slave labor) as well as the mill workers strike in 1862, where Lancashire mill workers stood in solidarity with enslaved workers on the US plantations as they refused to touch raw cotton picked by the enslaved. These seemingly fragmentary anti-colonial resistances against colonial capitalism, and the anti-colonial resistance formations in the colonial metropoles of Europe are part of the history of global abolition as well as demonstrate that abolitionist organizing has a long history in Europe as well.

Much of current abolitionist organizing within Europe stands in this tradition, while at the same time attending to the conditions of an increasing production of surplus populations against the background of neoliberal crisis and climate catastrophe, though an international approach can still be strengthened. What is important with regard to many of these radical formations is that they do not only challenge the murderous implications of reform or humanitarianism (better police, humane border or prisons), but also transform more traditional class politics by attending to surplus resistance. This means that they go beyond the organization of labor in the form of strikes or reductive class struggle, as labor exploitation is not the sole societal mechanism through which racial capital accumulates.

In France, the *Black Vests* movement's collective actions can be understood as accounts of surplus politics and resistance because they attend to and spring from the growing surplus classes. Inspired by the *Yellow Vests* movement, the *Black Vests* consists of several hundred undocumented migrant workers, mainly Black, and focuses on the conditions of undocumented racialized workers that occupy the lower strata of the workforce and bear the primary brunt of the expansion of the French carceral state. Some of their interventions include mass public acts such as the occupation of a terminal of the Charles De Gaulle airport in protest of deportations of illegalized and undocumented migrants. The further protest against the *Lager* (camps) system and detention centers. Their mobilizations also include struggles against horrific working conditions and union busting, and they organize for labor rights such as permanent contracts and decent wages, as their many protests and strikes in Paris show. On July 12, 2019, the *Black Vests* occupied the Pantheon in Paris with 700 people and demanded legalization, an end to their super-exploitation, decent work and wages as well as the right to housing for all. On their leaflets distributed at their claiming of the Pantheon, they stated:

> We don't just want papers, we want to break the system that also creates undocumented migrants. We must organize actions, occupations, demonstrations, strikes, blockades. We will only win the papers, the end of the prison-houses, dignified housing and wages for all and the destruction of the detention centers by force. Against racism and exploitation. For our dignity and our freedom.[39]

The *Black Vests* are not only fighting against borders or policing in a reductive sense, both methods of racial capitalism, but against the system that relies on these methods. They mobilize strikes and blockades of large corporations, thereby connecting the condition of super-exploitation to the production of people rendered surplus. They struggle against a system that puts profit over people, and functions through the production and exploitation of difference. In their demands and organizing against carcerality, for legalization, and for decent wages for all, we can see a move that characterizes many radical migrant workers' activisms as they connect struggles against carcerality with labor struggles from the perspective of the sub-proletariat, the marginalized and super-exploited sections of the working class-aspects which can't be separated for this segment of the global working class and working poor in the first place. Their emphasis on organizing actions, occupations, demonstrations, strikes and blockades speak to their multi-approach of surplus resistance, a multitude that opens rather than closes mass mobilizations and the varieties of class struggle. They further wage struggle against what they call the heart of French imperialism and its "plundering of Africa," Paris business district:

> Suez steals his water. Société Générale steals his money and finances the pollution of Africa with coal-fired power plants, Thales build the weapons with which they wage war. The same people who destroy our lives over there are waging war here.[40]

The direct emphasis on neo-colonialism as well as climate destruction shows that the *Black Vests* are mobilizing an encompassing abolitionist politics. In their squads and during their strikes, their blockades and actions, they further organize liminal structures of support and re-distribution, thereby also putting into practice how a different world could look through practicing it in the here and now.

These abolitionist liminal infrastructures are also crucial for the organizing of a feminist abolitionist group called *Women in Exile & Friends*.[41] Founded more than 20 years ago in Brandenburg, Germany, the collective started to engage in practices of police abolition and the abolition of detention centers as well as practices of transformative justice long before abolition gained renewed attention in 2020.[42] Organizing for the abolition of *Lagers*, policing, and borders, as well as struggling against sexualized and gendered violence within camps, and for access to health structures, work permits, wage justice and labor rights, *Women in Exile & Friends* shows clearly how state violence is connected to what Ruth Wilson Gilmore calls organized abandonment, and that abolitionist organizing must attend to these connections. They organize bus tours to *Lagers* in order to fight the isolation of people rendered refugees and to support them in building organizing structures. By also engaging in reproductive justice, they attend to the multi-directional violence that especially women and non-binary refugees are exposed to through the border and policing system. While this is often described as "care," *Women in Exile & Friends* and other abolitionist feminist collectives remind us, in the tradition of Third World Marxists Feminists, that care is also feminized labor, and should rather be collectively distributed instead of romanticized.

Mobilizing in *Lagers* in Germany, Switzerland and other countries, supporting rescue missions in the *Black Mediterranean*[43] and organizing collective health care, *Women in Exile & Friends* practices abolition as a transnational movement and presence. They see their work directly connected to the border system, not only because many had to flee themselves from conditions of war and catastrophe, linked to neo-imperial relations and capital accumulation, and survived crossing one of the most deadly border regions and surveilled carceral seascapes of the world, but because they understand that borders are flexible regimes that operate at the so-called outside as well as so-called inside of carceral geographies.

These forms of abolitionist organizing and struggle present surplus projects of resistance because they attend to the conditions of "surplus populations" ranging from displacement, criminalization of movement and migration, organized abandonment and super-exploitation. Their struggles are not limited to wage questions, but rather encompass the facets of exploitation and violence that surplus populations, often racialized and migrant, are exposed to in this conjuncture of carceral racial capitalism.

They do not only broaden the vectors of labor struggles but highlight the multiplicity of class struggle expressed in abolition. This approach to struggle against racial capitalism is in conversation with anti-colonial approaches. As Frantz Fanon once argued, "a Marxist analysis should always be slightly stretched when it comes to addressing the colonial issue."[44] For Fanon, this did not only concern the analysis of exploitation in the colonies and the function of colonialism for the constitution and reproduction of a capitalist world market, but also the analysis of coercive and brute violence as method, as well as the mapping of resistance. From a perspective of the colonial condition, he argued, the classical proletariat of the developed industrial capitalist societies, or even the marginalized colonized proletariat in the colonial cities, cannot be considered as the central forces of class struggle because in the colonies this does not make up the force that can be most resistant to colonial capitalism, and also because of the lack of industrialization as well as the closeness of the proletariat to the colonizing forces. Hence, he argues that the so-called lumpenproletariat in the colonies and the peasantry are the central forces of class struggle.

In a similar vein, though in a different stage of racial capitalism, Stuart Hall and his colleagues state in their analysis of the role of the Black working class and sub-proletariat, that due to the structural position of the racialized sub-proletariat, wageless and chronically unemployed, super-exploited, or highly precarious, they "have a critical political and ideological significance in terms of growing cohesion, militancy and capacity for struggle of the class."[45] They show that the politics of the Black sub-proletariat have never been able to function exclusively with the advanced industrial vanguard, or to develop exclusively around the point of production. In these struggles, the politicization of the unemployed and wageless became key factors for the mobilization against capital. Whereas Westernized Marxist approaches emphasize the role of the classical proletariat due to its position in processes of production as the source of surplus value and its power to disrupt the processes of production and profit generation, Hall and his colleagues, as well as various other Black radical scholars and organizers, recognize the power of the so-called underclasses in terms of mobilizing force as well as militancy.

When considering the expansion of wagelessness and pauperism, as well as the expansion of carceral techniques, the focus on the resistances of the so-called underclasses and the sub-proletariat, the ever-growing part of the population rendered surplus, becomes even more important. As the practices of the *Black Vests* and *Women in Exile & Friends* demonstrate, they do not only focus on labor organizing, but combine struggles of labor with struggles of people rendered surplus, who often cannot withdraw their labor, and therefore mobilize their bodies to disrupt capitalist infrastructures and flows (blockades and occupations), as well as the operation of its methods, such as a bordering and policing. A focus on just (nationalized) labor, though powerful, actually undermines the surplus power of an abolitionist multitude.

While these collectives are organizing within Europe, their work is also shaped by transnational dimensions, like the abolitionist work of collectives around detention centers and border regimes on the African continent demonstrate. The movement *Refugees in Libya* started mass protests in October 2011, when Libyan police and military forces raided many of the shelters in the Gargaresh area in Tripoli, home to many refugees and migrants. Thousands were detained and brutally beaten. The movement engaged in protest and blockading of the UNHCR after the mass raid and issued a manifesto soon thereafter. A passage from their manifesto reads:

> We are Refugees and we live in Libya.
>
> We come from South, East, Central, and West African countries, the Maghreb region, and the Middle East. We are fleeing from civil wars, persecutions, climate changes, and poverty back in our countries of origin. We were all pushed by circumstances beyond human endurance.
>
> We all had left our homes seeking a second chance for our lives and therefore arrived in Libya. Here we became the hidden workforce of the Libyan economy: we lay bricks and build Libyan houses, we repair and wash Libyan cars, we cultivate and plant fruit and vegetables for Libyan farmers and Libyan dining tables, and we mount satellites on high roofs for the Libyan screens, etc.
>
> Apparently, this is not enough for Libyan authorities. Our workforce is not enough. They want full control of our bodies and dignity.[46]

The movement makes clear the labor exploitation of people rendered surplus is mediated through brute violence and force. They further show that struggles against exploitation cannot be separated from struggles against the border system and modes of policing. As people are rendered surplus, displaced and forced to migrate, their struggle against the border system shows that the border is not only a labor regime, but a regime of premature death of the poor, who cannot exclusively organize around labor, but literally, by any means necessary as people rendered surplus. Linking these struggles transnationally, the movement has grown across different contexts throughout Northern Africa and across Europe. Refugees in Libya call for the evacuation to lands of safety, the abolition of detention centers and border regimes, the dismantling of neo-imperial externalization of borders and an end to the exploitation of migrant workers. Through organizing protests and campaigns, refugee support structures and solidarity marches, the movement draws on transnational mobilization to not only get the voices of those rendered surplus heard, but also to contribute to the transnational dimension of abolition.

ABOLITION AS SURPLUS MULTITUDES

In the last few years, we have witnessed an increase in abolitionist organizing around borders and policing, both methods of racial capitalism. As discussed above, much of this organizing addresses the struggle and resistance of relatively "surplus" populations: the wageless, the working poor, the criminalized, and those rendered idle. Against the background of the current stage of racial capitalism, radical organizing can no longer simply be reduced to the struggle of labor in a more classic sense as those rendered surplus, wageless, and idle have nothing to lose and everything to gain. Though it seems that this shrinks the power of the globally exploited, anti-colonial theories and struggles have shown that the resistance of the wretched of the earth must take many forms.

Abolition is thus in conversation with approaches that emphasize the heterogeneity of class relations and focus on the de-homogenization of the classical proletariat. I understand surplus abolitionist organizing as surplus multitudes. Michael Hardt and Antonio Negri define the global multitude of the poor as "multiplicity, a plane of singularities, an open set of relations, which is not homogeneous or identical with itself and bears an indistinct, inclusive relation to those outside of it."[47] Surplus multitudes, however, do not simply organize around different forms of labor, but combine economic as well as extra-economic forms of violence and abandonment.[48] Abolitionist surplus struggles draw on, as the *Black Vests* remind us, the multiplicity of struggle, the revolt, the blockade, the strike, the action, and the subversion. Putting these struggles in transnational relations more strongly, and strengthening the connections between the segments of surplusification, of those in the warehouses, the criminalized working poor districts, the jails, prisons and detention centers, the border scapes, the houseless streets, the cobalt mines, the gendered textile factories, the surrogacy homes, the abandoned farmlands, the reservations, those struggling to save the forests and seas in danger, would put into internationalist motion the creation of abolition worlds.

NOTES

1. www.theguardian.com/world/2022/jun/30/a-bloodbath-refugees-reel-from-deadly-melilla-mass-crossing
2. www.theguardian.com/world/2022/jun/30/a-bloodbath-refugees-reel-from-deadly-melilla-mass-crossing
3. Étienne Balibar and Immanuel Maurice Wallerstein, *Race, Nation, Class: Ambiguous Identities*. New York: Verso, 2011; Stuart Hall, Claus Critcher, Tony Jefferson John Clarke, and Brian Roberts, *Policing the Crisis. Mugging, the State and Law and Order*. London: Macmillan, 2013; Ida Danewid, "Policing the (Migrant) Crisis: Stuart Hall and the Defence of Whiteness." *Security Dialogue* 53(1), 2022: 21–37.
4. https://counter-investigations.org/investigation/the-pylos-shipwreck
5. Harsha Walia, *Border and Rule: Global Migration, Capitalism, and the Rise of Racist Nationalism*. Chicago: Haymarket, 2021.
6. Stuart Hall, "The Great Moving Right Show," *Marxism Today*, January 1979, pp. 14–20.
7. Neville Alexander, "An Illuminating Moment: Background to the Azanian Manifesto." In A. Mngxitama, A. Alexander, and N. Gibson (Eds), *Biko Lives! Contesting the Legacies of Steve Biko*. New York: Palgrave Macmillan, 2008, pp. 157–170; Cedric Robinson, *Black Marxism: The Making of the Black Radical Tradition*. Chapel Hill: University of North Carolina Press, 1983.
8. Ian Shaw and Marv Waterstone, "A Planet of Surplus Life: Building Worlds Beyond Capitalism." *Antipode* 53(6), 2021: 1788.
9. Parts of this analysis have been published in my previous work policing, breathing, and racial capitalism.
10. Mark Neocleous, *The Fabrication of Social Order: A Critical Theory of Police Power*. London: Pluto, 2000; Walia, *Border and Rule*; Radhika Mongia, "Race, Nationality, Mobility: A History of the Passport," in *After the Imperial Turn. Thinking and with and through the Nation*, ed. Antoinette Burton. Durham: Duke, 2003.
11. Neocleous, *The Fabrication of Social Order*.
12. Walia, *Border and Rule*, 35.
13. Ann Laura Stoler, *Duress. Imperial Durabilities in Our Times*. Durham: Duke University Press, 2016.
14. Fabian Georgi, "Toward Fortress Capitalism. The Restrictive Transformation of Migration and Border Regimes as a Reaction to the Capitalist Multicrisis." *The Canadian Review of Sociology* 56(4), 2019.
15. Giovanni Picker, *Racial Cities. Governance and the Segregation of Romani People in Urban Europe*. New York: Routledge, 2017; Rohit Jain, "Von

der 'Zigeunerkartei' zu den 'Schweizermachern' bis Racial Profiling."
In: Mohamed Wa Baile, Serena O. Dankwa, Tarek Naguib, Patricia
Purtschert, and Sarah Schilliger (Eds), *Racial Profiling. Struktureller Rassismus und antirassistischer Widerstand*. Münster: Transcript, 2021, pp.
43–65.

16. Giovanni Picker, *Racial Cities*; Simone Browne, *Dark Matters*. Durham:
    Duke University Press, 2015.

17. Walia, *Border and Rule*, 2021.

18. Gilmore, *Golden Gulag*; Cedric Johnson, *After Black Lives Matter. Policing
    and Anti-Capitalist Struggle*. London: Verso, 2023.

19. Browne, *Dark Matters*, 2015; Loick, *Kritik der Polizei*. Frankfurt: Campus,
    2018; Vanessa E. Thompson, "From Minneapolis to Dessau, from Moria
    to Tripoli, from the shores to the land and the sea: Global geographies of
    abolition" In: Menna Agha and Sara Salem (Eds), *Disembodied Territories Project*, 2022.

20. Hall, "The Great Moving Right Show."

21. Adam Elliott-Cooper, *Black Resistance to British Policing*. Manchester:
    Manchester University Press, 2021. Fatima El-Tayeb and Vanessa E.
    Thompson, "Alltagsrassismus, Staatliche Gewalt und koloniale Tradition." In: Mohamed Wa Baile, Serena O. Dankwa, Tarek Naguib, Patirica
    Purtschert, and Sarah Schilliger (Eds), *Racial Profiling. Struktureller Rassismus und antirassistischer Widerstand*. Münster: Transcript, 2021, pp.
    311–328; Pascal Blanchard, "The Colonial Legacy of French Policing."
    In: Jacques de Maillard and Wesley G. Skogan (Eds), *Policing in France*.
    London: Routledge, 2020.

22. Fabian Georgi, "Toward Fortress Capitalism."

23. Gilmore, *Golden Gulag*.

24. Fabian Georgi, "Toward Fortress Capitalism." Elliott-Cooper, *Black
    Resistance to British Policing*. Loïc Wacquant, *Punishing the Poor: The
    Neoliberal Government of Social Insecurity*. Durham: Duke University
    Press, 2009. Kendra Briken and Volker Eick, *Urban (In)Security. Policing
    the Neoliberal Crisis*. Ottawa: Red Quill Books, 2013.

25. Hall et al., *Policing the Crisis*.

26. Gilmore, *Golden Gulag*; William I. Robinson, *Global Capitalism and
    the Crisis of Humanity*. Cambridge: Cambridge University Press, 2014;
    Julia Sudbury, *Global Lockdown: Race, Gender, and the Prison-Industrial
    Complex*. London: Routledge, 2014.

27. Gavin A. Smith, "Selective Hegemony and Beyond-Populations With
    'No Productive Function.' A Framework for Enquiry." *Identities* 18(1):
    2–38.

28. Robinson, *Global Capitalism and the Crisis of Humanity*.

29. Walia, *Border and Rule*; Gilmore, *Golden Gulag*; Daniel Loick and
    Vanessa E. Thompson, *Abolitionismus. Ein Reader*. Berlin: Suhrkamp,
    2022.

30. William I. Robinson, "Accumulation Crisis and Global Police State," *Critical Sociology*; see also Georgi, "Toward Fortress Capitalism," 2019.
31. Harsha Walia, *Undoing Border Imperialism*. London: AK Press, 2013.
32. Jackie Wang, *Carceral Capitalism*. Cambridge: MIT Press, 2018.
33. Vanessa E. Thompson, forthcoming.
34. Robinson, *Black Marxism*, 1983; Balibar and Wallerstein, *Race, Nation, Class*, 2011; See also Satnam Virdee "Racialized Capitalism: An Account of its Contested Origins And Consolidation." *The Sociological Review*, 67(1), 2019: 3–27. Satnam Virdee, "The *Longue Durée* of Racialized Capitalism. A Response to Charlie Post." *Brookly Rail*, 2021. https://brooklynrail.org/2021/02/field-notes/The-Longue-Dure-of-Racialized-Capitalism-A-Response-to-Charlie-Post
35. Mike Davis, *Planet of Slums*. London: Verso, 2006, p. 11.
36. Ian Shaw and Marv Waterstone, "A Planet of Surplus Life: Building Worlds Beyond Capitalism." *Antipode* 53(6), 2021: 1790.
37. Ibid., 1788.
38. Sandro Mezzadra and Brett Neilsen, *Border as Method, or, the Multiplication of Labor*. Durham: Duke University Press, 2013.
39. www.thevolcano.org/2020/12/16/immigrant-self-defence-only-the-struggle-will-give-us-documents/
40. www.marxist.com/france-gilets-noirs-take-over-the-pantheon.htm
41. See *Women in Exile* in this volume.
42. www.women-in-exile.net/
43. S. A. Smythe, "The Black Mediterranean and the Politics of Imagination." *Middle East Report* 2018: 3–9.
44. Frantz Fanon, *The Wretched of the Earth*. New York: Groove Press, 1963.
45. Hall et al., *Policing the Crisis*, 284.
46. www.refugeesinlibya.org/manifesto
47. Michael Hardt and Antonio Negri, *Empire*. Cambridge: Harvard University Press, 2000, p. 103.
48. Gilmore, *Golden Gulag*.

4

#AbolishICE, #AbolishFrontex, abolish borders

Toward an abolitionist border study and struggle

Josue David Cisneros

In June of 2021, a coalition of activists and organizations across Europe held coordinated protests (including in Austria, Belgium, Canary Islands, Germany, Morocco, the Netherlands, and Switzerland) targeting the European border and coast guard agency Frontex. This coalition, organizing under the banner #Abolish-Frontex, released an "open letter" addressed to the EU goverment in Brussels criticizing the violent policing and detention of migrants by "Fortress Europe," and articulating the group's vision and demands:

> We don't want to see more lives lost at sea or in the desert; lives wasted in detention or in inhumane refugee camps. We oppose a world increasingly divided by fortified borders to protect the wealth of the rich from the desperation and righteous anger of the poor and oppressed. We believe in freedom of movement for all; in providing support and shelter for people on the move, and in working toward a world where people are no longer forced to flee their homes and can live where they choose to. In this context, Frontex cannot be reformed. It must be abolished.[1]

Over the next six months, #AbolishFrontex continued to hold direct actions and release further statements and policy analyses decrying the European Union's border and detention policies and calling for the abolition of Frontex and the freedom of movement of all immigrants.[2]

Three years earlier, in June of 2018, a similar call took shape in the United States: #AbolishICE (Immigration and Customs

54

Enforcement, one of the main US law enforcement agencies targeting immigrants). Emerging from networks of anti-criminalization and anti-deportation movements, #AbolishICE was popularized in 2018 in opposition to Trump's "zero tolerance" or "family separation" policy, and it also drew broad public attention during the 2020 Democratic presidential nomination campaign, helping to bring abolition into public consciousness.[3] In the words of organizer Tania Unzueta, the call to #AbolishICE – along with other slogans such as #AbolishCBP (Customs and Border Protection, the US border patrol agency) – is a "radical" and "abolitionist" demand "that no one should be subject to the harm of immigration enforcement."[4] As with #AbolishFrontex, the call to #AbolishICE has spurred protests and direct actions across the United States, helping movements to "connect local efforts to defund the police with the broader call to defund ICE and Border Patrol."[5]

#AbolishFrontex and #AbolishICE represent recent expressions of increasingly networked movements for the abolition of the border industrial complex that also recognize its connection to the prison-industrial complex.[6] Because of space, this chapter cannot provide a comprehensive discussion of these networks. However, these movements provide provocations for thinking about what an abolitionist approach to border studies and "no-border" activism could look like.[7] I write for border studies scholars and no-border activists from my position as a scholar of borders and migration who is also involved in activism for prison/police abolition and migrant justice. Abolition can serve as a framework for analysis, a radical horizon, and as praxis for border studies, creating a community of study and struggle that strives for the elimination of borders/bordering in all their manifestations.[8] Ultimately, an abolitionist framework reorients how we think about and study borders/bordering and redirects the objective and praxis of our work as a community of activists, artists, scholars, and writers.

BORDER STUDIES, NO-BORDER POLITICS, AND ABOLITIONISM

Formal studying and theorizing about borders, at least in the Western world, stems from the nineteenth century, in the context of colonialist nation-state borders and sovereignty. However, in the last 40 years, a critical, interdisciplinary field called border studies bloomed, as claims of a globalized and "borderless world" gave way to the reality of proliferating borders.[9] Border studies scholars emphasize that the border should be thought of as a place, practice, and perspective.[10] The border is a place of social division and space-making, where identity and belonging are created and delimited; it is a place where sovereignty is performed and made; and a place of division and expulsion as well as one of crossing and filtering.[11] Bordering *practices* draw social divisions and enact modes of racial and social governance, capitalist labor exploitation, and more.[12] These practices reach inside and beyond the nation-state's frontiers, and into the bodies and psyches of individuals.[13] As a *perspective*, the border attunes us to the margins, interstices, and liminalities of identity and power; and to the forms of connection, circulation, and culture that exist in the borderlands.[14] For example, the US–Mexico border is a place as well as a bundle of technologies and practices of social division and exclusion which produces racial-capitalist exploitation, yet it is also a space of contact and crossing that creates unique and hybridized border cultures and perspectives.[15]

There is an inherent anti-border politics of border studies expressed in a number of different ways, including libertarian calls for free and open borders, anarchist anti-state networks organizing against border controls, demands for status for all, and those who emphasize the "autonomy" and subjectivity of migrant movements and experiences.[16] Speaking of these various perspectives, my goal in this chapter is to push border studies and no-border movements toward an abolitionist framework. In a sense, abolition here serves as a crucial modifier, defining the scope and aim of no-border struggle and study, and linking it with the broader abolitionist movement.

#AbolishICE and #AbolishFrontex illustrate the degree to which anti-border politics increasingly embrace an abolitionist approach. This work inspires and is fueled by activist scholars such as Bridget Anderson, Nandita Sharma, Harsha Walia, and others, who increasingly clarify the stakes of an abolitionist approach to border studies and no-border politics. Drawing on this work, I argue that such an abolitionist framework necessarily reorients how we think about borders and deepens the praxis of border studies and anti-border politics. An *abolitionist* no-border study and struggle understands borders in relation to other forms of criminalization, dispossession, incarceration, and exploitation, which are necessary to the production and maintenance of racial capitalism. Furthermore, this approach provides a more focused critical and political praxis for anti-border theorizing and action; an abolitionist no-borders perspective calls not only for the end of borders but also the conditions that necessitate borders as a spatial and racial fix. Abolitionist perspectives also add specificity to no-border calls for "freedom of movement," noting that the freedom to move must interlock with the freedom to stay and to return to stolen lands as part of a "revolutionary" restructuring of our present world.[17]

AN ABOLITIONIST ANALYSIS OF BORDERS

The contemporary abolitionist movement stems at least as far back as the mid-twentieth century, though some scholars trace its roots even further to the transnational and networked movements for the abolition of slavery.[18] This movement posits abolition both as a radical horizon and as a praxis for challenging mass incarceration, criminalization, and the crises that engender them. In doing so, it also provides an analytic for understanding the role of prisons and policing within broader racial capitalism and colonialism. Abolitionism argues that carceral logics/institutions are the causes of violence rather than their solutions and that the only response is to dismantle these institutions and practices, not seek to reform them. "Carceral" is used here not just in the sense of police, prisons, and jails, but also more broadly as a reference to a kind of violence and containment integral to racial-capitalist and colonial statecraft. Abolitionist scholar and activist Dylan Rodriguez urges us to "imagine the U.S. prison not as a discrete institution, but, rather, as an abstracted site – or, if you will, a prototype – of organized punishment and social, civil, and biological death."[19] This recontextualizes carceral institutions like the prison (and, as we shall see, borders) within a broader legacy of "civilizational" regulation and violence, including land enclosures and vagabond laws, racial slavery, colonialism, internment, poor houses, psychiatric hospitals, and more.[20] In the neoliberal era, carcerality serves, to borrow from Ruth Wilson Gilmore, as a spatial fix to forms of organized abandonment and organized violence necessary for the maintenance of racial and colonial capitalism.[21] For example, "housing depravation" is a form of organized abandonment and organized violence (involving criminalization, vagrancy laws, gentrification) that is funneled through carceral institutions like policing, courts, and prisons.[22] Likewise, the immigration industrial complex – border policing, immigration law enforcement, immigration courts, detention – sits alongside the prison-industrial complex as an arm of racial-capitalist governance.[23]

Such an abolitionist framework pushes us to think of borders in both a more specific and a broader perspective than has recently been advanced in border studies. A tendency among some scholars has been to *expand* the border as an explanatory concept for the global/globalized world. For example, one recent self-professed *Theory of the Border* goes so far as to attempt to write the history of human civilization from the point of view of the border.[24] Yet the danger of expanding borders in this way is that it risks abstracting borders into "bio-ethno-social constants,"[25] ignoring everything that is most important about how borders function in the contemporary conjuncture. Balibar is right that "nothing is less like a material thing than a border," for it is not an ontological reality but rather a set of relations that structures labor, power, mobility, space, and being.[26] A competing tendency among border scholars is to *multiply* the border on ever-more mobile technologies and diffuse aspects of "everyday life," including biometrics, traffic regulation, environmental management, television, and pop culture.[27] This is an important move so long as it continues to understand these multiple everyday expressions of borders/bordering as part of the broader carceral landscape. Borders, like prisons, are a "spatial fix" for contradictions in capitalism, racial governance, and colonialism.[28] They create and manage crises through regimes of (im)mobility, displacement, and dispossession, ensuring the stability of racialized territorial governance and exploitable labor.[29]

Just as abolitionist writers and scholars remind us to distinguish carceral logics from the space of the prison, we must recognize the border as one of the "multifarious forms of boundaries that criss-cross the entire social body along the hierarchical lines of class, race, cultural difference," gender, ability, and more.[30] Just as prison abolitionists urge us not to take the bait and assume that so-called "criminal justice" systems are about preventing "crime," we should understand that border regimes are not really about managing human mobility, or at least are only concerned with doing so in the course of securing a much broader global system of racial and economic domination. As Canadian activist and scholar Harsha Walia writes,

> The border ... is less about a politics of movement per se and is better understood as a key method of imperial state forma-tion, hierarchical social ordering, labor control, and xenophobic nationalism ... [S]hared logics of border formation – displacing, immobilizing, criminalizing, exploiting, and expelling migrants and refugees – [are used] to divide the international working class and consolidate imperial, racial-capitalist, state, rul-ing-class, and far-right nationalist rule.[31]

#AbolishFrontex centers such an abolitionist framework on the European migration "crisis," linking the border policing of Frontex and "Fortress Europe" to broader legacies of colonialism and racial capitalism, and organizing around the recognition that EU borders create crises rather than responding to them. In their call to #AbolishFrontex, they argue that border regimes manage human mobility while securing a much broader global system of racial and economic domination.[32]

The #AbolishICE movement also exemplifies such an aboli-tionist perspective. For example, in a recent article entitled "The Immigrant Justice Movement Should Embrace Abolition," Silky Shah, the executive director of *Detention Watch Network*, explic-itly links calls to #AbolishICE in 2018 and to #defundthepolice in 2020 noting that "the criminal punishment and immigration enforcement systems are fully intertwined" through collaborations between ICE and "local police" to detain and deport immigrants, and through ICE "subcontracting" to use "empty prison and jail beds" as spaces for immigrant detention. Rather than accepting frames of illegality, national identity, or citizenship/membership, Shah productively resituates migration restriction and border control within the context of racial criminalization and white supremacy.[33]

A border industrial complex, analogous to the prison-industrial complex, involves multiple "public and private sector interests" invested in the maintenance and proliferation of bordering, the criminalization of migrants and refugees, and the caging and forced removal of people.[34] These include not only politicians and law enforcement agencies but also media conglomerates and think tanks that create moral panics around so-called "border crises," and private prison and security corporations that house migrants and refugees and provide technology and training for border enforcement from Mexico to Palestine.[35] In fact, I would note tangentially that carceral comes from the Latin word *carcer*, not just meaning prison/jail but also enclosure, illustrating that, even etymologically, the border is a technology of the carceral state and "the prison is itself a border."[36] This abolitionist analysis points to the vast network of carcerality within which border regimes are entwined and helps us to recognize and combat borders and other interlinked forms of human caging and immobilization.

AN ABOLITIONIST NO-BORDERS HORIZON

Border studies and no-borders struggles also need an abolitionist horizon, by which I mean both the telos toward which our work aims and the purpose that bounds and defines our perception and understanding of border struggles. Abolition functions as such a radical horizon for many activists and scholars because, to quote Rodriguez again, "it entails a radical reconfiguration of relations of power, community, collective identity, and sociality that does not rely on carcerality and its constitutive, oppressive forms of state and cultural violence."[37] This means, of course, dismantling structures of incarceration and global organized violence and abandonment. More broadly, however, abolition is also the building up of alternative structures and conditions that are life-affirming, where no one is disposable. In this sense, it entails alternative visions of community safety and accountability for harm that are not based on punishment or banishment but rather are transformative, creating healing for those harmed as well as those who harm, and addressing the conditions that lead to harm in the first place.[38]

As Mark Akkerman notes, #AbolishFrontex exemplifies such a horizon in their call for both abolishing the EU border regime and for "the building of a society where people are free to move and live." This entails not only an end to deportation and border policing but also health care, housing, employment, education, efforts to tackle climate change, and reparations for Europe's continuing colonialism and imperialism. Similarly, Walia writes that a specifically *abolitionist* no-borders politics "calls on us to transform the underlying social, political, and economic conditions giving rise to what we know as 'the migration crisis'" including "the brutalities of conquest, the voraciousness of capital, and the wreckages of climate change."[39]

Border studies and no-border movements often position free or autonomous movement as horizon – as the obverse of a world of borders. An abolitionist perspective enriches and complicates that horizon, taking it beyond the idea of free or autonomous movement, and pointing toward the necessity of "a global reshaping of economies and societies in a way that is not compatible with capitalism, nationalism, or the mode of state-controlled belonging that is citizenship."[40] As I have argued elsewhere, a better statement of this horizon could be, "Free to move, free to stay, and free to return," a slogan popularized by the Canadian collectives of the global radical network *No One is Illegal.*[41] The freedom of a no-border politics is something more than the freedom to move unrestricted, like the cosmopolitan frequent flyers of the global elite.[42] An abolitionist no-border politics struggles for "the freedom to stay and resist systemic displacement, the freedom to move in order to flourish with dignity and equality, and the freedom to return to dispossessed lands and homes."[43] An abolitionist horizon pushes border studies and no-border politics not just toward the critique of bordering practices and logics but also toward the end of broader structures that undergird this system of state-sanctioned caging and forced mobility.[44] The activist demand "freedom to move, freedom to stay, and freedom to return," points to a praxis of making connections and coalitions that link border struggles to other struggles against racial capitalism, settler colonialism, and the carceral state, which are the conditions that cause displacement just as much as immobilization.

THE PRAXIS OF ABOLITION

Finally, abolitionism provides a praxis for border studies and no-border struggles – a way by which our theories and knowledges are put into practice (which also feeds back dialectically on theory). Praxis here refers to an orientation toward research and political action that is engaged with and centers voices of the most affected communities, and whose goal is oriented toward community liberation and empowerment; it stems from the recognition that spaces of knowledge production and theorizing, including the university itself, are also sites of political struggle.[45] Abolitionist praxis provides a political program for all of those engaged in studying and resisting borders, in the academy and beyond, pushing us to disinvest from and dismantle the academic industrial complex and its relation to broader carceral regimes, such as through policing local communities or extracting their resources, contributing to securitization and militarization with research, or perpetuating carceral forms of pedagogy. According to the authors of "Abolitionist University Studies: An Invitation," this involves "reckoning with universities' complicity with a carceral, racial-capitalist society while creating an alternative, abolition university."[46] More specific to border studies, an abolitionist praxis pushes scholars to break down the borders between research and political activism, between the university and the community, and between objective knowledge production and subjective activism.[47]

Of course, a full discussion of the relationship between scholarship and activism is beyond this short chapter, but what this calls for is becoming what Gilmore calls "oppositional intellectuals," putting theory into practice for the liberation of those who are most subject to border and carceral regimes.[48] Concretely, such organic praxis might manifest in a number of ways, including funneling resources from our institutions to support abolitionist struggles and knowledge-making in affected communities; translating our no-borders scholarship into no-borders advocacy; and/or providing "abolitionist sanctuary" to those who are most subjected to the violence of borders.[49] Just as there are "carceral geographies" of borders and cages, including on our campuses and communities, so too are there "abolition geographies," or everyday spaces and experiments of living otherwise, which are happening all around us, including in the Sans Papiers and sanctuary networks, no-border collectives and hunger-striking migrants in detention, transnational activist networks such as #AbolishICE and #AbolishFrontex, and in the classrooms and study halls of university campuses.

Beyond the university, abolitionist movements provide a vibrant and extensive body of writings, campaigns, organizations, and experiments in study and struggle that can inspire our no-border activism. As discussed above, an abolitionist commitment highlights the importance of struggles that target borders and bordering within broader networks of carcerality and criminalization, rather than isolating border and migration issues from these broader struggles. Both #AbolishFrontex and #AbolishICE signal this networked praxis, targeting different nodes in the border and immigration industrial complex, from detention centers or local jails to arms and technology companies. During the No Border Camp 2022, the first week of August in Rotterdam, demonstrations targeted Detention Centre Rotterdam, airports, and companies that are shareholders in the EU border regime.[50] Likewise, *Detention Watch Network* pursues its abolitionist vision by seeking to shrink the size and scope of the carceral regime and to provide alternatives for detention. Many of their tactical demands – such as "ending family detention; ... phasing out private prisons to ICE private contracts; ... ending the use of expedited removal altogether; [and] fully ending the Migrant Protection Protocols" – demonstrate the aim of organizing against multiple nodes of the border/carceral apparatus.[51] Efforts to shrink the size and scope of these carceral regimes not only affect migrants and refugees but all of those who are criminalized and forcibly caged.

These movements also demonstrate the tactical lesson of distinguishing so-called "non-reformist reforms" from "recuperative reforms." The former are reforms that tear down carceral systems and build toward transformational change, whereas the latter do not center the most affected and/or legitimate and strengthen broader systems that we oppose.[52] Many abolitionists point to the fact that the modern prison was itself a recuperative reform and thus counsel against pushing for incremental changes that legitimate walls, cages, or criminalization.[53] For example, Shah (of *Detention Watch Network*) points to the limitations of efforts to achieve rights for immigrants or refugees by emphasizing their "worthiness" or distinguishing them from "criminals" or other "undeserving" members of the nation, arguing that this rhetorical strategy upholds logics and institutions of criminalization and racial management that legitimate bordering and immigrant incarceration.[54] An abolitionist praxis warns against these kinds of reformist tactics that sacrifice some people for the sake of incremental changes, demanding instead non-reformist struggles that resist borders and bordering practices *en face* and ensure that no one is made disposable.[55] As #AbolishFrontex member Taylor argued in a 2021 press release, "We are not asking for a better European migration policy: we are demanding the abolition of Frontex and the demilitarisation of the borders. And we are taking action to achieve this."[56]

A specifically *abolitionist* border studies and an *abolitionist* no-border politics are emerging in the transnational activist networks of #AbolishICE and #AbolishFrontex and in the recent work of activist scholars on whose work I have relied throughout this chapter. These networks of activists and intellectuals organized against all forms of carcerality call us to reassess how we understand and organize against borders and other forms of immobilization. Theory and praxis, study and struggle must go together here, for, as the old saying goes, the point of interpreting the world is to change it.

NOTES

1. "Abolish Frontex Open Letter." June 9, 2021. https://abolishfrontex.org/blog/2021/06/09/abolish-frontex-open-letter/
2. For further discussion, see Akkerman in this volume.
3. Nicole Narea, "How 'Abolish ICE' Helped Bring Abolitionist Ideas into the Mainstream." *Vox*, July 9, 2020. www.vox.com/policy-and-politics/2020/7/9/21307137/abolish-ice-police-immigrant-black-lives-matter

4. Tania Unzueta, "We Fell in Love in a Hopeless Place: A Grassroots History from #Not1More to Abolish ICE." *Medium*, June 29, 2018. https://medium.com/@LaTania/we-fell-in-love-in-a-hopeless-place-a-grassroots-history-from-not1more-to-abolish-ice-23089cf21711

5. Silky Shah, "The Immigrant Justice Movement Should Embrace Abolition." *The Forge*, March 4, 2021. https://forgeorganizing.org/article/immigrant-justice-movement-should-embrace-abolition

6. Tanya Golash-Boza, "The Immigration Industrial Complex: Why We Enforce Immigration Policies Destined to Fail." *Sociology Compass* 3(2), 2009: 295–309.

7. Akkerman in this volume.

8. The phrase "study and struggle" is borrowed from the Mississippi-based abolitionist collective of the same name. See www.studyandstruggle.com/

9. Thomas M. Wilson and Hastings Donnan, "Borders and Border Studies." In: Thomas M. Wilson and Hastings Donnan (Eds), *A Companion to Border Studies*. Hoboken: Wiley-Blackwell, 2012, pp. 1–25.

10. Corey Johnson, Reece Jones, Anssi Paasi, Louise Amoore, Alison Mountz, Mark Salter, and Chris Rumford, "Interventions on Rethinking 'the Border' in Border Studies." *Political Geography* 30(2), 2011: 61–69.

11. Étienne Balibar, "What is a Border?" In: *Politics and the Other Scene*. London: Verso, 2002, pp. 75–86; Barbara J. Morehouse, "Theoretical Approaches to Border Spaces and Identities." In: Barbara Morehouse, Vera Pavlakovich-Kochi, and Doris Wastl-Walter (Eds), *Challenged Borderlands: Transcending Political and Cultural Boundaries*. Farnham: Ashgate, 2004, pp. 19–39.

12. Maribel Casas-Cortés et al., "New Keywords: Migration and Borders." *Cultural Studies* 29(1), January 2, 2015: 55–87. doi: 10.1080/09502386.2014.891630; Harsha Walia, *Border and Rule: Global Migration, Capitalism, and the Rise of Racist Nationalism*. Chicago: Haymarket, 2021, Chapter 4.

13. Kent A. Ono, "Borders That Travel: Matters of the Figural Border." In: D. Robert DeChaine (Ed.), *Border Rhetorics: Citizenship and Identity on the US-Mexico Frontier*. Tuscaloosa: University of Alabama Press, 2012, pp. 19–25; Reece Jones and Corey Johnson, "Where Is the Border?" In: Reece Jones and Corey Johnson (Eds), *Placing the Border in Everyday Life*,. Routledge, 2016, pp. 18–31.

14. Mary Pat Brady, "Border." In: Bruce Burgett and Glenn Hendler (Eds), *Keywords for American Cultural Studies*. New York: NYU Press, 2007, pp. 29–32; José David Saldívar, *Border Matters: Remapping American Cultural Studies*. Berkeley: University of California Press, 1997.

15. Gloria Anzaldúa, *Borderlands/La Frontera: The New Mestiza*, San Francisco: Spinsters/Aunt Lute, 1987; Nicholas De Genova, "Borders, Scene and Obscene." In: Thomas M. Wilson and Hastings Donnan (Eds), *A*

Companion to Border Studies,. Chichester: Wiley-Blackwell, 2012, pp. 492–504.

16. See Harald Bauder, "The Possibilities of Open and No Borders," *Social Justice* 39(4), 2012: pp. 76–96; Reece Jones (Ed.), *Open Borders: In Defense of Free Movement.* Athens: University of Georgia Press, 2019.

17. Bridget Anderson, Nandita Sharma, and Cynthia Wright, "Why No Borders?" *Refuge* 26(2), 2009: 11–12.

18. Angela Y. Davis, *Are Prisons Obsolete?* New York: Seven Stories Press, 2011, ebook.

19. Dylan Rodriguez, "(Non) Scenes of Captivity: The Common Sense of Punishment and Death." *Radical History Review* 96, 2006: 9.

20. Dylan Rodríguez, "Abolition as Praxis of Human Being: A Foreword." *Harvard Law Review,* 132, 2018: 1587; see also Robert T. Chase (Ed.), *Caging Borders and Carceral States.* University of North Carolina Press, 2019.

21. Ruth Wilson Gilmore, *Golden Gulag: Prisons, Surplus, Crisis, and Opposition in Globalizing California.* University of California Press, 2007.

22. Charmaine Chua, "Abolition Is a Constant Struggle: Five Lessons from Minneapolis." *Theory & Event,* 23(5), 2020: 133.

23. Kelly Lytle Hernández, "Amnesty or Abolition." *Boom,* 1(4), November 1, 2011: 54–68. doi: 10.1525/boom.2011.1.4.54; James W. Kilgore, *Understanding Mass Incarceration: A People's Guide to the Key Civil Rights Struggle of Our Time.* The New Press, 2015, Chapter 5.

24. Thomas Nail, *Theory of the Border.* Oxford: Oxford University Press, 2016.

25. Vladimir Kolossov and James Scott, "Selected Conceptual Issues in Border Studies." *Belgeo: Revue Belge de Géographie* 1, 2013, https://journals.openedition.org/belgeo/10532, para. 40.

26. Balibar, "What is a Border?," 81.

27. Corey Johnson and Reece Jones (Eds), *Placing the Border in Everyday Life.* New York: Routledge, 2014.

28. Walia, *Border and Rule,* 14; see also Brenda Chalfin, "Border Security as Late-Capitalist 'Fix.'" In: Thomas M. Wilson, and Hastings Donnan (Eds), *A Companion to Border Studies.* Chichester: Wiley-Blackwell, 2012, pp. 283–300; Jones and Johnson, "Where Is the Border?," 8.

29. Jenna M. Loyd, Matt Mitchelson, and Andrew Burridge, "Introduction: Borders, Prisons, and Abolitionist Visions." In: Jenna M. Loyd, Matt Mitchelson, and Andrew Burridge (Eds), *Beyond Walls and Cages: Prisons, Borders, and Global Crisis.* Athens: University of Georgia Press, 2013, p. 2.

30. Charles Heller, Lorenzo Pezzani, and Maurice Stierl, "Toward a Politics of Freedom of Movement." In: Reece Jones (Ed.), *Open Borders: In Defense of Free Movement.* Athens: University of Georgia Press, 2019, p. 77.

31. Walia, *Border and Rule,* 1–2, 6–7.

32. "Abolish Frontex: End the EU Border Regime." 2021. https://abolish frontex.org/wp-content/uploads/2021/06/ENG_Abolish-Frontex-demands.pdf; see Akkerman in this volume.

33. Shah, "The Immigrant Justice Movement Should Embrace Abolition."

34. Golash-Boza, "The Immigration Industrial Complex," 296.

35. See, for example, Todd Miller, *Empire of Borders: The Expansion of the US Border Around the World.* London: Verso, 2019, ebook.

36. Angela Davis and Gina Dent, "Prison as a Border: A Conversation on Gender, Globalization, and Punishment." *Signs: Journal of Women in Culture and Society* 26(4), July 2001: 1236.

37. Rodríguez, "Abolition as Praxis of Human Being," 1612.

38. Jenna M. Loyd and Ruth Wilson Gilmore, "Race, Capitalist Crisis, and Abolitionist Organizing: An Interview with Ruth Wilson Gilmore, February 2010." In: Jenna M. Loyd, Matt Mitchelson, and Andrew Burridge (Eds), *Beyond Walls and Cages: Prisons, Borders, and Global Crisis.* Athens: University of Georgia Press, 2012, pp. 42–54.

39. Walia, *Border and Rule*, 213–214.

40. Anderson, Sharma, and Wright, "Why No Borders?," 12.

41. Josue David Cisneros, "Free to Move, Free to Stay, Free to Return: Border Rhetorics and a Commitment to Telos." *Communication and Critical/ Cultural Studies* 18(1), 2021: 96.

42. Ibid.

43. Harsha Walia, *Undoing Border Imperialism.* Oakland: AK Press, 2014, p. 77.

44. Jenna M. Loyd, "Prison Abolitionist Perspectives on No Borders." In: Reece Jones (Ed.), *Open Borders: In Defense of Free Movement.* Athens: University of Georgia Press, 2019, 94; see also Andrew Burridge, "'No Borders' as a Critical Politics of Mobility and Migration," *ACME: An International Journal for Critical Geographies* 13(3), 2014: 463–470.

45. William G. Tierney and Margaret W. Sallee, "Praxis." In: Lisa M. Given (Ed.), *The SAGE Encyclopedia of Qualitative Research Methods.* London: SAGE, 2008. doi: 10.4135/9781412963909

46. Abigail Boggs, Eli Meyerhoff, Nick Mitchell, and Zach Schwartz-Weinstein, "Abolitionist University Studies: An Invitation." *Abolition Journal*, August 28, 2019. https://abolitionjournal.org/abolitionist-university-studies-an-invitation/

47. Bryan J. McCann, "Borders of Engagement: Rethinking Scholarship, Activism, and the Academy." In: JongHwa Lee and Seth Kahn (Eds), *Activism and Rhetoric: Theories and Contexts for Political Engagement.* London: Routledge, 2019, pp. 18–19.

48. Ruth Wilson Gilmore, *Abolition Geography: Essays Towards Liberation.* London: Verso, 2022, p. 87.

49. A. Naomi Paik, *Bans, Walls, Raids, Sanctuary: Understanding US Immigration for the Twenty-First Century.* Berkeley: University of California

Press, 2020, Chapter 4. For examples of this work, see Sandro Mezzadra, "Abolitionist Vistas of the Human. Border Struggles, Migration and Freedom of Movement." *Citizenship Studies*, 24(4), May 18, 2020: 424–440; A. Naomi Paik, "Universities, Unjust Law, and Campus Sanctuaries." *Departures in Critical Qualitative Research* 9(1), 2020: 95–100.

50. Documentation of No Border Camp 2022 is available at https://nobordercamps.eu

51. Bob Libal, Setareh Ghandehari, and Silky Shah, "Communities Not Cages: A Just Transition from Immigration Detention Economies." *Detention Watch Network Report*, 2021. www.detentionwatchnetwork.org/sites/default/files/reports/Communities%20Not%20Cages-A%20Just%20Transition%20from%20Immigration%20Detention%20Economies_DWN%202021.pdf

52. Popularized in the context of abolition by Ruth Wilson Gilmore, the concept's origins are drawn from French labor theorist André Gorz. Gilmore, *Golden Gulag*, 242.

53. See Davis, *Are Prisons Obsolete?*

54. Shah, "The Immigrant Justice Movement Should Embrace Abolition."

55. See Reina Gossett, Dean Spade, and Hope Dector, "No One is Disposable: Everyday Practices of Prison Abolition." *Barnard Center for Research on Women*, February 7, 2014, video. https://bcrw.barnard.edu/no-one-is-disposable/

56. "With Actions in Eight Countries a New International Movement Rises to 'Abolish Frontex.'" Press Release, June 10, 2021. https://abolishfrontex.org/wp-content/uploads/2021/06/PR-10June2021-2.pdf

5

"For Black immigrants, it's a different America"

An interview with *Black Alliance for Just Immigration*

What is the Black Alliance for Just Immigration?

Abraham Paulos for BAJI: At the *Black Alliance for Just Immigration* (BAJI) we fight for the rights of Black migrants and African Americans. We do this through legal work, organizing, advocacy, policy, and some narrative building. We try to advance racial justice and migrant rights at the same time. We've been around since 2006 and BAJI has organizers in New York, Miami, LA, and Atlanta. So, we do local work in those spaces. We're headquartered out of Brooklyn and that's where I'm at.

Could you talk a bit about the general perception of migration in the US and how BAJI challenges that in terms of shifting people's understanding of who is a migrant and how that plays out along racial lines?

BAJI: The US has a very funny history around migrants and, first off, shout out to the Indigenous community that was here from the start. I think when people think of immigrants it was mostly white people coming from Europe and that was actually the case for a very long time with the exception of people from Mexico – we always say a lot of the country *was* Mexico.

The biggest shift that happened was Black people in this country: African Americans, challenging white supremacy through the Civil Rights Movement. So, in 1965, the Voting Rights Act came out, but also what was called the Immigration Act of 1965 – and what it did is that it leveled the playing field for people to come from outside of the United States. In 1965 about 80 percent of immigrants were white people from Europe but by the 1970s and 1980s it flipped and about 80 percent of immigrants coming to the country were Black and Brown people coming from Africa, Asia, Central and South America. Black people coming into this country was a recent phenomenon – recent meaning in the last like six decades. That was one transition that happened.

The second is that most people have the idea that immigration is primarily a Latinx issue, and for good reason: they took Mexico. Up to a certain moment, this is true, because Black people weren't coming. We weren't coming during Jim Crow. There was no way that Black people were like, "We saw the Civil Rights newsreels, sign us up." I was born in Sudan and my family came in the 1980s. There were probably about 800,000 Black immigrants from Africa and the Caribbean then. Today we're about 4 or 5 million. So, there's been a demographic shift in immigration. BAJI feels it's important to have a narrative around Black immigrants: we have a different story to tell. When you're looking at Europeans and even to a certain extent to the Latinx community, there's a narrative around assimilating into America or the American dream. All of that is whiteness. For Black immigrants, it's a different America. We are here, moving through Black America, which is a different kind of conversation and that conversation I think is different on a couple of levels, especially around citizenship.

When people think about immigration rights many think of it as a recent sort of phenomenon like in the 1980s with the Immigration Responsibility Act and former president Ronald Reagan's amnesty which legalized many people who arrived before 1982. For us this whole idea of citizenship started with Black people being forcibly brought here (slavery) but also with the 14th Amendment which says that if you are born in the US, you are a US citizen. So, we find that the fight for citizenship in this country did not start with Reagan but is actually a 300- or 400-year-old fight. That's a fundamental difference that we see citizenship as a different kind of issue.

Finally, people might look at immigration frequently as a Latinx issue, but when we look at deportations and detention we realize that it is a very Black issue. Seventy-six percent of Black people get deported because of contact with the criminal system.

Overrepresentation in detention and deportation and anti-Blackness holds true for immigrant populations as well, correct?

BAJI: Absolutely because it involves law enforcement. When you have law enforcement and a racist country like the US, it's going to ensnare mostly Black people. Eighty-eight percent of Jamaicans get deported because of contact with the criminal system. Our Black immigrant experience is centered around the police state that the US has already built up where Black women are held longer, bonds are higher, and Black migrants are thrown in solitary confinement a lot longer.

Let's switch from the carceral state to its abolition. How do you all think about abolition and how has it shaped your political practice and ideas around border abolition?

BAJI: Let me start with abolition and BAJI and then I'll address border abolition. BAJI started doing detention work and seeing that this is horrible, partly because it's so administrative. You don't get a lawyer but you are stuck in the legal system. The conditions are fucking terrible. And then we got to a point where we asked ourselves: Why are people even being locked up? Why not just send a letter and tell people to show up in court? Which is what they used to do. So, we saw this bal- looning happening with mass incarceration and detention and then we got to a point where we decided we didn't want any detention. We were focused around immigration detention and we were challenged on that. Because then folks that work against mass incarceration asked: What about regular prisons, the county, state and feds? And we were like "Damn actually, we got to think about this a little longer." We're like "Yo, 86% of these cats are actually innocent, haven't been convicted!" and then we started talking about the violence: "What about violent offenders and what have you?" and so I think we just came to a point. We were like "No matter what the problem is, locking somebody up is not a solution." It's just not. There is not a legit problem that throwing a cage over someone is an answer for.

So, we got there through that road and that's when we started calling ourselves abolitionists. We got there by understanding that we want solutions to problems and by understanding that resources are the issue: to make sure that Black people and Black communities have the resources to be able to have a dignified life.

This leads to abolition and borders. We started using the term state violence and it's like "What the fuck is the state?" And then it was like "Well, what's a border?" I think that was our road to abolition. We don't believe in open borders, we believe in no borders. We got checked on that too. You know, there's a lot of smart people in BAJI and they were like "What do you mean when you say open borders – what about no borders, like the dismantling of them?"

For us the starting point was "What is a border?" I went all the way back to the Treaty of Westphalia. Most people are like "I don't need to know about that," but it's important because it's 1648. Only a couple hundred years after Columbus pulled up and the Treaty of Westphalia was trying to solve a problem. The Thirty Years War or whatever it was right? That's a straight-up white people problem. So, we were like: "From the beginning borders were a solution white people came up with for a white-person problem." How the hell did this come to us? Answer: colonialism and the slave trade. We started understanding the history of borders. Let's take Africa, for instance. Every border in Africa was made by Europeans. In 1884 at the Berlin Conference, nobody Black was there and if they were, they were working, not talking. This was a decision made without us. During the African Liberation Movement in the 1960s, part of the conversation was "What are we going to do about these borders?" They're not ours. We're fighting over them. The African Union got together and there were two camps: one was like "We're just gonna destroy the borders and start all over" and then another camp was like, "Well, we might need to respect these borders." The fear was that if the borders weren't respected all hell was going to break loose and so they decided to respect the colonial borders. Even the term self-determination: every country had to go make an argument at the UN that we don't want to be occupied or colonized any more. I'm like "That wasn't self-determination!" In BAJI, that was part of the road to abolition. We also started having experiences on the US/Mexico border and saw that borders are the same there: an imposition. So, we said "We're abolitionists, we're gonna have this abolitionist approach to this issue. We don't need borders." Obviously, there's always going to be issues and things that have to be worked out. I just feel like if these motherfuckers were smart enough to make borders, I believe that they can work it out to live without them.

I'm wondering what you think some of the complications of border abolitionist organizing are? Either from your lived experience or from the kind of thinking and research that you've done.

BAJI: Great question. I think it's racism. Because if you think about it, what is a border? Who lives in a borderless world? With a United States passport you could go to a 190 countries almost visa-free. That passport is essentially a no-border passport. So, there is a version of no borders that some people are actually living already. So, what if we just ask for that? This idea that it's so complicated, well ... Even the idea of what a border is; when you look physically in certain places, if there is a road, it is obvious, but in a mountain range, who knows? To people who say it is complicated, I say how about the US passport? It is not that complicated. No borders just means freedom of movement.

The reason why somebody says I'm Nigerian and somebody says I'm Kenyan was because of a white person. The reason that there are Black people in Jamaica and Black people in Brazil and Black people in Colombia is because of slavery. The border didn't make us, the culture did. And sometimes people will say "What do you mean no borders? I'm this and I'm that." And it's like "Yeah, bro, but that's just your papers. Your papers say that and that's kind of all it is to me."

There are complicating factors here and one of them to note is resources and land. Indigenous people have been fighting for land. So, I think we got to check that. We have to discuss whether we are colonizing them again in one way or another and that is complicated. However, in terms of the mechanisms and structures for no borders, they already exist for some.

All this becomes more complicated with Black people. For instance, they gave that Silicon Valley Bank hundreds of billions of dollars in two days in 2023 when it needed a bailout. But when *we* ask for things, the answer is "Oh, it's complicated." They need to set up a whole office and go on a whole academic journey. And that's the complicated part race plays in all this, because why would they give Black people the freedom to move freely?

One last question. What does it look like to be doing abolitionist or border abolitionist work where you are and what are some of the difficulties and challenges of that?

BAJI: I think we all want to be a part of something, that's what makes us whole. I think organizing is talking to that part of our spirit as a human being. I want to be a part of something because there's a problem here and I want to address it, but I can only do it with other people. And so, you're like "What's the problem? What's the issue? Let's get some people together."

We organize those directly affected; so, we organize Black people. That is who we work with. We work with those who have been locked up, deported, or who are coming back because they have experienced the violence of a border. If someone has been locked up in a detention center or been shackled on a plane, then they understand what the border has done to them. It's a lot of violence. And the same for Africans, the violence has been detrimental. Organizing is one part of the healing process. It's to understand that as people, we've been through a lot of violence. We want to organize ourselves to stop the violence, to end the war on Black people. When I say the war, I mean prisons and border enforcement. And I didn't come up with that concept myself. The US Congress called it "the war on drugs," they called it "the war on poverty," "the war on terrorism." These are their words. They're letting us know how they feel about us. Although other folks might not see it that way, this is what these folks explicitly say in the halls of power!

Another example: when the Ukraine war started in 2022, the foreign minister was in the US and I remember a reporter asked them, "What do you need from the US?" and he was like, "Weapons, weapons, weapons." And it's funny because we go to City Council meetings in Miami, New York, or LA and that's all the police say: "We need weapons, weapons, weapons." The only difference is that one knows that they're in a war and the other one is trying to play games like they are not.

Organizing is a healing kind of vibe: it brings you back to your dignity. It brings back your awareness and you're only here for a small amount of time. Societies don't transform by themselves – societies are transformed by people going through a transformation. And that's abolitionist too, I am transforming from one thought and one person into another. And so once that one person transforms, they understand what a border actually is and it's easier for them to understand we don't need borders and get on this road to abolitionism, which is a journey, we understand that.

What are our challenges when it comes down to organizing those that are directly affected? First, we are fighting something that has endless resources. We are fighting something that we feel is more powerful than us. But we have to look at that and say "If we feel powerless, we're really not gonna win" and it's hard to feel anything but powerless when the border has been very violent for one way or another and for generations.

Even the 2023 war in Sudan is basically over a fucking border. That border was actually put there through the British protectorate back in the day and now they're fighting over it and whatever have you.

And so, I think that the challenge for us organizing is making sure that people feel that they're not powerless.

I think a challenge as an organizer in the no borders movement or even just in certain spaces of abolitionists is that they are sometimes low-key anti-Black. It's one of those things that we have to navigate. We want to get shit done. But in the US and also in Europe to a certain extent when you look at open-border academics these cats are mostly white. So that's a challenge. You think it would be easy: those that are denied freedom, know freedom the most. When Black people say "Rush the gates, rush the border …" it's a different vibe. I'm like "Yo, get on those boats. Fuck it." Either you realize that there really isn't a border or we're gonna make you realize that and one of the things that we always have is bloodshed, our bodies. When I heard about the Haitians stranded in Puerto Rico or the Haitians dying in the Atlantic Ocean in 2022, I felt like, "Damn that Atlantic Ocean is still eating up Black lives."

I think one of the challenges right now is to fight for our freedom. I don't even think we need allies right now, I think we need family and friends. Because in that type of relationship there's communication, there's honesty and there's trust. An example is what happened last year at the Del Rio bridge crossing between the US and Mexico where a mass of Black migrants had camped out in Mexico. And it was like, "Okay, now we are really talking about no borders." You have these Haitians that are like we are almost inside. What was funny, though, was that the conversation – after the US stormed the encampment

– was about these white dudes on horseback, law enforcement, whipping Black people. And there needs to be a conversation about that but it was like we couldn't talk about anything else. People would ask us for our opinion and we'd say that part is not a surprise to us. The other part, though, is how many people were under that bridge? Thousands. They showed one image of Black people under a bridge being like we don't believe in this border and you guys already destroyed our country Haiti. And then three days later: there was no one there. There's no trash, not even a plastic bag. Like one flapping in the wind. And to me that's the image we need to talk about. They were like, "What? Black people at the border?" Boom. Ajax'ed it down. We had our allies and everybody yelling about folks on horsebacks and whipping. It was funny because this was right around the same time as the disastrous US exit from Kabul when they didn't have enough planes to evacuate everyone. I was like "Well, now I know where the planes are." I challenge those that talk about border abolition like "Yo, let's talk about that – the second part of Del Rio." I feel that in BAJI right now that's an area that we're really trying to talk about. It's really about understanding that border abolition is also about Black liberation.

CONSTELLATION II

Abolitionisms Against the Border Complex

6

The place of asylum and empire in contemporary abolition

Jenna M. Loyd

The Emirates Humanitarian City (EHC) sits within an industrial district of Abu Dhabi dotted with malls, residences, and a hospital, but its proximity to seaports and the airport is its main selling point. This "city" was purpose-built by the United Arab Emirates (UAE) in 2011 to serve as a logistics hub for humanitarian response in the Persian Gulf and Horn of Africa region. It operates as a "free zone" for nearly 90 non-governmental and parastatal organizations, like the United Nations High Commissioner for Refugees (UNHCR), and for commercial entities that are provided facilities for on-site operations. EHC boasts 135,000 meters of office and warehouse space in which teams of people and machines can rapidly assemble large aid kits that can be sent by cargo plane to areas of need, such as following the 2023 earthquake in Turkey.

The international humanitarian hub took on a major new role during the COVID-19 pandemic. This simultaneously connected and contained zone served as a useful place to construct residential quarantine facilities where citizens of different Arab nations stayed when their countries arranged for their return from China. In 2021, EHC's residential spaces took on yet another role as a significant node in the geopolitics of asylum. EHC became one of the "lily pads" through which the United States government and private groups evacuated Afghan citizens with whom they had worked when the US withdrew from Afghanistan.[1] Since then, some 10,000 Afghans who stayed at EHC have been able to resettle in a different country, but as of this writing almost two years later, approximately 2,100 Afghans remain stuck there in legal limbo.[2] Afghans living on site have protested their confinement on multiple occasions, and human rights monitors have issued reports condemning the situation. At one protest, children held signs reading in English, "Kids are not for jail" and "I don't want to be here for more time."[3] While the UAE and US State Department have denied that human rights abuses are routine at EHC, Afghans living there describe how the protracted waiting steals "hope for the future."[4] They also call into question the meaning of humanitarianism, equating the space to a jail: "It doesn't matter if we are safe ... Psychologically, physically, mentally, medically, we will die. This is a slow death."[5]

The protracted confinement and apparently arbitrary nature of administrative decisions facing Afghans at EHC have drawn considerable international media attention. Much of this coverage treats the situation as an extension of the chaos pervading the withdrawal or as a betrayal of US-stated obligations to its allies.[6] In this telling, the situation at EHC represents a break from the norm of responsibility and care. But abolitionists have taught us to ask whether the system is broken or working as designed. Accordingly, EHC is better understood as a window into the state of refugee rights for people who have been displaced. While outrage on the part of outside observers at the uncertainty and sense of betrayal is real, the situation facing Afghans is not a departure from the existing refugee protection system. As I spell out more fully below, the right to asylum and possibility of refugee resettlement have been steadily eroded since the end of the Cold War.[7] Even before the US withdrawal, Afghan refugees faced protracted displacement, with millions living in Iran, Pakistan, and other neighboring countries. The UNHCR stopped accepting applications from Afghan citizens for resettlement in 2013, meaning that doors to formal resettlement in Europe or North America have been virtually closed to them for at least ten years. Nor did the Special Immigrant Visa (SIV), established in 2006 by the US Congress for Iraqis and Afghans whose lives were in danger by virtue of their association with the US, offer a timely protection process. While Congress legislated a nine-month screening time (involving medical and extensive security checks), actual processing times have been significantly longer, with reports ranging from nearly two to more than four years.[8] Given this backlog, many of the evacuated Afghans who did arrive in the US were granted "humanitarian parole," which means that while they are physically present on US soil, they were not admitted to the US for purposes of immigration law. Two years later, the number of SIV applications in the system is seven times greater than in 2021 and advocates warn that at the current pace, it will take 20 years to get through the backlog.[9]

This confusing mix of legal categories and administrative procedures should elicit outrage, but rather than view it as a problem for this group in this moment alone, the situation for Afghans should be understood as part of a broader transnational dynamic to restrict rights to refuge and freedom of movement more broadly. Within our world's interstate system, nation-states have the authority to decide who comes and goes and with what rights.[10] These decisions are not made simply at nation-state boundaries, but are distributed across transnational spaces, transpiring in encounters with migration police, migration authorities, smugglers, the International Organization for Migration (IOM), UNHCR, and more. Spaces like EHC are where the "coloniality of asylum," which Fiorenza Picozza defines as the "differential, racialized and classed distribution of the freedom of movement," transpires.[11]

For philosopher Kelly Oliver, states have turned the so-called refugee crisis into "a matter of humanitarian aid or charity, on one hand, and national security, on the other, justifying military interventions."[12] Humanitarian logics overtake "properly political solution[s]" to the political problems of empire, rights, and claims on the future.[13] Within this context, states treat asylum and refugee rights as gifts bestowed by benevolent states, which then position refugees not as rights claimants, but as needy, powerless supplicants.[14] Oliver refers to such places as spaces of "carceral humanitarianism."

If abolitionists situate asylum, and migration more broadly, within colonial and imperial dynamics, as I believe we should, then we can also understand asylum through abolition's anti-imperial commitments. My questions for this piece are: how is the EHC an abolitionist question and how might theories of imperialism inform our answers? In the remainder of this essay, I will outline the importance of two strands of (anti-)imperial analysis to abolitionist thought. Then I will analyze EHC and freedom of movement more broadly within the context of imperialism, thereby extending abolitionist analyses of imperialism to the transnational regime of refugee and migrant controls. Spaces like EHC must be abolished not simply because they are carceral but because they uphold an empire of rights for some and rightlessness for others.[15]

WHAT DO WE MEAN WHEN WE SAY IMPERIALISM?: FIGURING CAPITALISM AND THE STATE

Meanings of imperialism are varied and debated on the broadly thought left. Historian Salar Mohandesi suggests there are two main tendencies.[16] One prominent line of analysis builds on the English economist and journalist J. A. Hobson's account of European nations busily competing to carve up the territories of the Earth in the late nineteenth to early twentieth century. He argued that these countries' thirst for profit fed the race to possess or rule over other people's lands, from which they aimed to extract raw materials and create markets for the goods imperial nations manufactured. Their ambitions created the conditions for international rivalries and ultimately war. This definition of imperialism – colonial rivalry turning into war among capitalist rivals – was shared by many subsequent thinkers, including Hannah Arendt, and Marxists from Rosa Luxemburg to V. I. Lenin to David Harvey. This definition has held sway because it fits Marxist understandings of capitalism, namely that capitalism has tendencies toward expansion (capital is value in motion), unevenness (capital accumulation in some places is linked to extraction and exploitation of others), and crisis (capitalism is inherently unstable because firms compete for highest level of profits, but this process routinely undermines the profitability and ecology of particular places, so some firms and places inevitably lose out). In this telling, imperialism is essentially equivalent to capitalism as it expands globally.

Others on the left have sought to foreground the role of the state in their theorizations of imperialism. For them, the classic Marxist focus on economic dynamics reduces states to instruments of capital. Treating the state as a direct auxiliary of corporations can lead to functionalist understandings of state violence, such that

imperial wars get boiled down to the profits they make for particular sectors or firms. It's not that war for oil is not objectionable or
that security firms don't make money from war, but that this scale
of analysis doesn't explain geopolitics, including efforts to maintain
international hierarchies rooted in colonialism. Nor does it explain
the "complex" of the military- (or prison-) industrial complex,
which also involves societal organization to make violence.[17] This
strand of analysis brings focus on the workings and meanings of
state and state-sanctioned violence in their own right.

This focus on the state does not mean that its relationships with
capitalism disappear or are unimportant. Instead, the perspective helps open the "black box" of "the state" to an understanding
that states comprise different apparatuses, arms of which are often
in conflict, *and* which are sites of class struggle. For Laleh Khalili,
states' roles in imperialism include "entire legal and administrative
apparatuses that ensure the subjugation or exploitation of some in
the globe by others."[18] Rather than inexorable tendencies of capitalism, this perspective entails a historically and geographically
specific, or conjunctural, analysis.[19] One pertinent example is James
O'Connor's theorization of post-Second World War United States as
a "welfare–warfare state," whose militarily backed empire sustained
broader social investments and distribution of wealth at this time
(also called the golden era, or Keynesianism).[20] Abolitionist geographer Ruth Wilson Gilmore built on this concept to explain how
in the 1980s these welfare–warfare arms of the state shifted. While
many early analysts of capitalist globalization and neoliberalism
thought the state was shrinking, Gilmore diagnosed how institutions of domestic and international war-making (including policing
and prisons) expanded even as the welfare arm of the state was disinvested. She called this new state "post-Keynesian militarism."[21]
Another excellent example is Stuart Hall and colleagues' analysis
of the "domestic" politics of empire in *Policing the Crisis.*[22] They
demonstrated how social conflict over (invited) immigration from
Britain's former colonies in the Caribbean and South Asia transpired through increasingly restrictive migration policy *and* a moral
panic over "mugging" that resulted in increased policing of Black
youth. Rather than accept the state's domestic-foreign, inside-out-
side divides as natural and unchanging, these accounts all offer

dialectical accounts of the shifting relationships between "domestic" politics, policy, and law and transnational imperial relations.

IMPERIALISM WITHIN ABOLITIONIST THOUGHT AND PRACTICE

Both strands of imperial analysis have informed abolitionist thinking and action. Analyses of bordering as a racialized, gendered, and sexualized tool that facilitates exploitation by capital have been well developed by Harsha Walia, Nicolas de Genova, and thinkers in this book.[23] These analyses are crucial for countering the claim that the border is race (or gender, nation, religion, etc.) neutral and for showing how racist nationalism or xenophobia in the name of citizens' jobs fails to challenge capitalist power, among other reasons. In leaving aside the state-capitalism question and foregrounding the state and state violence in this analysis, I want to bring the transnational workings of imperial power into the abolitionist frame as sites of violent nation-building and dispossession.

This internationalist imperative has long been part of anti-imperial movements and radical thought. Take the Black Panthers who regarded the policing of their neighborhoods and Native reservations as parallel to the military occupations that the US was engaged in in Southeast Asia and elsewhere. Or David Gilbert, a member of the Weather Underground who was imprisoned for 40 years: "[W]e don't have a chance of abolishing the PIC [prison-industrial complex] without opposing imperialism. The warfare and security states go together and reinforce each other."[24] Or Angela Y. Davis on the torture that was revealed in the early days of the United States' "global war on terror." While many critics viewed torture, and its photographic evidence, as an aberration of American democracy, Davis situated the practice within the context of a nation that was "willing to treat human beings as refuse."[25] While "torture is extraordinary," she continued, if "we consider the various forms of violence linked to the practice of imprisonment – circuits of violence linked to one another – then we begin to see that the extraordinary has some connection to the ordinary."[26]

The importance of linking forms of imperial violence across borders became urgent following the attacks of September 11,

2001. The United States (and allies) responded by launching two massive wars in Afghanistan and Iraq and establishing the Department of Homeland Security, which consolidated previously separate law enforcement and migration agencies, and expanded the security state's tools of surveillance. To understand this new conjuncture of war and heightened domestic repression of Muslim and Arab communities in particular, Davis turned to W. E. B. Du Bois's *Black Reconstruction in America*.[27] In this text, Du Bois argues that the project to abolish slavery, which led to the US Civil War, was not complete. Radical Reconstruction had been thwarted by a counter-revolution of Southern planters and Northern capital. This counter-revolution was not confined to the US South. He argued that late nineteenth-century US imperial claims to Puerto Rico, Hawai'i, and the Philippines were military actions that also helped cement "a racial state domestically: the consolidation of Jim Crow, the industrialization of the South …"[28] The related extension of the "color line" around the world linked societies with legacies of slavery and ongoing colonialism. That is to say, the counter-revolution against Reconstruction was advanced through domestic terror *and* imperial war.

Du Bois's call for abolition democracy would build the "host of democratic institutions [that] are needed to fully achieve abolition."[29] In the context of the "global war on terror," Davis saw in Du Bois's idea of abolition democracy a concept that could link efforts to dismantle institutions of state violence to projects to build life-affirming institutions. Gilmore likewise advanced this strategy in her analysis of the restructuring of the welfare-warfare state into post-Keynesian warfare, of which the expansion of prisons in California was a part.[30] For Gilmore, this meant that not only would prisons be sites of abolitionist struggle, but so would arms of the state where folks could mobilize to redirect violence spending into education, housing, health care and the like.[31] In this reading, and as others in this collection contend, abolition is also class struggle, about building non-capitalist futures.

Another significant contribution to anti-imperial abolitionist analyses grew out of efforts to link anti-war efforts to opposition to increased racist surveillance and anti-immigrant policies. INCITE! Women of Color Against Violence became leading theorists of the connections between imperial wars abroad and the "wars at home."[32] One rationale that the George W. Bush administration gave for invading Afghanistan is that the war would liberate women from the Taliban. This refrain was repeated by liberal and conservative feminists. INCITE! challenged the patronizing conceit that the West would rescue and bring rights to Afghan women through war by drawing on Valerie Amos and Pratibha Parmar's concept of imperial feminism and Leila Ahmed's idea of colonial feminism.[33] INCITE! refused the imagined imperial geography that war "over there" would extend the protections women enjoyed at home. They insisted that the "war on terror" "intensifies violence against women of color, third world women, and our communities," communities that crossed national boundaries.[34] One of the most powerful aspects of their analysis is their feminist, anti-imperial account of violence. Like Davis, they linked different forms of violence together, including sexual assault on the part of militaries and border patrol agents, increased poverty as a consequence of prioritizing military spending, the health and disability consequences of war, legal attacks on and targeting of communities of color by Homeland Security, and increases of racist assaults on communities of color in the US. In their rejection of an imagined binary of the peaceful home front facing the dangerous world outside, they showed instead interlinkages of racial and gendered violence across domestic and international space that made some women of color and their communities more vulnerable to violence rather than secured from it.

While memory of the UN World Conference Against Racism in Durban has been overshadowed by 9/11, the movements against racism and Zionism that coalesced there were part of what enabled INCITE! and other women of color feminists to articulate criticisms of militarism and the carceral state as connected transnationally.[35] Nadine Naber, a scholar and longtime activist, has written extensively about her research with and involvement in Arab-American and women of color feminist organizations, including with INCITE!, both before and after 9/11. In the San Francisco Bay Area, for example, Naber observes that, a common tendency among activists of color ... throughout the 1990s was to implicitly accept the notion that anti-imperialist, anti-war, international solidarity organizing takes place within national community boundaries – Koreans or Asian Pacific Islanders work in North Korea, Filipinos in the Philippines, and Arabs on Palestine. Alternately, the dominant approach was to assume that organizing around domestic issues – the prison industrial complex, police brutality, welfare, and gentrification – takes place within broad-based, multi-racial "people of color-led" coalitions.[36]

For organizers working in people of color coalitions, Naber argues that this tendency shifted to a view that "U.S. imperialism is an extension of U.S. domestic policies," which enabled unified fights against racism and war.[37] From this perspective, imperial war and ramped-up surveillance of immigrant communities in the US were connected across space *and* connected to the policing of Black and brown neighborhoods that was already happening. For Naber, the multiscalar political understandings that Black and Arab feminists working in coalition have created stand to transform "dominant frameworks that define radical feminist and queer concerns solely with US 'domestic' issues and reduce the struggles of women globally to simply 'foreign'" ones.[38]

I want to draw four conclusions from this focus on the state in radical and women of color feminists' analyses of imperialism. First, approaching imperialism with attention to the state does not mean capitalism is not an issue, simply that state violence in all its forms is a problem to be confronted in its own right. Second, instead of accepting state attempts to divide the domestic from the imperial, these groups saw linkages, if not dialectical relations, across domestic and international space. Third, it is through their analyses of state violence, in all its forms, that women of color feminists drew linkages of racialized and gendered state violence across geographic scales and across national boundaries. The home (or neighborhood) can be a site of imperial violence through state surveillance and policing *and* through interpersonal violence, which is not private, but rather is linked systemically to war and other expressions of state violence.[39] Finally, women of color feminist critiques of imperial feminism and the carceral state did not stop at stating what should be obvious (war does not save women; prisons don't make women safer), but also name the violence in forms of state protection that proclaim to be caring and protective. I bring these analyses to bear on Emirates Humanitarian City.

EMIRATES HUMANITARIAN CITY AS A NODE OF GLOBAL APARTHEID

So, why is Emirates Humanitarian City an abolitionist issue? Building on Mohandesi's contention that imperialism "has to be broadly understood as a relationship of domination between states rather than a synonym for capitalist expansion," I view migration controls as transnational exercises of imperial rule because they shape the mobility of not only their nations' citizens, but the majority of the world's population.[40] This is a form of state domination because imperial states create geopolitical and economic conditions in which other nation-states can exercise their sovereignty over their citizens' mobility. Imperial states also create geopolitical and economic conditions within which less powerful states work in concert with imperial states to extend migration controls into spaces far beyond formal national boundaries. Accordingly, the majority of people in the world are rendered imperial subjects whose formal rights under international law have been dispossessed.

Emirates Humanitarian City is one place where imperial controls of mobility are starkly evident. I turn to poet and activist scholar, Rafeef Ziadeh, who researched the facility that preceded the EHC. She refers to EHC as a space where "humanitarian, commercial and military logics play interchangeable and mutually reinforcing roles – militaries and logistics firms serve as humanitarians, and humanitarianism helps to expand and grow military power and commercial reach."[41] The role UAE crafted for itself grew out of its place as "an important node within the wider circulatory networks of British colonialism in the Gulf region."[42] Since its foundation as an independent state in 1971, the UAE and the United States have maintained a strong geopolitical relationship. The US military has military personnel stationed in the UAE and firms in UAE have been important contractors for US wars in Afghanistan and Iraq.[43] The US does not dominate, in Mohandesi's sense, the UAE. Rather, both nations dominate through their geopolitical ties and tensions. UAE has been establishing a military presence in the region, a geo-political power in the region, and is one of the largest international aid donors in the world. For Ziadeh, the UAE's stake in humanitar-ian logistics "operates alongside and helps to strengthen the UAE's wider regional projection of power."[44]

It was in this context, where the UAE has a good deal of political power and logistics capabilities, that the UAE allowed the United States military and privately contracted flights to evacuate Afghans through the EHC. For Khalili, parastatal complexes, like EHC where private and public institutions are tightly connected, are key to understanding imperialism. In places like this, one can examine where the boundary of "naming things as public or private, sov-ereign or not" transpires.[45] In the case of Afghans who found themselves at EHC, this dividing line is consequential, making the difference between access to rights or consignment to the private (i.e., nonpolitical) realm of humanitarianism. CNN reported that the people still at EHC in 2023 largely had been evacuated by private groups and then "left in a legal limbo with seemingly no clear path to the US – or anywhere else."[46] One American who organized private flights for Afghans recounted to CNN that a State Department official told him, "Not our plane, not our problem," even though President Biden publicly praised the efforts of private groups at the time.[47]

The EHC's humanitarian node model is a parastatal twist on the US's long history of using its own military bases both to evacuate civilians and to confine asylum seekers en route to US territory.[48] As at EHC, the humanitarian face of these operations has not meant that people were afforded their right to claim refuge. As mentioned at the outset, the use of geographic strategies of border external-ization and refugee containment has become more apparent since the end of the Cold War. For refugee studies scholar B. S. Chimni, this has transpired because "refugees no longer possess ideological or geopolitical value" for the world's superpowers.[49] Accordingly, the "universal and protective label 'refugee' has, as a result, frag-mented and translated into the curtailment of rights. Those who now seek refuge find that they represent security threats to states and regions and that all roads lead quickly home."[50]

EHC must be understood as part of this geography of imperial migration controls and the proliferation of deadly borderlands in seas and deserts. This geography goes by many names and encapsulates many dynamics: global apartheid, border imperialism, refugee containment, non-entrée regime, border externalization, deterrence. Together, they explain a series of interlocking policies and practices that aim to keep people on the move from reaching countries of the Global North. US agreements and funding of Mexican and Central American border patrols, for example, have created what people on the move call the "vertical border."[51] EU nations also have been externalizing their border enforcement to countries in Africa in exchange for development aid and payment for border policing and detention. Turkey, likewise, has used its position as the border of Europe to negotiate the terms of its accession to the EU. Not to be outdone, Australia has made agreements with Nauru and Papua New Guinea to confine people claiming asylum without a chance to enter Australia.[52] And more.

The languishing Afghan population at the EHC has put the UAE in the spotlight, with Human Rights Watch calling the situation "arbitrary detention."[53] Some analysts have cited this negative attention and the UAE's disapproval of the evacuation process as a reason for its cooling relationship with the United States. But this imperial situation is not so simple (if they ever are). In the context of a "multipolar" world, the UAE has fostered political and economic ties with other global powerhouses, which makes it increasingly independent from US interests.[54] That is, our anti-imperial analysis needs to include multiple empires in their competition (and cooperation). The UAE's military and financing roles in conflicts in Yemen, Libya, and Sudan have come under increasing scrutiny, with critics contending that the UAE's support of R.S.F., one of the two major armed factions in Sudan, gives the UAE priority access to natural resources.[55] Other critics contend that the UAE and the international community are complicit in R.S.F.'s policing of migration to Europe following the Khartoum agreement.[56] And UAE's own record of treating immigrant workers is far from spotless.[57] From this vantage, EHC no longer appears as an exception, but rather part of the broader imperial mobility regime coordinated by states that serve to benefit from migration controls even as they compete for other forms of power and resources. The ad hoc humanitarian nature of EHC betrays this as a space of rightlessness, rather than one of migration and refugee law.

CONCLUSION

My focus on tracing state violence across space compliments analyses that link bordering to the workings of racial capitalism and reproduction of heteropatriarchy. I brought EHC into the abolitionist frame as a place that is linked not only to war-making, but also as a place that enacts imperial power of bordering across transnational space. This echoes Picozza's views on the coloniality of asylum as a "border struggle" that actively produces both refugees and Europe (and the Global North more broadly) as a space of "postcolonial 'good' whiteness, premised on liberal, democratic and humanitarian discourses."[58]

Approaching migration controls as imperial forms of domination that deepen historically rooted colonial and racialized inequalities helps us to see how drawing a line between migrant and asylum seeker is also part of interlocked humanitarian–military logics that animate contemporary imperialism. While this division has real effects in terms of how people on the move can navigate their encounters with state authorities, both groups are subject to national security threat logics and screenings that have become increasingly more intrusive. In this way, the global war on terror persists not just in war zones and their deep lasting effects, but also in how most of the people in the world, as imperial subjects, may move across state borders. Asylum – and freedom of movement more broadly – is an anti-imperial abolitionist issue because migration controls are also political sites where people contest how imperial legal regimes facilitate war-making while dispossessing them of even modest claims to refuge. Or a future. This suggests that activists should also reject the false binary states and media enact dividing refugees from other migrants. Rather than seeing defense of asylum rights as undermining broader rights to mobility, we can recognize that imperial efforts to undermine asylum are part of constraining human mobility.

EHC is a site where imperial power is exercised through the production of rightlessness. Does this mean that the abolitionist answer is more rights? For Naomi Paik, rightlessness as a condition is not solely the dispossession of rights, but exists on a continuum that also includes the forms in which one may make claims about whether they will be listened to.[59] For Paik, the point is "not that rights are good, rightlessness is bad," but that rightlessness is produced by rights regimes.[60] I take this to mean that rights struggles will necessarily continue as "overdetermined at the source" sites of political struggle.[61] For Dean Spade, the securing of rights or legal recognition is not a goal in itself, rather "law reform [is] a tactic to dismantle systems of state violence."[62] The abolitionist conclusion that Paik draws from this situation is "not a future where everyone has their rights recognized. The goal is a future where rights are no longer necessary."[63]

EHC should be abolished as part of dismantling the entire non-entrée regime of global apartheid. Homing in on forms of state violence enables us to recognize the violence of humanitarianism and subject it to political critique. Abolition feminism and women of color analyses of imperialism (and their overlaps) in particular provide a *politics* for doing so because they have developed strong analyses of the violence that states and their private or nonprofit proxies routinely do in the name of protection and care. These analyses equip us to parse through the public-private divide through which the US and UAE work to allocate or dispossess rights *as a space of political struggle*. By recognizing the political construction of this division, abolitionists can reject the boundary as a false one and thereby also make political the ostensibly apolitical workings of humanitarianism. This is bordering via humanitarianism. The violent hierarchies and paternalism it enacts also demand abolition.

ACKNOWLEDGMENTS

Thank you to the *Border Abolition Now* collective for their gracious and thoughtful engagement with this piece. It is better for this collective thinking, while errors and (provisional) analyses remain my responsibility.

NOTES

1. Rebecca Beitch, "Can't Go Home, Can't Enter the US: Thousands of Afghans Remain Stuck in Between." *The Hill*, August 31, 2022. https://thehill.com/policy/international/3615871-cant-go-home-cant-enter-the-us-thousands-of-afghans-remain-stuck-in-between/; Leo Shane, III, "Vets Group Plead for More Action from White House on Afghanistan Evacuations." *Military Times*, August 23, 2021. www.militarytimes.com/flashpoints/afghanistan/2021/08/23/vets-groups-plead-for-more-action-from-white-house-on-afghanistan-evacuations/
2. For context, 125,000 Afghan people were airlifted out of Afghanistan in 2021. By the end of that year, there were 3.5 million Afghans displaced within their country and 2.6 million people displaced outside the country. "Afghanistan Refugee Crisis Explained," *UNHCR*, July 18, 2023. www.unrefugees.org/news/afghanistan-refugee-crisis-explained/; "Afghan Refugees in UAE Protest against Uncertainty and 'Prison-like' Conditions." *Middle East Eye*, August 24, 2022. www.middleeasteye.net/news/afghanistan-refugees-protest-uae-uncertainty-prison-like-conditions; Haley Britzky, "Thousands of Afghans Escaped the Taliban with the Help of Private Veteran Groups. Today, Many Remain in Limbo, Held in a Compound in the UAE." *CNN*, May 7, 2023. www.cnn.com/2023/05/07/politics/afghan-evacuees-stuck-uae-private-evacuation/index.html
3. "US Officials Meet Afghans Stranded in UAE, Apologizes for Delays." *Al Jazeera*, March 4, 2022. www.aljazeera.com/news/2022/3/4/us-official-meets-afghans-stranded-in-uae-apologises-for-delays
4. Beitch, "Can't Go Home."
5. Global Detention Project and Migrant-rights.org, "'THIS IS A SLOW DEATH': An Urgent Appeal on the Plight of Afghan Refugees Indefinitely and Arbitrarily Detained in the UAE. Global Detention Project." *Global Detention Project*, March 13, 2023. www.globaldetentionproject.org/urgent-appeal-plight-of-afghan-refugees-indefinitely-and-arbitrarily-detained-in-uae
6. Britzkey, "Thousands of Afghans Escaped."
7. B. S. Chimni, "The Geopolitics of Refugee Studies: A View from the South." *Journal of Refugee Studies* 11(4), 1998: 350–374; Alison Mountz, *The Death of Asylum: Hidden Geographies of the Enforcement Archipelago*. Minneapolis: University of Minnesota Press, 2020.
8. "Processing Delays in the Special Immigrant Visa Program." *International Refugee Assistance Project*, last updated 2020. https://refugeerights.org/wp-content/uploads/2020/05/Processing-Delays-in-the-SIV-

Program-Summary.pdf; "Fact Sheet: Overview of the Special Immigrant Visa Programs." *National Immigration Forum*, June 22, 2021. https://immigrationforum.org/article/fact-sheet-overview-of-the-special-immigrant-visa-programs/

9. Jack Detch and Robbie Gramer, "Afghan Special Immigrant Visas Surge amid Taliban Crackdown." *Foreign Policy*, March 8, 2023. https://foreignpolicy.com/2023/03/08/afghanistan-special-immigrant-visa-biden-taliban-crackdown/; Grace Segars, "The U.S. May Break its Promise to the Afghan Allies it Left Behind." *The New Republic*, March 16, 2023. https://newrepublic.com/article/171182/afghan-allies-visa-backlog-taliban

10. Historian Frederick Cooper reminds us that the alignment of rights with nation-states is of recent origin and has been contested throughout colonial and decolonial eras. Frederick Cooper, "Afterword: Social Rights and Human Rights in the Time of Decolonization." *Humanity*, 3(3), Winter 2012: 473–492.

11. Fiorenza Picozza, *The Coloniality of Asylum: Mobility, Autonomy and Solidarity in the Wake of Europe's Refugee Crisis*. Lanham: Rowman & Littlefield Publishers, 2021, xxiii.

12. Kelly Oliver, *Carceral Humanitarianism: Logics of Refugee Detention*. Minneapolis: University of Minnesota Press, 2017, 7.

13. Oliver, *Carceral Humanitarianism*, 7.

14. Mimi Thi Nguyen, *The Gift of Freedom: War, Debt, and Other Refugee Passages*. Durham: Duke University Press, 2012.

15. A. Naomi Paik, *Rightlessness: Testimony and Redress in US Prison Camps since World War II*. Chapel Hill: UNC Press Books, 2016.

16. For a more thorough discussion, see Salar Mohandesi, "The Specificity of Imperialism." *Viewpoint Magazine*, February 1, 2018. https://viewpointmag.com/2018/02/01/the-specificity-of-imperialism/

17. Ruth Wilson Gilmore, *Abolition Geography: Essays toward Liberation*. New York: Verso, 2022.

18. Khalili's definition of imperialism brings the capitalist economic and state analysis perspectives together, comprising in addition "structures of economic extraction and exploitation; asymmetric forms of capital accumulation; [and] modalities of military control." Laleh Khalili, "How Empire Operates: An Interview with Laleh Khalili." *Viewpoint Magazine*, February 1, 2018. https://viewpointmag.com/2018/02/01/empire-operates-interview-laleh-khalili/

19. Mohandesi, "The Specificity of Imperialism."

20. James O'Connor, *The Fiscal Crisis of the State*. New York: St. Martin's, 1973.

21. Ruth Wilson Gilmore, "Globalisation and US Prison Growth: From Military Keynesianism to Post-Keynesian Militarism." *Race & Class* 40(2–3), 1998: doi: 10.1177/030639689904000212

22. Stuart Hall, Chas Critcher, Tony Jefferson, John Clarke, and Brian Roberts, *Policing the Crisis: Mugging, the State and Law and Order*. London: Red Globe Press, 2013 [1978].

23. Nicholas De Genova, *Working the Boundaries: Race, Space, and "Illegality" in Mexican Chicago*. Durham: Duke University Press, 2005; Harsha Walia, *Undoing Border Imperialism*. Oakland: AK Press, 2014; Harsha Walia, *Border and Rule: Global Migration, Capitalism, and the Rise of Racist Nationalism*. Chicago: Haymarket Books, 2021.

24. David Gilbert, "A System within the System: The Prison-Industrial Complex and Imperialism." In: CR10 Collective (Ed.), *Abolition Now!* http://criticalresistance.org/wp-content/uploads/2012/06/Critical-Resistance-Abolition-Now-Ten-Years-of-Strategy-and-Struggle-against-the-Prison-Industrial-Complex.pdf, 38.

25. Angela Davis, *Abolition Democracy: Beyond Empire, Prisons, and Torture*. New York: Seven Stories Press, 2005, p. 50.

26. Davis, *Abolition Democracy*, 62.

27. W. E. B. Du Bois, *Black Reconstruction in America, 1860–1880*. New York: Free Press, 1998 [1935].

28. Du Bois, *Black Reconstruction*, quoted in Davis, *Abolition Democracy*, 83.

29. Davis, *Abolition Democracy*, 96.

30. Ruth Wilson Gilmore, "Fatal Couplings of Power and Difference: Notes on Racism and Geography." *The Professional Geographer*, 54(1), 2002: 15–24.

31. Clément Petitjean, "Prisons and Class Warfare: An Interview with Ruth Wilson Gilmore." *Solidarity* XXX 2019. https://solidarity-us.org/prisons-and-class-warfare-an-interview-with-ruth-wilson-gilmore/

32. INCITE! Women of Color against Violence, "Anti-Militarism Resources," last accessed August 10, 2023. https://incite-national.org/anti-militarism/

33. Valeria Amos and Pratibha Parmar, "Challenging Imperial Feminism." *Feminist Review* 17(1), 1984: 3–19; Leila Ahmed, *Women and Gender in Islam*. New Haven: Yale University Press, 1993.

34. INCITE!, "Anti-Militarism Resources."

35. Maylei Blackwell and Nadine Naber, "Intersectionality in an Era of Gobalization: The Implications of the UN World Conference against Racism for Transnational Feminist Practices – A Conference Report." *Meridians* 2(2), 2002: 237–248.

36. Nadine Naber, "So Our History Doesn't Become Your Future: The Local and Global Politics of Coalition Building post September 11th." *Journal of Asian American Studies* 5(3), 2002: 234.

37. Naber, "So Our History," 234.

38. Nadine Naber, "Arab and Black Feminisms: Joint Struggle and Transnational Anti-Imperialist Activism." *Departures in Critical Qualitative Research* 5(3), 2016: 123.

39. For an excellent discussion of how the "false division between the public and private spheres" is mobilized by the state, see Angela Y. Davis, Gina Dent, Erica R. Meiners, and Beth E. Richie, *Abolition. Feminism. Now*. Chicago: Haymarket Books, p. 70.

40. Mohandesi, "The Specificity of Imperialism."

41. Rafeef Ziadah, "Circulating Power: Humanitarian Logistics, Militarism, and the United Arab Emirates." *Antipode* 51(5), 2019: 1697.

42. Ziadah, "Circulating Power," 1690.

43. Ziadah, "Circulating Power," XXX; Sharp, "The United Arab Emirates (UAE): Issues for U.S. Policy." *Congressional Research Service*. Last updated January 30, 2023. https://crsreports.congress.gov/product/pdf/RS/RS21852/146

44. Ziadah, "Circulating Power," 1693.

45. Khalili, "How Empire Operates."

46. Britzkey, "Thousands of Afghans Escaped."

47. "Not Our Plane." In: Britzkey, "Thousands of Afghans Escaped"; Shane, "Vets Group Plead for More Action."

48. Yến Lê Espiritu, *Body Counts: The Vietnam War and Militarized Refugees*. Oakland: University of California Press: 2014; Jenna M. Loyd and Alison Mountz, *Boats, Borders, and Bases: Race, the Cold War, and the Rise of Migration Detention in the United States*. Oakland: University of California Press: 2018.

49. B. S. Chimni, "Globalization, Humanitarianism and the Erosion of Refugee Protection." *Journal of Refugee Studies* 13(3), 2000, p. 244.

50. Chimni, "Globalization," 245.

51. Wendy Vogt, *Lives in Transit: Violence and Intimacy on the Migrant Journey*. Oakland: University of California Press, 2018.

52. Mountz, *The Death of Asylum*.

53. "UAE: Arbitrarily Detained Afghans Stuck in Limbo." *Human Rights Watch*, March 15, 2023. www.hrw.org/news/2023/03/15/uae-arbitrarily-detained-afghans-stuck-limbo

54. Sharp, "The United Arab Emirates"; Rafeef, "Circulating Power."

55. Nasim Ahmed, "Sudan Bloody War Shows UAE is an Agent of Chaos and Instability." *Middle East Monitor*, April 26, 2023. www.middleeastmonitor.com/20230426-sudan-bloody-war-shows-uae-is-an-agent-of-chaos-and-instability/

56. Bayan Abubakr, "Sudan Will Not Be Left for Dead." *New York Times*, July 7, 2023. www.nytimes.com/2023/07/07/opinion/sudan-war-conflict.html?smid=nytcore-ios-share&referringSource=articleShare

57. Philippe Fargues, Nasra M. Shah, and Imco Brouwer, "Working and Living Conditions of Low-Income Migrant Workers in the Hospitality and Construction Sectors in the United Arab Emirates: A Survey among Migrant Workers through Focus Group Discussions." *Migration Policy Center*, 2019. https://hdl.handle.net/1814/65986; Maya Gebeily, "'They

Told Us They Hate Africans': Hundreds Detained, Deported from Abu Dhabi." *Reuters*, September 3, 2021. www.reuters.com/world/middle-east/they-told-us-they-hate-africans-hundreds-detained-deported-abu-dhabi-2021-09-02/
58. Picozza, *Coloniality of Asylum*, xxii, xxiii.
59. Paik, *Rightlessness*.
60. In Dylan Rodríguez, "Public Thinker: A. Naomi Paik on a Future without Rights." *Public Books*, January 10, 2020. www.publicbooks.org/public-thinker-a-naomi-paik-on-a-future-without-rights/
61. Gilmore, "Fatal Couplings," 21.
62. Dean Spade, "Toward a Critical Trans Politics." *Upping the Anti* 14, 2012: 37–51. www.deanspade.net/wp-content/uploads/2013/03/upping-the-anti-interview-2012.pdf
63. In Rodríguez, "Public Thinker."

7

Abolition, not relocation

Moving from humanitarian containment toward camp abolition

Simon Campbell

"GOOD" AND "BAD" CAMPS

In March 2021, I participated in a demonstration against camps in Freiburg, a small city in the South West of Germany. It was a relatively sunny spring day and the march gradually picked up people as it threaded its way from the office of the camp administration, toward the camp itself, the Landeserstaufnahmeeinrichtung für Flüchtlinge, known by its acronym LEA. The demo had started with speeches from the local Black Lives Matter group and an anti-deportation collective, and as around a hundred of us rolled up to the camp gates with placards and bicycles, a sound system was set up again. Residents from the camp started to share their experiences of the repression they faced, the cramped living conditions, the bureaucracy and surveillance, restrictive curfews, endless waiting or impromptu transfers, and the constant overhanging threat of deportation. Cops, camp security and a few CCTV cameras looked on gormlessly.

Banners were hung on the fences calling for "no more camps," "no borders," and some marking out the German state, the European Union (EU), the United Nations High Commissioner for Refugees (UNHCR), and the International Organization for Migration (IOM) as perpetrators. Placards and chants also drew out solidarity with people in camps outside of Germany, such as Lipa in Bosnia-Herzegovina and Moria on the Greek island of Lesvos, two prominent locations in the EU's violent externalization policy. Speaking to the system of state-run transit and reception centers across Europe, the protestors called out a border regime which hinges on keeping people in contained, securitized, and industrial-size spaces, shut away from others. Moreover, the call for "camp abolition" was more than just about closing down the LEA, it was about undoing the racist violence that migrants face in the city from police and locals, the precarity of jobs for those able to stay, and the dangerous routes crossed to get to Germany. Starting to map out a place to live in, next to the fences of the place that ought to be destroyed, you could feel a buzz about the crowd, that energy demos often impart, even if just for a fleeting moment.

But this mood was soon punctured. Toward the end of the speeches, the microphone was passed onto an organizer involved in local government. A back and forth ensued, caught on that sticky word that makes liberals so often start to sweat. Abolition. According to them, it didn't make sense to call for the closure of the camp, after all, what would happen to the people housed inside? Yes, he admitted, the conditions weren't ideal, but that's why they were lobbying at the local level to change them. Notably, he stressed that the camp would be needed to accept more people currently stuck at the EU external border in places "like Moria and Lipa," and after all, despite the problems people were raising, it wasn't the *worst* camp. To speak of abolition was counterproductive, he said.

Later, speaking to folks from the demo, I found this to be a discourse that organizers were facing regularly. The dominant municipal-led organizing strategy leaned heavily toward retaining and reforming the camp, bringing its management further under the mandate of local government. Activists who took a more radical abolitionist stance were being criticized for naivety, and even for damaging the situation of refugees in Germany. Some were actually told LEA was not a camp at all, as one organizer shared with me in an interview:

Some representative was not happy that we used the term "*camp*" to describe LEA. There were two arguments actually. There was one argument saying "*you're putting LEA in the same area as concentration camps*," which is just absurd I think. But the other was like, "*No, the camps in Europe they are in Moria. Here you cannot compare to Moria,*" which we aren't doing of course.

The reference to institutions of the Nazi period is particular to the German discourse on camps. However, these remarks do provide insight into a wider comparative approach which scales camps on a continuum of repression to care. This logic suggests there are two different types of camps at either pole. First, contemporary ones like the LEA in Freiburg, a reception center, serviceable enough and connected with a "fair" asylum process, in reality, not a "real" camp at all. Second, "bad" camps, places awful enough to credit the word "camp" and its connection with incarceration, exploitation and genocide. According to this line of thought, if there were real camps, today it would be places like Moria on Lesvos, or Lipa in Bosnia-Herzegovina. Since this discussion, I have been looking at this insistence on "good" and "bad" camps, and the type of discourses and neo-colonial geographies it reproduces.[1] In doing so, I have been learning from abolitionists who are paving new analytical and material alternatives to camps, and whose interventions challenge their very existence, rather than scaling them from worst to best.

In the first section of this chapter, I look at how border abolition unmasks the reformist logics of humanitarianism, a supposed system of care which actually reproduces camps as spaces of containment. I explore how "humanitarian relocation" retains the specter of a redeemable, caring, "good" camp – using this as a way of moving people between camps, rather than questioning their logic as spaces. In particular, I highlight the decolonial and transnational outlooks of abolitionism which helps us to understand camps as differentiated networks of carcerality, and ones which perform distinct labor in the process of what Piro Rexhepi describes as "white enclosure."[2] Here, an abolitionist analytic signals how reformist calls for "relocation" widen the carceral state, and entrench neo-colonial polarities that position "bad" camps at Europe's racialized periphery, and "good" camps at its self-proclaimed *white* liberal core. Thus camp abolition is not just a process of withdrawing consent from carceral systems, but also from the reproduction of imperial borderlands.

In the second part of this chapter, I look at the ways abolitionist praxis is being employed not only to critique camps, but also to map non-bordered spaces of care beyond them. In particular, I highlight the way migrant-led and community activism take up critical positionalities to camps, developing autonomous spaces of mutual aid, while also probing the options and pitfalls of abolitionist reform. Rather than a "good/bad" analysis, which enables the continuity of carceral camps, these movements call on intersectional feminist, decolonial, anti-capitalist, and transnational solidarities to rehearse a world of no camps. In the final section, I ask what this means for European solidarity activism, myself being someone who has participated in movements and organizations co-opted by reformist humanitarian logics. This is an effort to explore what the no-borders struggle can (un)learn, moving from a stance of "refugees welcome" to an "abolitionist welcome" which critiques the racialized positioning of Europe as host.

RELOCATION TO WHAT?

To pursue an abolitionist intervention on camps we need to dig a little deeper into how the understanding of "good" and "bad" camps has come about, and the role of humanitarianism in systems of encampment. Masking itself in the language of post-political care, humanitarianism is in fact a construct entwined with imperialism.[3] Thus while feigning to offer neutral forms of aid, humanitarianism has been mobilized over time by European states as a tool to contain and exploit colonial subjects. As Hanno Brankamp has described, humanitarian encampment is a form of racialized incarceration developed by imperial powers, a technology used to govern internal movement in colonies, carry out processes of enclosure, control workforces, and suppress anti-colonial rebellion.[4] As such, camps are forms of enclosure tightly bound up with the historic formation of borders, colonial governance of labor, and contemporary developments in humanitarian militarism.[5] Yet encampment (in its various different forms) continues to be narrated as a supportive form of infrastructure, owing to the civilizing ethos of humanitarianism and its roots in white supremacy.[6]

Much of today's formal camp infrastructures work on a variation of the same humanitarian twist. Posing as interventions of care, camps primarily function to warehouse and filter bodies in service of racial capitalism. The system of encampment underpinning the EU's externalization policy is one prime example of this conceit. Externalization, a process by which bordering takes place at the edges or outside of EU territory, is a neo-colonial extension of migration governance. In particular, the industrial growth in camps as the main form of reception for migrants, notably since 2015, signals how tools of the colonial state have been reanimated to control contemporary mobility. These reception infrastructures (see Marchi in this volume) intersect directly with repressive augmentations in the EU asylum and labor regime, making camps part of a wider pipeline of containment, to extraction, to deportation. Administering this is an ever-expanding alliance of state organs, NGOs, and sub-contractors – agents of the "humanitarian border"[7] – which interlock heavily with police and prison services. An abolitionist analytic draws attention to this carceral web, its roots in racism and imperialism, and the role of neoliberalism in infrastructures of encampment.

So where does "good" and "bad" come into it? Well, it's true that camps at the EU external border have particularly repressive conditions, and intentionally so. These camps are an intrinsic part of the system of organized abandonment,[8] drawing containment into a violent nexus together with pushbacks and border killings.[9] Moria, a camp on the Greek island of Lesvos, stood for a long time as the prime example of this explicit effort to contain and repress migrants moving at the outer borders of the EU. Until it burned down in 2020, Moria was an overcrowded and poorly maintained set of improvised shelters where migrants crossing by boat from Turkey were held. In its wake came a new set of closed camp facilities across the Greek islands, replacing the already repressive "hotspot" approach with a network of bluntly carceral spaces. Another demonstrative part of the EU's externalization policy is Lipa, a camp in the Northwest of Bosnia-Herzegovina, where migrants violently pushed back from nearby Croatia have been kept. This site has developed as a key node in the containment of migrants crossing the Balkan Route, holding people outside of the EU external border in fenced-off containers.

Looking across the EU's outer border, carceral encampment is a key instrument employed in sites like the Spanish enclaves of Melilla and Ceuta, the Italian islands in the Mediterranean, the Polish–Belarussian border, and the Kent coast in the United Kingdom. Moreover, it is also important to understand that externalization is not a linear process that takes place solely at the border, but one which involves neo-colonial intervention of states and NGOs in a range of humanitarian encampment practices in states outside the EU. Under the New Pact on Migration and Asylum proposed by the EU,[10] there is set to be further emphasis on the use of carceral encampment at the external border to govern access to the territory, as well as deeper cooperation between states on deportation. This comes alongside other tools such as the EU's long-standing use of accession processes, visa and citizenship regimes, policy synchronization, and initiatives in non-member states (such as recent Frontex deployments) to control mobility. Addressing externalization tactics in the Balkans, Marta Stojić Mitrović and Ana Vilenica describe this as "European imperial and neo-colonial attempts to filter the flow of migrants by imposing operations of security and control to the territories from which the migrants come or pass through."[11]

In response to this system of violence at the EU's outer borders, activists across Central and Northwest Europe have channeled solidarity through calls of "refugees welcome" and "*wir haben platz* [we have space]," signaling a willingness to receive more people in their countries. For example, groups like Seebrücke have organized around the notion of "safe harbours," campaigning for local authorities in Germany to declare more reception capacity. This kind of organizing has been very successful in mobilizing people, but also poses questions about the limits of solidarity premised on relocation. While we should rightly challenge violent encampment practices, an overemphasis or exceptionalism of carceral violence at the edge of Europe can and has spurred liberal humanitarian responses which reinforce encampment across the rest of the continent.

The growth of movements calling for the "relocation" or "evacuation" of migrants from the EU external border is still often hinged on the idea of camps being a reformable model that can be done "better" somewhere else – that somewhere else being *inner* Europe. This humanitarian facilitation of movement is seen as a way to enter people into the "accessible" and "orderly" reception processes of Central and Western Europe, despite this reception system being a key gear in the border regime. Such an intervention doesn't actually depart much from the EU narrative on externalization. Rather, it reproduces the notion of a threshold of deterrence at Europe's periphery, counterposed by the "fairness" of camps and asylum systems in countries like Germany. This further fuels discourses on the bounds of care and deservingness, with the "good" and "bad" camp working in tandem with the distinction between "good refugee" and "bad migrant." What such a binary view of encampment fails to address is the staged system of containment which connects places like Moria, Lipa, and the LEA, sites which form part of a cohesive network of encampments integral to the EU's racialized order of "liberal violence."[12] In a rush to get people out of camps at the external border, relocation activism risks normalizing encampment across all contexts, rather than challenging its application as the norm.

As the encounter at the demonstration in Freiburg highlights, the reproduction of camp space has often been expressed through the municipal lobbying of activists aiming to bring the administration of more "humane" camps under the purview of city authorities.[13] Abolitionism directly questions this practice, first by marking camps as inherently carceral, but also through critiquing the false promise of decentralizing encampment, a process which only embeds and widens containing infrastructure at the local level. Thinking through activist commitments from an abolitionist stance, we can peel away at the idea of camps as a necessary form of accommodation to meet the "emergency" of migration. Instead, encampment is a spatial response contingent on multiple structures of exclusion and exploitation related to housing, citizenship and labor. As such it is a historically rooted form of mobility governance under racial capitalism.

Camp abolition also challenges the humanitarian practice of separating encampment at the EU's outer border from encampment in Western and Central Europe, not least because these systems are jointly coordinated and funded. Part of connecting up the different aspects of carcerality is seeing, thinking, and acting beyond singular instances of border violence. Encampment is a historically relational phenomenon, a network of spaces which stage differentiated but interlocking processes of warehousing and moving people, working in concert with prisons, policing, asylum institutions, and labor markets.[14] As such, "relocation" is not an act of reprieve that separates people from camps, but instead a sinew that moves people between them. Whether through humanitarian means, deportation, or autonomous movement; relocation works as an inbuilt part of Europe's dense network of encampment. Here, abolitionist writing on prisons helps us to see how carcerality under bordered racial capitalism is not only about the fixing of movement, but the intersections of this fixing with the incitement of precarious labor[15] (see Whitener in this volume). Therefore, the humanitarian call to relocate camp residents, from external to internal camps, from supposed "bad" to "good," only has an insulating function for a regime of mobility already working as intended, what Barbara Beznec and Andrej Kurnik describe as "the management of the hierarchical porosity of EUropean borders."[16]

Challenging this "good/bad" binary is not just important to dispel the myth of an alternate and caring "good" camp, or to draw attention to the systemic relations of camps through relocation. Challenging the binary is also crucial in undoing the racialized bordering that humanitarianism reproduces. The focus of North and Central European activism with the bad conditions in camps at the EU external border (though fully warranted of solidarity) reaches a level of preoccupation which too often spills over into white saviorism. In doing so, it entrenches the idea of "bad" camps as only located in a periphery from which people need to be relocated (even "saved"), ignoring the systems of carcerality that they are moved on toward.

These solidarities premised on relocation reinforce a particular neo-colonial gaze, demarcating Europe's periphery as an inherent space of violence and repression, counterposed by discourses of an orderly core. As Marijana Hameršak, Sabine Hess, Marc Speer, and Marta Stojić Mitrović write, European attention toward the Balkan Route has often focused on particular camp conditions and pushbacks, but "this spectacularization was rarely directly attributed to the externalization of border control but rather more readily linked to a presumed inability of the Balkan states to manage migration, or to manage it without the blatant use of violence."[17] Thus the EU simultaneously outsources racialized border violence to the external border, while also portraying this bordering as unruly, and in itself a pretext for further securitarian and humanitarian intervention. As Rexhepi points out, the multiple forms of border externalization in the Balkans, including the carceral encampment of migrants funded by the EU, is part of a wider history of Euro-Atlantic white enclosure.[18] This is a multiscalar process which interfaces the racialization of migrants from Africa and Asia, with the racialization of people from the Balkan region itself, producing nesting hierarchies of nominal whiteness which serve EU mobility and market regimes.

> The Balkan route reemerges here not as a separate set of supposedly independent nation-states submerged in interethnic conflicts but as collaborative, interdependent, and protracted forms of modern/colonial regimes of power that facilitate the filtering of refugees for the Euro-American inner core through parallel processes of interpolicing their own racialized populations.[19]

Far from challenging this process, the call for humanitarian relocation to the "good" camp acts as a supportive narration of this racialized system, charting and constructing the distinction between an inner *white* liberal European "host,"[20] and its uncaring periphery, the outer threshold from which people are "saved." An abolitionist attention to the colonial histories enfolded in the idea of Europe and its periphery puts this discourse into relief. It also further challenges our unproblematized use of "refugees welcome" and "we have space." What kind of welcome? What kind of space? Willkommenskultur [Welcome Culture], which entered the German popular discourse in 2015, is perhaps the most acute example of this dehistoricized humanitarian reception which reconstructs colonial asymmetries of power and whiteness for the hoster,[21] while normalizing containment in camps as the given form of refuge for arriving migrants.

CAMP ABOLITION IN PRACTICE

As Jenna Loyd, Matt Mitchelson, and Andrew Burridge remind us, abolition is about connecting up intersecting dimensions of carceral state violence not just analytically, but also through the collaboration of resistance movements in breaking them and building up new revolutionary spaces of community.[22] Supporting anti-camp movements, who are refusing to fall for the reformist promise of migrant relocation, forges alternatives to humanitarianism. Instead of a "contained welcome" – which carves out the space for more camps – abolitionist organizers are challenging the idea of encampment altogether and its neo-colonial geographies. In doing so, they are growing community infrastructures of care which reject the idea of safety as something enforced by border guards, prison officers, police, or camp security.

A feminist stance is integral to camp abolition

The work of groups like *Women in Exile* (see Ngari and Dede in this volume), a migrant-led women's collective campaigning against camps in Germany, has been at the forefront of this struggle. Since 2002 they have been organizing around the call of camp abolition: meeting with women in camps across the country, documenting conditions inside different sites, and holding awareness workshops and demonstrations. Their intervention makes clear that it is the "compulsory collective accommodation system"[23] as a whole that is at fault, rather than any particular aspect of camps that can be remedied to make them "safe" for women and queer migrants. This work reminds us that a "good" camp is a fiction of reformist politics, and we need to remove our consent from policies which seek a liberal gender parity under the persistence of carceral institutions. While humanitarian efforts divert attention to the specter of facilities abroad, or bury actual transformation in small-scale changes to "soften" containment, abolitionists are working on radical actions which connect encampment with the wider struggles against carceral borders and heteropatriarchy (see Cowan et al. in this volume), building on the radical praxis of Black feminism which informs and strengthens the abolitionist struggle.[24]

In her writing on movements in the Kreuzberg district of Berlin, Napuli Langa describes how the feminist anti-camp movement has taken the issue of camps and border violence into the street: occupying schools, public squares like Oranienplatz, political institutions and even the Brandenburg Gate. As Langa emphasizes:

> Underlying all these actions were three demands: Abolition of the *lagers*, abolition of the obligation of residence ("Residenzpflicht" in the German language), which forbids us to leave the city where we are accommodated so that refugees are to move only 40 kilometres and not more, and the cessation of deportations.[25]

Here we see how camp abolition brings together the fight on different aspects of border violence, moving the dial from a simple critique of accommodation, to a focus on the way encampment meshes with policing everyday movement, gatekeeping asylum and feeding deportation policies. Migrant feminist activism is central to this work, drawing attention to the intersectional oppressions of the camp which disproportionately impact women and LGBTQ+ migrants. The call of "No *Lager* for Women! Abolish all *Lagers!*"[26] (see Ngari and Dede in this volume) is a refusal of the system in its entirety, reminding us that abolition is not a segmented struggle which relies on "winning one set of (apparent) privileges through reinforcing someone else's oppression."[27]

Mutual aid is a process of care against and beyond camps

Ending encampment also means attending to the structures of care which need to be built up in opposition to and beyond carceral frameworks. Activism around camps can act to rethink housing, labor, healthcare and social space – important aspects of abolitionist organizing which build community strength and bust the myth of camps as necessary protective structures for migrants. In Freiburg, the networks built up by migrants from the camp, together with local activists, speak to these potential shifts from humanitarian aid to mutual aid. Setting up food-sharing, community kitchens, and social events outside of camps are practical steps in the withdrawal of consent from the humanitarian industrial complex.[28] This mutual aid praxis creates revolutionary spaces of learning toward an abolitionist future.[29] It also develops radical alternatives of care to the system of encampment which uses constant relocation as a tool to prevent the building of community.

With this in mind, abolitionist mutual aid is not simply about the commoning of physical resources, but also the building of political autonomy and anti-carceral networks which go beyond just camps. This can take many forms: like court support, translation work, demo organizing, anti-deportation mobilization, coalition building with movements in other cities and countries, engaging in labor struggles, as well as supporting local anti-racist and feminist campaigns. One key dimension of this abolitionist organizing has been the growth of Camp-watch groups, building from the radical tradition of Cop-watch and detention visitors groups which monitor policing and prisons. This is an example of how information networks connect migrants and other solidarians in an effort to understand the problems being faced within carceral-deportative regimes. Documenting and publishing information about camps engages activists with the challenges of highlighting institutional violence in order to hasten its end, while also risking the reform of conditions which retain the institution. But this work on abolitionist reforms is also a necessary step to chip away and reveal contradictions in the system, and when combined with independent mutual aid structures embraces the diversity of tactics needed to dismantle carceral systems.

Camp abolition is also anti-colonial, or it is not abolitionist

Solidarity to people facing the oppression of encampment should not be predicated on the arc of containment which humanitarian relocation offers. This reformist approach does the work of separating and obscuring the violence of encampment in Western and Central Europe, while exceptionalizing camps at and beyond the EU external border. Camp abolitionism works to dismantle the notion of *white* European solidarity activists as "the good hosts," challenging this colonial gaze of Europe's periphery and highlighting the reciprocal relationship of encampment across different locations. Instead of insisting on conditions in camps like Lipa and Moria as being an isolated part of an otherwise "welcoming" system, abolitionist activism attacks the border politics of the EU which brings these supposed opposite poles into a connected system of containment.

Importantly, this does not mean a relativism which sees all camps as the same or diminishes the particular violence of externalization. Decolonial abolition works from the situated organizing of migrants and comrades across different contexts. This is based on the experience and knowledge of people who have faced differentiated regimes of encampment through (intersecting) processes of imperialism, fascism and humanitarianism. Taking cues from migrant-led organizing in camps, no-borders groups and activist networks such as *Transbalkanska solidarnost*[30] who support people along the Balkan Route, we can reposition solidarities in service of local movements working at the EU external border. These abolitionist formations build feminist, anti-fascist, anti-capitalist and migrant-led horizons of care, informed by historic and ongoing counter-hegemonic struggles against the neo-colonial projects of Western states in the Balkans.[31] In this way, rather than replicating an imposed and securitized "help" from the outside,[32] we can reconsider what solidarity means in the abolitionist struggle, foregrounding the work of people fighting at the interface of carceral state violence, imperialism, racial capitalism and EU hegemony.

Thinking through these geographies of solidarity allows us to understand the ways "externalization" has been internalized by the "refugees welcome" movement, and how we might think and act outside of this. Thus, rather than falling for humanitarian relocation, decolonial abolition can build stronger and more positioned solidarity against camps, critically addressing histories of Euro-white saviorism and taking the lead from regional mobilizations which have particular lived experiences of encampment. In these ways, abolition invites us to attend to the threading of the local with the transborder, an ongoing and contextual process which requires us to share in radical care across space and time, while actively acknowledging and fighting the system of imperial racial capitalism which unevenly impacts us.

AN ABOLITIONIST WELCOME

Following Ruth Wilson Gilmore's call that "Freedom is a place"[33] an abolitionist approach to camps engages us with the question of how to build this place and how we conceive of solidarity. What would an "abolitionist welcome" look like, as opposed to the contained encampment implicit to "refugees welcome"? In critically addressing these positionalities of care we need to think who the "we" is that is offering space, and to what kind of spaces are people "welcome"? Looking at systems of encampment it is clear that freedom is not a place that people can be simply relocated to, nor is it counterposed by a place from which people must be saved. Thus an abolitionist welcome asks us to move beyond Europe as host, a racialized humanitarian logic that serves the constant reanimation of imperial borderlands and the reproduction of carceral spaces. In re-aligning what we mean by "welcome," we can learn from migrant-led and regional no-borders struggles which critically address camps as non-reformable infrastructures of the border regime. This activism in and against camps draws out the need for anti-carceral solidarities which attend to the EU reception system as a whole, solidarities which are attuned to the way this system functions through differentiated and interlocking processes of containment and relocation.

More than just a reflexive approach to solidarity, camp abolition is an active and growing praxis which opens spaces and alliances grounded in decolonial, feminist and mutual aid organizing. In fighting to dismantle the carceral border regime, these mobilizations look to thread the local with the transborder, creating welcomes that exceed the confines of nation-states, the EU and humanitarian infrastructures. The work of groups like *Women in Exile* bring this to the fore in their local campaigning actions on camps, as well as their transnational engagements with wider struggles against EU border externalization, such as their launching of the Sea Watch 5 vessel in January 2023.[34] These un-bordered rehearsals work toward abolitionist futures, guided by those experiencing and organizing against the intersection of encampment with neo-colonialism, heteropatriarchy and racial capitalism (see Thompson in this volume). In building solidarity against and beyond camps, we see how abolition is not an isolated campaign goal to end a certain institution, but a revolutionary praxis which connects up and resists the carceral border regime in its entirety.

NOTES

1. Thanks to Elife Krasniqi for introducing me to many of the texts and ideas which this chapter draws on, and to Anela, Bekim, Arberie, Silke, and Taylor for our long class discussions. Thanks also to Marijana Hameršak, Clara Bauer and the *Border Abolition Now* editorial team for their thoughtful revisions.

2. Piro Rexhepi, *White Enclosures: Racial Capitalism and Coloniality along the Balkan Route, On Decoloniality*, Durham: Duke University Press, 2022.

3. Michael Hardt and Antonio Negri, *Empire*. Cambridge: Harvard University Press, 2000.

4. Hanno Brankamp, "Camp Abolition: Ending Carceral Humanitarianism in Kenya (and Beyond)." *Antipode* 54(1), 2022: 106–129.

5. Athena Athanasiou, "Reflections on the Politics of Mourning: Feminist Ethics and Politics in the Age of Empire." *Historein*, 5, 2005: 40–57.

6. Polly Pallister-Wilkins, "Saving the Souls of White Folk: Humanitarianism as White Supremacy." *Security Dialogue* 52, 2021: 98–106.

7. William Walters, "Foucault and Frontiers: Notes on the Birth of the Humanitarian Border." In: U. Bröckling, S. Krasmann, and T. Lemke (Eds), *Governmentality: Current issues and Future Challenges,*. London: Routledge, 2010, pp.138–364.

8. Ruth Wilson Gilmore, *Golden Gulag: Prisons, Surplus, Crisis, and Opposition in Globalizing California*. Oakland: University of California Press, 2007.

9. Lois Becket, "A System of Global Apartheid: Author Harsha Walia on Why the Border Crisis Is a Myth." *The Guardian*, April 7, 2021. www.theguardian.com/world/2021/apr/07/us-border-immigration-harsha-walia

10. European Commission, "Political Agreement on the New Pact on Migration and Asylum." Accessed June 30, 2023. https://ec.europa.eu/commission/presscorner/detail/en/statement_23_3183

11. Marta Stojić Mitrović and Ana Vilenica, "Enforcing and Disrupting Circular Movement in an EU Borderscape: Housingscaping in Serbia." *Citizenship Studies* 23(6), 2019: 540–558.

12. Arshad Isakjee, Thom Davies, Jelena Obradović-Wochnik and Karolína Augustová, "Liberal Violence and the Racial Borders of the European Union." *Antipode* 52(6), 2020: 1751–1773.

13. Helge Schwiertz and Felix Keß, "Safe Harbours: The Cities Defying the EU to Welcome Migrants." *OpenDemocracy*. Accessed June 30, 2023.

www.opendemocracy.net/en/safe-harbours-cities-defying-eu-welcome-migrants/

14. Jenna Loyd, Matt Mitchelson and Andrew Burridge (Eds), *Beyond Walls and Cages: Prisons, Borders, and Global Crisis*. Athens: University of Georgia Press, 2012.

15. Ruth Wilson Gilmore and Craig Gilmore, "Restating the Obvious: Ruth Wilson Gilmore & Craig Gilmore." In: Micheal Sorkin (Ed.), *Indefensible Space: The Architecture of the National Insecurity State*. New York: Taylor & Francis, 2012.

16. Barbara Beznec and Andrej Kurnik, "Old Routes, New Perspectives. A Postcolonial Reading of the Balkan Route." *Movements. Journal for Critical Migration and Border Regime Studies* 5(1) 2020, p. 47.

17. Marijana Hameršak, Sabine Hess, Marc Speer, and Marta Stojić Mitrović, "The Forging of the Balkan Route. Contextualizing the Border Regime in the EU Periphery." *Movements. Journal for Critical Migration and Border Regime Studies* 5(1), 2020, p. 21.

18. Rexhepi, *White Enclosures*.

19. Ibid., p. 9.

20. Nataša Kovačević, "Europe as Host/Hostage." *Interventions* 14(3), 2012: 361–376.

21. Fiorenza Picozza, *The Coloniality of Asylum: Mobility, Autonomy and Solidarity in the Wake of Europe's Refugee Crisis*. Washington: Rowman and Littlefield, 2021.

22. Loyd, Mitchelson, and Burridge, *Beyond Walls and Cages*, 9.

23. *Women in Exile*, "Asylum Seeking Women Organising and Empowering Themselves." 2013, p. 3, accessed July 20, 2023. www.women-in-exile.net/wp-content/uploads/2013/12/wie_infobroschuere_31.10.13_for_refugee_women.pdf

24. Angela Y. Davis, Gina Dent, Erica R. Meiners, and Beth E. Richie, *Abolition. Feminism. Now.* New York: Penguin, 2022, p. 16.

25. Napuli Langa, "About the Refugee Movement in Kreuzberg/Berlin." *Movements. Journal for Critical Migration and Border Regime Studies* 1(2), 2015, p. 3.

26. *Lager* is the German word used for camp.

27. Loyd, Mitchelson, and Burridge, *Beyond Walls and Cages*, 9.

28. Deanna Dadusc and Pierpaolo Mudu, "Care without Control: The Humanitarian Industrial Complex and the Criminalisation of Solidarity." *Geopolitics* 27(4), 2020: 1205–1230.

29. Aviah Sarah Day and Shanice Octavia McBean, *Abolition Revolution*. London: Pluto Press, 2022.

30. Transbalkanska solidarnost. Accessed July 6, 2023. https://transbalkanskasolidarnost.home.blog/

31. Beznec and Kurnik, *Old Routes, New Perspectives*.

32. Nidžara Ahmetašević and Gorana Mlinarević, *People on the Move in Bosnia and Herzegovina in 2018: Stuck in the Corridors to the EU.* Sarajevo: Heinrich Böll Stiftung, 2019.
33. Ruth Wilson Gilmore, *Abolition Geography: Essays Towards Liberation.* New York: Verso, 2022.
34. Women in Exile & Friends, "We Are the Godmothers of Sea-Watch 5." Accessed July 6, 2023. www.women-in-exile.net/en/wir-sind-die-patinnen-von-sea-watch-5/

8

"Alternatives to detention" and the carceral state in the UK

Lauren Cape-Davenhill

In 2021, the UK introduced GPS tagging for immigration purposes. The new GPS ankle tags monitor the wearer's location 24 hours a day in an increasingly technologized approach to the control and confinement of non-citizens that extends borders deep into everyday life. GPS tagging is an example of the adaptation and expansion of "Alternatives to Detention" (ATDs): a range of practices, policies and technologies used by governments to manage people subject to immigration control in the community as opposed to closed confinement. ATDs are expanding globally, with more than 250 examples identified in over 60 countries.[1] While often promoted as a more "humane" alternative to immigration detention by mainstream advocacy and human rights organizations, ATDs reinforce and extend the carceral state, functioning as part of a continuum of social control of migrants which also includes detention and deportation.

This chapter takes an abolitionist perspective, using the UK as a case study to outline how ATDs form part of the "immigration enforcement detention and surveillance regime"[2] in three key ways. First, ATDs expand the reach of the carceral state through drawing new populations under state surveillance and control, and increasing the tools and technologies available to immigration enforcement. Second, ATDs contribute to the (re)production of the carceral state through generating profits and reinforcing the political economy of the immigration-industrial complex; disciplining and controlling migrants; and reproducing the discourses and logics underpinning immigration control. Finally, ATDs qualitatively change the nature of carceral control through extending the reach of immigration enforcement into the most intimate and personal areas of people's everyday lives. The chapter is based on data from UK Home Office policy and guidance documents; inspection reports; and findings from qualitative research with people subject to ATDs in the UK from 2021 to 2022. It argues that abolitionist organizing must pay attention to ATDs as part of the struggle to dismantle the systemic violence of the carceral state.

ABOLITIONISM AND THE CARCERAL STATE

Abolitionism is ultimately emancipatory, seeking rich lives and human flourishing for all through the transformation of society. This includes the dismantling of mass incarceration, policing, and border control as dominant responses to social issues; addressing the root causes of violence and harm through education, healthcare, and other social provision; and the envisioning and building of new forms of justice "based on reparation and reconciliation rather than retribution and vengeance."[3] This chapter draws on abolitionist understandings of the carceral state to unpack the functioning and effects of "Alternatives to Detention." The idea of the "carceral state" draws attention to the systemic and relational aspects of mass incarceration, showing that carceral institutions such as prisons and detention centers do not exist in isolation. Mass incarceration serves a range of political and economic interests, with carceral institutions forming part of a dense network of relationships, actors, entities and companies.[4] This systems-orientated lens enables analysis of ATDs as part of a carceral continuum and in relationship to other forms of incarceration and enforcement.

Following from an understanding of the carceral state as a system of economic and social relations, a key question for abolitionists becomes whether any given reform serves to challenge this system and increase the possibilities for further transformation in the future; or whether it leaves this system intact, or even reinforces the oppressive structures it seeks to improve.[5] This is encapsulated in the idea of "reformist" versus "non-reformist reforms," originally articulated by André Gorz[6] and developed in discussions around prison abolition by Ruth Wilson Gilmore and others. ATDs in the UK act as "reformist reforms," a set of practices which, while superficially progressive, serve to reinforce the carceral state. This chapter sets out the specific ways in which ATDs extend and deepen the reach of the carceral state as part of a carceral continuum along with detention, deportation, and other forms of enforcement and surveillance.

"ALTERNATIVES TO DETENTION" AND THE CARCERAL STATE: THE INTERNATIONAL CONTEXT

While there is debate over the precise definition of ATDs, they broadly enable "asylum-seekers, refugees, and migrants to reside in the community while their migration status is being resolved or while awaiting deportation or removal from the country ... subject to some restrictions on movement or liberty."[7] ATDs are becoming increasingly widespread internationally. In 2014, the UN High Commission on Refugees (UNHCR) launched a global strategy to end immigration detention. One of the strategy's main goals was to ensure that ATDs were legally available and implemented in practice. As part of this strategy, ATDs have been implemented or expanded in countries including Indonesia, Mexico, Canada, the UK, Bulgaria, and Lithuania.[8]

The expansion of ATDs must be understood in the context of intensifying hostility toward migrants and restrictive approaches to immigration enforcement. Globally, people on the move have been increasingly framed in political and public discourse as an existential threat to national security and identity; notably following 9/11 and the "global war on terror." The past three decades have been characterized by increasingly coercive and violent measures to contain, control or expel migrants, including externalization; pushbacks; the expansion of inland border controls; a plethora of restrictive immigration policies making it ever harder for non-citizens to gain asylum, residency, or citizenship; and the expansion of immigration detention. Immigration detention has become routine in many countries, with over 1,300 detention centers identified globally as of March 2023.[9] In neoliberal states such as the US and UK, the expansion of immigration detention and the criminalization of migrants is intimately connected with the rise in mass incarceration, whereby prison and policing form increasingly dominant responses to populations marginalized by neoliberalism.[10]

This context of hostility toward migrants and a hardening of approaches to immigration control has been reflected in government approaches to ATDs, which have generally been interpreted through a lens of control and enforcement.[11] Nevertheless, ATDs are still promoted as a more "humane" approach to immigration enforcement by a range of mainstream human rights and advocacy organizations as well as governments. The language of "alternatives" to detention gives the illusion of a clear distinction between ATDs and incarceration, suggesting an anti-carceral potential and deflecting attention away from the harms and state violence of ATDs. It is thus important for abolitionists to pay attention to ATDs as part of struggles against detention and deportation, as discussed below. The examination of ATDs as implemented and experienced in practice is also valuable analytically, contributing to abolitionist understandings of the ways in which the carceral state is expanding and adapting in specific contexts.

ATDS IN THE UK

The UK is a fruitful context to unpack the ways in which ATDs reinforce and extend the carceral state. In line with global trends, UK discourses and policies toward migrants have become ever more restrictive in recent decades, including the implementation of "Hostile Environment" policies designed to make life unlivable for people without documents. Detention has formed an increasingly important part of the UK's approach to immigration enforcement since the 1990s. The UK detains people without a time limit, making it the only country in Europe to deploy indefinite detention for immigration purposes.

Concerns around both the human impacts and escalating costs of detention have framed growing interest in ATDs in the UK. A 2015 cross-party parliamentary inquiry into immigration detention, and a 2016 independent review commissioned by the Home Office, both called for a reduction in the use of detention and an expansion in the use of alternatives. The Home Office has primarily interpreted ATDs through an enforcement lens, as part of "a suite of interventions to reduce illegal migration."[12] As such, the UK ATD landscape has been characterized by an expansion in coercive and surveillance-based approaches. ATDs currently used in the UK include immigration bail; restrictions on work, study and residence; reporting requirements; electronic monitoring; voluntary return schemes; and a small number of case management pilots. These restrictions reshape and extend the carceral state into communities and homes.

ATDS AS AN EXPANSION OF THE CARCERAL STATE: NEW PEOPLE, TOOLS, AND TECHNOLOGIES

ATDs in the UK first serve to expand the reach of the carceral state through drawing an ever-broader range of people into some form of state supervision; and increasing the techniques and technologies available to immigration enforcement. First, ATDs have a "net-widening" effect, supplementing rather than replacing immigration detention and drawing in new populations who would never have been detained. Reporting, going to "sign on" with the Home Office, is the most common ATD imposed alongside bail. From 2015 to 2018, between 75,000 and 90,000 people in the UK at any one time were required to report for immigration purposes.[13] This is far higher than the number of people detained, which numbers a maximum of around 3,500 at any one time.[14] Furthermore, people in the UK can be made subject to an ATD even if they cannot lawfully be detained, for example, because there is no prospect of their imminent removal due to documentation issues or other barriers to return. ATDs thus serve to expand the net of social control beyond that of immigration detention, through drawing in tens of thousands of people annually who would never have been detained.

The implementation of ATDs in the UK has also been characterized by an expansion in the criteria of people eligible for particular ATDs. This is particularly evident when considering the trajectory of one of the most coercive forms of ATD, electronic monitoring (EM), or tagging. EM for immigration purposes was first introduced through the Asylum and Immigration (Treatment of Claimants) Act 2004, with eligibility limited to people deemed "high harm" or at "high risk" of absconding. The 2016 Immigration Act expanded EM use, placing an obligation on the Secretary of State to impose EM conditions on *everyone* categorized as a "foreign national offender" and subject to immigration control. Tagging has also been expanded beyond people with convictions, with an ongoing pilot imposing EM for people arriving in the UK "irregularly" via boat.[15] This parallels trends in the US, where the use of EM for immigration purposes was originally limited to people with convictions, but has since expanded to people seeking asylum, including children.[16] This demonstrates the ways in which new digital technologies enable ever more people to be drawn into the regime of state surveillance and control.

Furthermore, EM provides a clear example of ATDs serving to expand the "technologies, tools and tactics available for immigration control."[17] New GPS tags, introduced in 2021, enable the wearer's location to be tracked 24 hours a day. This represents a significant increase in levels of surveillance and intrusion, with serious human costs, as discussed below. The transition to GPS monitoring for immigration purposes has been accompanied by new powers for the Home Office to collect, store, and access data indefinitely via private contractors. Of particular concern, the Home Office is able to use location data collected through GPS surveillance against people in their immigration claims. It is as yet unclear how frequently this is being done in practice, but has disturbing echoes of developments in the US, where data from electronic tags has been used as intelligence to inform immigration raids on workplaces.

ATDS AND THE (RE)PRODUCTION
OF THE CARCERAL STATE

ATDs also contribute to the (re)production of the carceral state. First, ATDs in the UK can be situated within the "immigration-industrial" complex. Private companies in the UK are increasingly involved in delivering ATDs, with a small number of companies contracted to deliver a range of contracts across the immigration system. G4S and Serco both have recent or current contracts for immigration detention, asylum accommodation, and EM. As in the US,[18] a small number of companies thus profit from whether people are detained or supervised via ATDs. EM is operated exclusively by the private sector, and is increasingly a source of profit for technology companies as well as security contractors. British technology company Buddi Limited was awarded a £6 million contract in 2022 to provide facial recognition smartwatches, as part of a new wave of EM devices. ATDs thus form an increasingly important part of the political economy of incarceration. Indeed, the pursuit of "alternatives" to detention is in keeping with neoliberal imperatives of efficiency, or what Hadar Aviram terms "humonetarianism."[19] For governments, the increasing popularity of ATDs reflects pressures on detention bed capacity and the desire to cut costs and conduct immigration enforcement in a more cost-effective way.

As part of the immigration-industrial complex, ATDs are one component in a system designed to discipline and control migrants which is partly exerted through the threat of deportation. Officially, ATDs and detention both exist to facilitate deportation, with staff at some reporting centers being given explicit targets for the number of removals they are supposed to complete.[20] For those who remain undeported, ATDs are one component of a system of social control. Migrant bodies circulate through various forms of incarceration including immigration detention and ATD supervision in a manifestation of "carceral churn."[21] This is illustrated by the "revolving door" between detention and reporting. Reporting centers are a common site where people are taken into detention, with the ostensible objective of facilitating removal. However, in practice many people detained are released back onto some form of ATD restriction in the community. Of over 2,500 people who were detained on reporting to the Home Office between April and September 2016, over two thirds had been released from detention within four months.[22] This "churn" serves to distress, exhaust and discipline migrants, reducing the potential for resistance.

Finally, ATDs reproduce the logics and discourses underpinning immigration enforcement and detention through reinforcing the associations between migrants and criminality. The immigration-industrial complex is premised on "the assumption that there is a perpetual enemy who must always be fought, but can never be conquered."[23] Criminalization and (racialized) "othering" are an integral component of the production of this "enemy." ATDs deploying techniques and practices drawn directly from the criminal justice system further inscribe migrants with associations of criminality. Electronic tags, in particular, are strongly associated with criminality and often experienced as highly stigmatizing, as discussed below. Given the majority of people subject to tagging for immigration purposes are racially minoritized men, this interacts with discourses around dangerous Black/foreign criminality. Such discourses and practices of exclusion serve to produce and maintain certain people and groups as "enemy" and therefore "detainable" or otherwise subject to immigration control.[24] This further strengthens the logics of immigration detention and enforcement.

QUALITATIVE CHANGES TO THE NATURE OF INCARCERATION: ATDs AS AN EXTENSION OF THE CARCERAL INTO EVERYDAY LIVES

Finally, ATDs in the UK qualitatively change the nature of carceral control, extending the reach of immigration enforcement into the most intimate and personal areas of people's everyday lives and function as a form of incarceration in the community. This is illustrated with data gathered from research with people facing deportation in the UK from 2021 to 2022.[25]

The consequences of not complying with ATD requirements include being detained (and ultimately deported), or even arrested, as a breach of conditions is considered a criminal offense. The fear of being detained or deported as a result of non-compliance with ATD requirements has a powerful disciplinary effect. An omnipresent sense of "deportability," the powerfully interiorized fear of detention and deportation,[26] leads people to structure their lives and everyday routines around meeting their ATD requirements. Often, reporting centers are far from people's homes, requiring time-consuming and expensive journeys. Reporting frequency varies, with some people being required to report monthly or less, while others are required to go weekly or even multiple times per week. As a result, particularly in cases of more frequent reporting, people's weeks are structured by their reporting requirements.

> Mentally, it's like you program, your week, you know where you're going Monday, and this Monday, this Monday, Monday, Wednesday, or Thursday …
>
> (Akin)[27]

Ensuring that electronic tags remain charged similarly elicits high levels of self-discipline. Reported charging times range from two hours to nine or ten hours due to technical issues; and in some instances, the tag's battery runs down again quickly, requiring multiple periods of charging within 24 hours.

> Yesterday, I didn't charge it, so today I have to wait two bloody hours in a wall, waiting for it to be charged, and you know, I just have to put the, you know, the coffee and tobacco in front of me, and the music quite low, and I listen to the radio and have one cigarette after the other …
>
> (Miguel)

People describe curtailing their social activities due to concerns about getting home in time to charge their tag, in further evidence of the powerful disciplinary impact of ATDs. Furthermore, in line with other research,[28] people subject to tagging report feeling uncomfortable with or avoiding social activities where their tag might be visible, due to high levels of stigma. They worry that the tag will lead others to perceive them as a "criminal" or "terrorist," again resulting in the self-limiting of everyday activities.

> Even my son, I can't even take him to the swimming pool because I don't want him asking me questions (about the tag) …
>
> (Lazarus)

The disciplinary impacts of EM have been compounded by the transition from radio to GPS tagging. Constant panoptic surveillance serves as a form of incarceration in the community, with people describing feeling monitored and observed, and drawing explicit parallels with prior experiences of incarceration.

> This is still a prison. Yeah, okay. I'm allowed out whenever I want. This tag – they know exactly what I do every single 24 hours ...
>
> (Miguel)

Furthermore, tagging extends the reach of immigration enforcement onto the body itself. Electronic monitoring is an ATD literally attached to the body through an ankle tag, and people on tag experience an inescapable embodied reminder of their restriction, as well as discomfort, and in some cases pain and injury. The tags attached to the ankle are bulky, and can rub, irritate or cause physical pain:

> ... the other tag have already, have caused me an injury on the other leg. I'm injured, and I'm still trying to get it fixed, and it's not healed yet ...
>
> (Luis)

The tags also vibrate when they are low on battery, acting as an intrusive embodied reminder of their presence, as well as generating anxiety about running out of charge.

Moreover, ATDs in the UK are an indefinite form of confinement. Unlike the use of community sanctions in the criminal justice system, which are typically time-limited, people on ATDs do not know how long they will be subject to their conditions.

> ... they do for you tag, but the problem, they don't tell you time. They don't tell you time. I don't know how long they going to take it off – maybe 1 year, maybe 3 months, maybe 4 months. They don't tell you time ...
>
> (Iyad)

As a result of the lack of time limitation and weak scrutiny of ATD use, people may be subject to ATD conditions for extremely long periods of time. For example, Paul spent 17 months in immigration detention following a 14-month prison sentence; and has since spent over eleven years on multiple ATDs, including being unable to work or study; having restrictions on residence; and reporting every week. Unsurprisingly, the mental health impacts of these restrictions are significant. ATDs thus represent an indefinite extension of immigration control into people's everyday lives and exert a powerful disciplinary effect underpinned by the fear of detention and deportation.

ABOLITIONISM AND THE NEED FOR
NEW FORMS OF JUSTICE

Abolitionists seek to challenge the systemic violence of the carceral state and build new forms of justice. As such, it is part of abolitionist work to challenge the social control and violence of both ATDs and detention, as part of the broader struggle against incarceration and borders. Abolitionists have long been active in campaigning against detention both in the UK and globally. It is important that organizing against detention incorporates explicit opposition to "alternatives" which simply extend the carceral state in new directions. Without this, there is a risk that anti-detention campaigning inadvertently bolsters the case for ATDs, given that ATDs are typically presented as more "humane" and, crucially, are cheaper than detention, making them particularly appealing for policy-makers.

Organizing against ATDs as part of the broader struggle against borders in the UK has become more visible in recent years, as exemplified by the "Abolish Reporting" campaign.[29] Abolish Reporting is coordinated by migrant-led campaigning and advice organization *Migrants Organise* and the grassroots campaign against detention *These Walls Must Fall*. The campaign is explicitly framed in abolitionist terms. It situates the demand to end reporting and electronic monitoring as part of the wider struggle to end immigration detention and enforcement, and the criminalization and surveillance of people subject to immigration control; and to fight for "dignity, justice and welcome for all migrants." Campaign activities have included a national day of action with protests outside six different reporting centers as well as online; building connections between groups challenging reporting conditions in different parts of the country; and compiling and sharing information sheets with practical advice for people subject to reporting conditions, and advisers and caseworkers, on how to challenge these conditions. Such tactics both try and improve the immediate situation of people subject to ATDs, through supporting them to challenge their conditions; while also challenging the broader system of which ATDs are a component. This campaign thus provides an important example of "non-reformist" organizing which challenges both ATDs and the broader immigration enforcement and surveillance regime.

CONCLUSION

Lessons from the realities of ATD implementation in the UK are relevant to other contexts, given the growing international interest in ATDs and tendency for carceral technologies, techniques and tools to circulate across borders.[30] This chapter has demonstrated that far from presenting an "alternative" to detention, ATDs in the UK form part of a continuum of incarceration and social control in a number of specific ways. ATDs draw in large numbers of people who would never have been detained into a form of carceral control in the community through "net-widening." They also expand the tools, technologies and techniques available to immigration enforcement, with GPS tagging enabling 24-hour surveillance and the collection of geolocation data which has the potential to be used against people in their own immigration cases. ATDs contribute to the reproduction of the carceral state as part of the "immigration-industrial complex," with an increasing range of private actors profiting from ATDs as well as detention and other forms of enforcement. They also contribute to the discipline and control of migrants, underpinned by the fear of deportation, and partly achieved through "carceral churn" as people are circulated through various forms of incarceration, including carceral control in the community. ATDs also help to (re)produce the rationales of the carceral state through reinforcing the associations between migrants and criminality. Qualitative data from recent research in the UK has illustrated how ATDs as a form of indefinite incarceration in the community qualitatively change the nature of carceral control, extending the reach of immigration enforcement deep into people's everyday lives and exerting a powerful disciplinary effect underpinned by the fear of detention and deportation.

Developments in ATDs in the UK thus illustrate the broader limitations of trying to "improve" elements of the immigration system without challenging borders themselves. ATDs premised on surveillance and control must be challenged as part of abolitionist organizing against detention, deportation and other manifestations of the carceral state. The recently launched campaign "Abolish Reporting" provides an important example of grassroots organizing which situates ATDs as part of a carceral continuum, and seeks to directly improve the lives of those subject to ATDs while challenging borders and enforcement more broadly. Beyond this, we must continue to seek new and radical forms of justice which contribute to the dismantling of the carceral state.

NOTES

1. International Detention Coalition, "There Are Alternatives," *IDC*, 2015, p. 1.
2. Sarah Sherman-Stokes, "Immigration Detention Abolition and the Violence of Digital Cages." *Boston University School of Law Research Paper* 23(6), 2023: 4.
3. Angela Davis, *Are Prisons Obsolete?* New York: Seven Stories Press, 2003, p. 107.
4. Ruth Wilson Gilmore, *Abolition Geography: Essays towards Liberation.* London: Verso, 2022.
5. Luke de Noronha and Gracie Mae Bradley, *Against Borders: The Case for Abolition.* London and New York: Verso, 2022, p. 151.
6. André Gorz, *Strategy for Labour: A Radical Proposal.* Boston: Beacon Press, 1967, pp. 7–8.
7. C. Costello and E. Kaytaz, *Building Empirical Evidence into Alternatives to Detention: Perceptions of Asylum-Seekers and Refugees in Toronto and Geneva.* Geneva: UNHCR, 2013, pp. 10–11.
8. UNHCR, "UNHCR Global Strategy Beyond Detention: Final Progress Report, 2014–2019," *UNCR*, 2020.
9. Global Detention Project, "Immigration Detention Centres," 2023. www.globaldetentionproject.org/detention-centres/map-view
10. Loïc Wacquant, *Punishing the Poor: The Neoliberal Government of Social Insecurity.* Durham: Duke University Press, 2009; Ruth Wilson Gilmore,

Golden Gulag: Prisons, Surplus, Crisis, and Opposition in Globalizing California. Berkeley: University of California Press, 2007.

11. Alice Bloomfield, "Alternatives to Detention at a Crossroads: Humanisation or Criminalisation?" *Refugee Survey Quarterly* 35(1), 2016: 40.

12. Stephen Shaw, "Assessment of Government Progress in Implementing the Report on the Welfare in Detention of Vulnerable Persons." *Home Office*, 2018, p. 115. https://assets.publishing.service.gov.uk/government/uploads/system/uploads/attachment_data/file/728376/Shaw_report_2018_Final_web_accessible.pdf

13. David Bolt, "An Inspection of the Home Office's Reporting and Offender Management Processes." *Home Office*, 2017, p. 5; David Bolt, "A Re-Inspection of the Home Office's Reporting and Offender Management Processes and of Its Management of Non-Detained Foreign National Offenders," *Home Office*, 2019, p. 10.

14. Stephanie Silverman and Melanie Griffiths, "Immigration Detention in the UK." *Migration Observatory*, November 2, 2022. https://migrationobservatory.ox.ac.uk/resources/briefings/immigration-detention-in-the-uk/

15. Home Office, "Equality Impact Assessment: GPS Electronic Monitoring Expansion Pilot," *Home Office*, 2022. www.gov.uk/government/publications/offender-management/equality-impact-assessment-gps-electronic-monitoring-expansion-pilot

16. Carolina Sanchez Boe, "Fighting Border Control in Three Sites of Confinement: Contestation and Visibility in Prison, Immigration Detention and Under Digital Confinement in New York." *Champ Pénal/Penal Field*, 2020.

17. De Noronha and Mae Bradley, *Against Borders*, p. 157.

18. Boe, "Fighting Border Control."

19. Hadar Aviram, *Cheap on Crime: Recession-Era Politics and the Transformation of American Punishment*. Berkeley and Los Angeles: University of California Press, 2015.

20. Bolt, "An Inspection of the Home Office's Reporting and Offender Management Processes," 10.

21. Nick Gill et al., "Carceral Circuitry: New Directions in Carceral Geography." *Progress in Human Geography* 42(2), 2018: 187.

22. Bolt, "An Inspection of the Home Office's Reporting and Offender Management Processes," 19–20. Statistics on reporting are not routinely released. These figures are from ad hoc inspection reports, and are the latest available at the time of writing.

23. Gilmore, *Abolition Geography*, 459.

24. Lauren Martin and Matthew Mitchelson, "Geographies of Detention and Imprisonment: Interrogating Spatial Practices of Confinement,

Discipline, Law, and State Power." *Geography Compass* 3(1), 2009: 468–469.

25. Data was collected as part of a broader qualitative PhD study on experiences of facing deportation after contact with the criminal justice system in the UK. 22 people with lived experience of ATD conditions were interviewed.

26. Nicholas De Genova, "The Legal Production of Mexican/Migrant 'Illegality.'" *Latino Studies* 2(2): 2004, 161.

27. Names and other identifying information have been changed to protect anonymity.

28. Boe, "Fighting Border Control"; Monish Bhatia, "Racial Surveillance and the Mental Health Impacts of Electronic Monitoring on Migrants." *Race and Class* 62(3), 2021: 18–36.

29. These Walls Must Fall, "Abolish Reporting," *Walls Must Fall*, 2022. https://wallsmustfall.org/abolish-reporting/#approach

30. Gill et al., "Carceral Circuitry."

9

Golden Gulag in Italy?

For the abolition of the reception-industrial complex

Francesco Marchi

Border humanitarianism nourishes the grandiose sovereign project of human mobility regulation. Border humanitarianism generates calls for more sovereignty rather than sovereignty's radical and emancipatory critique.

– Maurizio Albahari, *Crimes of Peace.*[1]

WHY RECEPTION NOW? ENVISIONING AN ABOLITIONIST POLITICS

Why reception[2]*? Why now? Why for so many people – especially for people of color?* These questions – which retrace the ones posed by Ruth Wilson Gilmore[3] on the expansion of the US prison-industrial complex – often go unasked, even in anti-racist and leftist circles. The common and taken-for-granted explanation is simple: for about a decade a series of emergencies, from the 2011 "Arab Uprisings" and the NATO military operation in Libya to the 2015 Syrian Civil War, caused an unprecedented flow of "forced migrants"[4] in need of reception in European countries. That is why, the taken-for-granted argument goes, we have witnessed an impressive growth of reception facilities.

In this regard, the Italian case, the focus of this chapter, is striking. If 6,284 people were in reception centers in 2007, this number skyrocketed to 66,066 in 2014 and reached a maximum of 183,681 in 2017.[5] About 50 reception centers were operative in 2008, while 12,275 facilities were active in 2018. From 2011 to

2018, public spending on reception increased by 900%. Is systemic and structural reception growth exclusively caused and related to a massive flow of "forced migrants?" Or, rather, do we have to analyze this phenomenon in counterintuitive ways? Are the key issues underlying *reception expansion* "moral" ones – or are they racial, economic, or political?[6]

Informed by Gilmore's insights, this chapter contends that *reception* expansion embodied a *fix* in a period of systemic socio-economic crisis. As the 1980s California prison expansion cannot be scrutinized without considering the profound and irreversible socio-economic crisis of the 1970s, reception expansion, which occurred in Italy during the 2010s, cannot be properly addressed without bringing back the 2008 Global Financial Crisis into the analytical framework. In the wake of the crisis, socio-economic arrangements went through a radical restructuring, with Italy risking default in 2011. Thus, one might argue that the socio-legal production of Global South people on the move as "forced migrants" to be confined within the reception system partly resembles the process of mass incarceration that occurred during the 1980s in California. Following this analytical suggestion, I refer to the reception-industrial complex in order to describe an array of interlacing elements – legal, socio-political, spatial, cultural and ideological – which converged and gave rise to a new infrastructure of government, which favored capital accumulation in a moment of cyclical stagnation, as well as the racial restructuring of society.

As such, this chapter contends that an anti-racist politics should envision an abolition of the reception-industrial complex. The humanitarian logic, the core principle of reception, indeed implies that Global South populations, prevented from an unconditional access to the sphere of citizenship and to the realm of the human, must require permission from the "white sovereign savior" in order to obtain partial socio-political recognition.[7] People are rendered applicants who, for a prolonged and undetermined period, are confined in reception centers while the humanitarian bureaucracy, according to arbitrary and changing parameters, divides between the "deserving ones," to be assimilated into the national order of things, and the "undeserving others," to be made deportable and undocumented. This racial politics of sorting the human(itarian) populations interlinks with the working of capital, which extracts profits and organizes its modes of accumulation around these bodies.

In similar ways to prison, *reception* operates as a political and economic *border* which reinforces, reproduces and naturalizes *longue durée* racial-colonial and gender inequalities rather than promoting and envisioning forms for their abolition.[8] In the Italian context, several social groups and advocates tended to promote a "good reception" versus "bad reception" discourse, *de facto* accepting and internalizing the existence of humanitarian logic, and the presence of the reception-industrial complex. Without denying differences and nuances in reception services, which can be grasped through ethnographic works, it is of pivotal importance to refuse this false binarism and engage with the racial – political and economic – premises of the reception-industrial complex.

THE GREAT RUPTURE: 2008–2011. THE RECEPTION-INDUSTRIAL COMPLEX IN RETROSPECT

Until the end of the Cold War, Italy was mainly an emigration and transit country. During the 1990s, due to the geopolitical reconfiguration and the progressive European integration process, a series of migratory waves, from Eastern countries and the Global South, impacted Italian society. The Italian response was differential, inconsistent, and characterized by a restrictive and humanitarian approach. Being at the forefront of the Mediterranean border, an increasing number of undocumented people entered the Italian territory and met variegated reactions from Italian authorities. Emblematic, in this perspective, was the brutal confinement, in 1991, of thousands of Albanian citizens into a football stadium in Bari, the Apulian capital city, and their partial repatriation. Of those who remained in Italy, 20,000 applied for asylum. Even though Albanians did not meet the selective parameters to obtain asylum status, they were granted an *ad hoc* humanitarian document allowing access to the labor market.[9]

From the 1990s onward, migration was mainly regulated through the restrictive programs of "working visa" (e.g., quota system), family reunification, student visas and through a politics of amnesty. Given the significant number of undocumented migrants, *ad hoc* measures favored their legalization. At the same time, Italian authorities often granted *ad hoc* humanitarian documents, with access to the labor market, to asylum seeker groups (i.e., people fleeing the ex-Yugoslavia conflict) with negligible chances to obtain asylum status.

The government of migration in Italy changed drastically in the wake of the 2008 global crisis.[10] Hit by the most dramatic socio-economic crisis since the Second World War,[11] Italy heavily restricted the already restrictive release of various types of visas. All those entering as undocumented – via the Mediterranean Sea and via the Balkan Route – were *de facto* channeled into the asylum procedure. Contrary to the previous socio-economic and political scenario, the "refugeeization" of undocumented people was coupled with the nationwide implementation and expansion of the reception system.

Before the 2008–2011 period, only a negligible percentage of asylum seekers were inserted into the very few facilities scattered around the country; the majority of them had a relative freedom to settle throughout the country, maybe by following social and family networks. In the wake of the 2008 crisis, due to a series of socio-legal and political changes, asylum seekers were automatically moved through and warehoused into a booming reception system. If before the 2008–2011 period the issue of reception of "forced migrants" remained somehow marginal and *ad hoc* legislative measures partly contributed to unloading the asylum system, after this period, due to a mixture of legal, political, socio-economic and racial arrangements, "forced migrants" were automatically and quasi-naturally inserted within the expanding reception system.

As outlined by various studies, 2011 represented a turning point in the history of Italian migratory management.[12] The "Arab Uprisings" and the NATO military operation in Libya provoked a geopolitical reconfiguration in the Mediterranean basin. In that year, a modest wave of people (about 63,000) reached the Italian island of Lampedusa and the Italian government declared a humanitarian state of emergency, known as the *North Africa Emergency* [*Emergenza Nord Africa*, ENA]. The reception of these undocumented people was entrusted to the Italian civil protection, which was responsible for their management. Given the shortage of available spots in the ordinary reception system (SPRAR) at that time, an emergency reception system (CAS) was implemented, which *de facto* became integrated with the former and regularly hosted the majority of asylum seekers.

The emergency discourse promoted by Italian authorities to govern this modest migratory wave was a socio-political construction instrumental to further policing Global South migration. Asylum became not only the pivotal regime for governing Global South populations, but it also emerged as a dispositif with different procedures and practices, when compared to previous conjunctures. *Why reception? Why now? Why for so many people – especially for people of color?*

Critical migration studies have rarely read the radical changes in migration management within the simultaneous broader socio-economic transformations. In the wake of the 2008 global financial crisis and the consequent crisis of European sovereign debts, Italy was at concrete risk of default. In November 2011, Prime Minister Silvio Berlusconi, leading a right-wing neoliberal government, resigned and Mario Monti, an economist with a distinguished degree in various European institutions, took over and formed a "technical government," which in the name of *austerity* further implemented a series of neoliberal reforms under the indirect supervision of European institutions. Other than assuring the stability of the Italian bank system, Monti's government reformed labor market policy with the aim to favor capital's needs for a flexible access to labor, raised the retirement age and continued the defunding of welfare services in a moment of severe social crisis. Since 2011, the Italian economy has been in recession. The social costs of the crisis mainly affected workers and families, and an increased percentage of young and old workers entered the infernal circle of short-term jobs/unemployment/short-term jobs.[13] After Monti's government, subsequent administrations continued the implementation of reforms in favor of flexible capital accumulation.

Between 2007 and 2013, more than 1 million people lost their jobs and GDP decreased by about 4.5%. In the 2010–2019 period,

37 billion euros were cut from public health services.[14] In 2011–2012, education funds decreased by more than 5%, marking one of the highest falls in the Eurozone.[15] In 2007, 1.79 million people were in absolute poverty, while in 2013 it was 4.42 million.[16] Manufacturing and construction entered an irreversible crisis, with a further "turn to service-work" of the Italian economy.[17] Within this overall tendency, marked by rampant inequality and welfare state defunding, reception boomed. While between 2005 and 2011 governmental funds amounted to a total of about 1 billion, from 2011 to 2017 14.4 billion euros were invested into reception. Thousands of new reception facilities opened around the country and an array of variegated service economies and racialized circuits of value came to light.

MASS REFUGEEIZATION AS MASS INCARCERATION?

The radical changes in migration management, which occurred in the wake of the great rupture (2008–2011), can be framed in terms of *mass refugeeization*.

The fact is that many who apply for asylum are not eligible for asylum status. When they arrive here, many would like to simply get a residency document, but since applying for asylum is the only way for them to get a paper, we need to sit, think and invent together a plausible story to present to the *commissione territoriale [the local authority which decides upon international protection demand]*, so some of them might get a document.

So Giorgio told me, a migrant activist who followed and supported for years those trapped in the asylum procedure. Given the legal preclusion from legitimate and unconditional access to the European Union progressively implemented by European and national institutions over the last decades, people coming from the Global South are indirectly forced to apply for asylum in order to legalize, albeit temporarily and conditionally, their stay in Europe.

The story of Noor, an engineer from Pakistan, well epitomizes the socio-legal and political process of *mass refugeeization*. In talking with me about his journey to Italy from Libya, where he worked as an engineer, a sense of disappointment and frustration invaded his words when remembering that he could not obtain a residency document, as anticipated by some friends in Tripoli:

> Noor: When I came here I didn't know anything about asylum seekers, nothing about it, because I don't have experience, my friends … my family is not in Europe, I didn't know what procedure … My friends in Libia told me "you go in Italia, you can get visa for 5 years … 2 years and after that you can go everywhere," that's why I decided to come here …

> Me: So when you arrived in Italy you didn't know that you had to apply for asylum?

> Noor: No, when I had my commission, in *prefettura [the provincial office of the Minister of Interior]*, the judge asked me if I have problems and I said no, I have no problems, my family everything is good … and so they gave me negative …

> Me: When you did your appeal in Venice did you change the story?

> Noor: No … no … why would I have to change it? … In Venezia judge talked with me 10 minutes easy and gave me humanitarian protection, 2 years …[18]

Noor arrived in Italy in 2014 and was transferred to Verona where he applied for asylum. As others who are indirectly channeled into the asylum procedure, he could not decide where to go and settle in the country. The Italian authority arbitrarily decides the province destination for asylum seekers, who are treated as dehumanized objects passively moved and warehoused within what Lorenzo Vianelli emblematically referred to as the *reception supply chain.*[19] It is not by chance that many "forced migrants" I met during my fieldwork used expressions like "I was moved to …" or "they moved me to …" when describing their reception experience in Italy. In this perspective, the logistical rationality of asylum partly resembles, in disturbing and revealing ways, the transportation of *black* bodies during the Atlantic slave trade.[20]

Noor's asylum application was rejected in *commissione* in 2015 and then he received a humanitarian protection document in 2017. At the end of 2021 he managed to convert his document into a work permit, which finally allowed him to go back to his family in Pakistan after seven years of being trapped in Italy. Between 2014 and 2021, Noor wandered through various "low-skilled" and underpaid jobs. He worked for years as a vegetable picker, paid 5 euros per hour; as a gardener, with a piecework payment of about 30 euros per day; and as a deliveryman for various companies.[21]

Noor's case, as many others, puts into question the meaning commonly associated with the notion of "forced migration." As noted by Francesco Della Puppa and Giuliana Sanò,

> if forcing exists, it should rather be framed within the processes of categorization, labelling, infantilization and cohabitation that are put in place when migrants arrive in destination countries (Feldman 2012) ... Based on these elements, we believe that to be correctly understood, the definition of "forced" must be applied to the context of arrival and not so much to the reasons for departure.[22]

Far from revealing and signaling an objective truth about the causes of migration, which are always multifarious, complex and unique, and putative moral management of European hosting countries, the figure of "forced migrant" embodies an opaque category of government which is reproduced through site-specific political, legal and cultural arrangements, and which reflects contingent socio-economic and political interests.

Seen from this perspective, the *mass refugeeization* of Global South people partly recalls the process of *mass incarceration* that occurred in the 1980s in the US context. In her illuminating book, *Golden Gulag*, Ruth Wilson Gilmore contends that the mass incarceration of racialized and impoverished people during the 1980s is incomprehensible without a profound engagement with structural socio-economic changes, repressive juridical reforms and the working of specific racial-punitive ideologies. Mass incarceration would have been simply unfeasible according to pre-existing legislation and the socio-economic order more broadly. Accordingly, the radical change in migration and asylum policy, coupled with a mutating socio-economic and political scenario, was crucial for mass refugeeization and the simultaneous expansion of the reception-industrial complex.

THE PRISON FIX

According to Gilmore, the process of mass incarceration represented a structural measure, a *fix*, to radically restore the California economy and society. Prisons embodied "partial geographical solutions to political economic crises, organized by the state, which is itself in crisis. Crisis means instability that can be fixed only through radical measures, which include developing new relationships and new or renovated institutions out of what already exists."[23]

During the 1970s, the Californian capitalist state entered an irreversible socio-economic crisis. The "welfare–warfare" industrial model of the Californian capitalist state (military–Keynesianism), based on a racial social contract with a relative presence of social guarantees, went through a profound transformation. Gilmore identifies four types of surpluses which came out from this socio-economic transition: state capacity, (racialized) population, lands, and financial capacity. Put simply, the erosion of secure forms of employment and the progressive dismantling of the manufacturing industry caused a systemic presence of working-class and racialized people in excess to labor demand. Contrary to the previous socio-economic order, this population needed to be "employed" and valorized differently in order to assure the reproduction and sustainability of society. Similarly, due to a series of economic and ecologic contingencies, lands could no longer be used for farming. State administration, no longer responsible for massive social planning, had a technical capacity to be directed toward other activities. Financial capital was looking for new investment channels as public projects in education, health, etc. progressively decreased.

In sum, state capital needed to re-valorize these surpluses through different arrangements and combinations. Here, according to Gimore, the prison represented a structural and site-specific *fix* in which these surpluses were made to converge, and the development of the prison-industrial complex gave rise to a new socio-economic model (neoliberal–punitive). Privatization and financialization of services, flexible and unguaranteed labor, on the one hand, and re-establishment of a white supremacist order, on the other. *Mass incarceration + prisons expansion* embodied a partial yet structural measure to establish a new socio-economic order. The development of the prison-industrial complex meant the creation of an array of economic activities: from prison building, maintenance, and financial investments to the variegated activities for managing the carceral population (jailers, basic services for prisoners, carceral state bureaucracy, etc.). This new economic model was built and based on pre-existent racial inequalities, with Blacks, Latinxs and Indigenous people being the most affected by these adjustments.

In convincingly outlining that "punishment has to be conceptually severed from its seemingly indissoluble link with crime,"[24] Gilmore offers an analysis able to highlight how and why prisons emerged as a gravitational center around which (state) capital, in this specific geo-historical context, based its new social and accumulation model. Attentive to avoid an economicist approach, Gilmore weaves together economic, political, ideological and legal processes in order to deliver a complex and multi-scalar account which pays attention to subjective resistances, thus escaping any conspiracist or totalizing effect.

THE RECEPTION-INDUSTRIAL COMPLEX

No jailer frees his prisoner, all the more so when the prisoner constitutes the raison d'être of the jailer.
   – *Enrico Beniamino de Matteis* (my translation).

Gilmore's framework can be intriguingly deployed in order to excavate the emergence of what I propose to call the reception-industrial complex. Clearly, I do not want to make a strict comparison between the two cases. Given the geographical, historical and societal diversity, I do not aim to provide a complete and exhaustive overview of the birth of the reception-industrial complex. Rather, I intend to offer a few insights and ideas with the aim to contrast a sort of taken-for-granted "moral" posture about what media and institutions named the European migratory or refugee crisis. Gilmore's gaze indeed represents a pivotal attempt to scrutinize the karstic connections between changes in population government and socio-economic transitions.

Far from being limited to the Italian case, I contend that a similar analysis can be applied to other European countries. In the wake of the crisis, the European socio-economic order was dramatically shaken and asylum became the crucial *dispositif* for governing Global South migration. Public spending on reception boomed in various European countries. As such, reception expansion needs to be seen as a socio-economic and racial measure implemented by different European countries during a period of systemic instability. Within this overall tendency, it is necessary to produce site-specific accounts able to highlight differences and assonances between supranational, national, and local contexts.

If we look at Italy in the wake of the "great rupture," we catch sight of a country in which entire economic sectors (construction, manufacturing) entered an irreversible decline, in which millions of (young) people faced prolonged and stagnant unemployment, in which rural and internal areas became the symbol of a broader trend of defunding in local welfare, in which entire territories became more and more impoverished and unproductive. In other words, that social formation could no longer "be reproduced on the basis of pre-existing system of social relations."[25] How did the state and capital react to this structural impasse? What kind of solutions did they implement in order to re-valorize, by other means, the above-mentioned surpluses – an increasing mass of unemployed people, as well as unproductive businesses and impoverished territories?

The radical and structural neoliberal reforming of the labor market, with flexible, fixed-terms and unguaranteed forms of employment and the further conversion of the industrial economy into a service-based model, attractive to private and financial investments, were among the structural measures implemented by various governments since 2011.[26] Within this scenario, reception expansion was *one of the solutions* to govern the transition to a social formation based on an aggressive, predatory and punitive accumulation model in a country in which neoliberal elements coexisted for decades with "welfarist" and "industrial" arrangements.

Since 2011, the nationwide and unprecedented expansion of reception, contributed to absorbing in different ways the above-mentioned surpluses. Tens of thousands of (young) social workers, cultural mediators, educators, psychologists, anthropologists, cleaners, cooks, and so on, found in the reception a form of precarious, unstable, and poorly paid work. Thousands of spaces dedicated to various businesses or institutional activities, such as failed hotels, abandoned military facilities, and private buildings, were converted into reception centers. In a moment of economic depression and structural cuts in social services, billions of euros passed from the state's coffers to a myriad of private actors. Finance capital invested heavily in reception, considered a highly profitable sector.[27] The creation of reception facilities in impoverished areas contributed to the development of a series of socio-economic activities, with reception embodying a partial yet effective fix for local communities.

Through a complex subcontracting system, the management of migrants' reception was outsourced to third-sector entities, cooperatives, consortiums and multinationals. In this regard, the systemic delays of state bureaucracy to decide upon asylum demands, which is often considered as a failure of the system, can also be considered an instrumental function which enables the sustainability of this reception economy, as private actors receive funds for any migrant they host on a daily basis. The prolonged and exhaustive stay of the migrants in reception facilities in waiting for a response to their asylum application, which is often framed as a form of organized social abandonment, needs also to be considered in terms of a *political economy of waiting*.[28]

It is also of pivotal importance to consider the "direct" exploitation of "forced migrants." Above-mentioned racialized circuits of value indeed imply an "indirect" employment of the migrants. Their "simple" presence sustains multiple economic activities. Other than that, as suggested by various reports, migrants inserted into the reception-industrial complex, due to a series of legal and social-political factors, became the ideal surplus racialized workforce in "low-skilled" sectors, such as agriculture and logistics. Enrica Rigo and Nick Dines referred to this process as the *refugeeization* of the workforce.[29] Nowadays, entire site-specific economies are dependent on the reception-industrial complex, as it assures the capture of flexible, just-in-time surplus racialized labor. Thus, the reception-industrial complex entertained a two-fold relationship with surplus populations.[30] On the one hand, it contributed to absorbing and attracting unemployed labor. On the other, it operated as an infrastructure assuring the reproduction of a highly precarious and exploitable migrant workforce to be channeled into an already racialized labor market in absolute need of contingent and semi-coerced labor. Overall, it is around this new figure of "forced migrant" that multifaceted and site-specific racialized circuits of value developed in almost every angle of the country. Reception embodied an important fix during the most severe socio-economic crisis since the Second World War.

In this regard, Miguel Mellino proposed to consider the contemporary right to asylum as a *neoliberal right*:

> the reception system became a business entirely incorporated into the "extractive" and "predatory" logic of neoliberal capitalism: characterized by an increasing *outsourcing, privatization* and *commoditization* of care and protection services, humanitarian government can be seen as one of the multiple forms of "accumulation by dispossession" (Harvey 2004). On the one hand, the management of the different services for asylum seekers and migrants by cooperatives, associations, NGOs and third-sector companies turned into an important *profit* and *revenue-making* machine, also through the exploitation of an increasingly precarious or unpaid workforce (social operators, cultural mediators, etc.). On the other hand, the humanitarian government, pursuing a continuous proliferation of different migrant statuses, directly aims to the production of a "docile" migrant workforce ... This new *neoliberal right to asylum* contributes to increase the "condition of deportability," vulnerability and precariousness of the migrants, legally reproducing them not only as highly exploitable subjects on the labour market, but exclusively suited to certain racialized "niches" of labour.[31]

The reception-industrial complex can be seen in terms of a *dispositif*, a peculiar infrastructure of government that contributed to assure the partial transformation of the socio-economic formation. According to Foucault, a *dispositif* is a "structure of heterogeneous elements" aimed at governing the social body, and distinct populations in situations of societal instability. We can think about it as a singular concatenation and integration of laws, spaces, actors, procedures, discourses and ideologies which contributed to "fix" the structural instability of Italian society. A *dispositif* does not simply replace old ones. It evolves and significantly transforms a repertoire of practices, techniques and discourses according to socio-political and economic contingencies. In this regard, Foucault's words are particularly relevant to our case:

> I understand by the term "apparatus" (*dispositif*) a sort of – shall we say – formation which has as its major function at a given historical moment that of responding to an *urgent need*. The apparatus thus has a dominant strategic function.[32]

As I, schematically and provisionally, tried to explain, in the wake of the great rupture, the Italian capital state had to confront *the urgent need* to ensure the consolidation of an aggressive, predatory and punitive model of accumulation through the partial re-valorization of certain surpluses and their alternative reintegration in the socio-economic sphere. Not only did asylum become the pivotal dispositif for governing Global South migration, but it evolved into a highly distinct dispositif, if compared with asylum during the 1990s. It is properly this dispositif that we call the reception-industrial complex.

The socio-economic restructuring via the reception-industrial complex went hand in hand with a specific repertoire of racial discourses and ideologies. This model was functional to the reproduction of a racial societal order where people from the Global South were socio-legally and economically segregated and prevented from direct and unconditional access to citizenship rights. Far from embodying a system of reciprocal care and mutual assistance antagonist to the racial and neoliberal order of things, the reception-industrial complex is one of the several and site-specific manifestations of the global apartheid[33] we are living in, where certain populations are not only repressed, dispossessed and exploited, but become the *raison d'etre* for the reproduction of this same racial order. That is why, it is argued, humanitarian quests to ameliorate the reception-industrial complex are destined to reinforce the racial foundations of neoliberal societies. Abolition is the only way forward for a real political anti-racism.

NOTES

1. Maurizio Albahari, *Crimes of Peace. Mediterranean Migration at the World's Deadliest Border*. Philadelphia: University of Pennsylvania Press, 2015.
2. Reception refers to the so-called asylum reception system, namely a network of various facilities, services, and support systems that are involved in the process of receiving and managing asylum seekers while their asylum application is processed by Italian authorities; a process that might last several years. Reception centers are not standard facilities, they rather are a heterogenous archipelago made by former apartments, military barracks, hotels, airport hangars, containers where asylum seekers are socio-spatially confined for a prolonged period of time. See: Giuseppe Campesi, "Between Containment, Confinement and Dispersal: The Evolution of the Italian reception System Before and After the 'Refugee Crisis.'" *Journal of Modern Italian Studies* 23(4), 2018a: 490–506; G. Campesi, "Seeking Asylum in Times of Crisis: Reception, Confinement, and Detention at Europe's Southern Border." *Refugee Survey Quarterly* 37(1), 2018b: 44–70; Paolo Novak, *Re-Producing the Humanitarian Border, Geopolitics*, 2022. doi: 10.1080/14650045.2022.2105699
3. Ruth Wilson Gilmore, *Golden Gulag. Prisons, Surplus, Crisis, and Abolition in Globalizing California*. Berkeley, Los Angeles, London: University of California Press, 2007.
4. I wittingly use the "forced migration" concept in quotation marks to insist on the ambiguities of this category of migration (see below).
5. Data on the Italian reception system that will be presented throughout this chapter are taken from: Commissione nazionale asilo 2022. Quaderno Statistico 1990–2020. www.libertaciviliimmigrazione.dlci. interno.gov.it/sites/default/files/allegati/quaderno_statistico_per_gli_anni_1990_2020.pdf; Eleonora Ghizzi Gola, *L'accoglienza dei richiedenti e titolari di protezione internazionale in Italia. Aspetti giuridici e sociologici*. Bologna: L'Altro diritto, 2015. www.adir.unifi.it/rivista/2015/ghizzi/index.htm; Lunaria, "Costi disumani. La spesa pubblica per il contrasto dell'immigrazione irregolare." Lunaria.org, 2013; Maria Silvia Olivieri, 2008, Rapporto Annuale Sprar 2007/2008. www1.interno.gov.

it/mininterno/export/sites/default/it/assets/files/15/0081_SPRAR_-_ Rapporto_Annuale_2007-2008.pdf; Openpolis. 2018. "Centri d'Italia." www.openpolis.it/esercizi/i-centri-di-accoglienza-in-italia-la-spesa-e-i-contratti-pubblici/; Carlo Valdes (Ed.), 2018. "Alcune implicazioni dell'immigrazione sui conti pubblici." Report Osservatorio conti pubblici italiani.

6. Ruth Wilson Gilmore, "Globalisation and US Prison Growth: From Military Keynesianism to Post-Keynesian Militarism." *Race & Class* 40(2–3), 1999: 171–188.

7. Teju Cole, "The White-Savior Industrial Complex." *The Atlantic*, March 2012. www.theatlantic.com/international/archive/2012/03/the-white-savior-industrial-complex/254843/

8. Angela Davis, and Gina Dent. "Prison as a Border: A Conversation on Gender, Globalization, and Punishment." *Signs* 26(4), 2001: 1235–1241.

9. Nadan Petrovic, *Storia del diritto d'asilo in Italia (1945–2020)*. Milano: FrancoAngeli, 2020.

10. Carlo Caprioglio, and Enrica Rigo, *Diritto, migrazioni e sfruttamento nell'agricoltura italiana*. In: Ilaria Ippolito, et al. (Eds), *Braccia rubate dall'agricoltura*. Torino: Seb27, 2021.

11. Carlo Bastasin, and Gianni Toniolo, *La strada smarrita*. Bari, Roma: Laterza, 2020.

12. Elena Fontanari, *Lives in Transit*. London: Routledge, 2019; Marchetti, Chiara. *Framing Emergency. Italian Response to 2011 (Forced) Migrations from Tunisia and Libya*. Paper presented at the "RSC 30th Anniversary Conference: Understanding Global Refugee Policy," Oxford, 2012.

13. Marta Fana, *Non è lavoro, è sfruttamento*. Bari, Roma: Laterza, 2017.

14. Gimbe, *Il definanziamento 2010–2019 del Servizio Sanitario Nazionale*. Report Osservatorio GIMBE n. 7/2019.

15. European Commission. Education budgets under pressure in Member States. https://ec.europa.eu/commission/presscorner/detail/it/IP_13_261, 2013.

16. Che cos'è la povertà assoluta. Openpolis, www.openpolis.it/parole/che-cose-la-poverta-assoluta/, 2021

17. Emilio Reynieri. *Le due grandi crisi del mercato del lavoro: gli anni trenta del XX secolo e gli anni dieci del XXI secolo a confronto*. in *La società italiana e le grandi crisi economiche (1929–2016)*. Istat. Anno 147, Serie XIII – vol. 2, 2019.

18. Noor [pseudonym], interviewed by the author, September 21, 2021, Verona.

19. Lorenzo Vianelli, "Warehousing Asylum Seekers: The *Logistification* of Reception," *EPD: Society and Space* 40(2), 2022: 1–19.

20. Stefano Harney and Fred Moten, *The Undercommons. Fugitive Planning and Black Study*. Wivenhoe, New York, Port Watson: Minor Composition, 2013.

21. Noor lived for about one month in a reception center and then he managed to move in a shared flat with other Pakistani people. Usually, asylum seekers tend to remain in reception centers for the whole duration of the asylum procedure, which often lasts for years. The overt racism of landlords, who do not usually rent to black and "non-white" racialized people, and the difficulty to obtain long-term and guaranteed job contracts, which are prerequisites to access the housing market, are among the various reasons behind asylum seekers necessity to remain in reception facilities, which de facto embody the "lesser evil" housing solution.
22. Francesco Della Puppa and Giuliana Sanò, "The Prism of New Mobilities. The Mobility Trajectories of Refugees and Asylum Seekers Outside the Italian Reception System." *Journal of Modern Italian Studies* 26(5), 2021.
23. Gilmore, *Golden Gulag*, p. 26.
24. Davis, Angela. *Are Prisons Obsolete?* New York: Seven Stories Press, 2003, p. 85.
25. Stuart Hall, and Bill Schwartz, "State and Society." In: *The Hard Road to Renewal*. New York: Verso, 1988, quoted in Gilmore, *Golden Gulag*, p. 54.
26. Christian Marazzi, *Diario della crisi infinita*. Verona: Ombre corte, 2015.
27. Stefano Liberti, "Il grande business dell'accoglienza." *Internazionale*. www.internazionale.it/reportage/stefano-liberti/2014/12/03/il-grande-affare-dei-centri-d-accoglienza; Rosy Battaglia, "La lunga mano della finanzia speculativa sull'accoglienza." *Valori*. https://valori.it/business-accoglienza-ors/
28. Ina Zharkevich, "'We are in the Process': The Exploitation of Hope and the Political Economy of Waiting Among the Aspiring Irregular Migrants in Nepal." *Environment and Planning D: Society and Space* 39(5), 2021: 827–843.
29. Nick Dines, and Enrica Rigo, "Postcolonial Citizenships and the 'Refugeeization' of the Workforce: Migrant Agricultural Labour in the Italian Mezzogiorno." In: Sandra Ponzanesi and Gianmaria Colpani (Eds), *Postcolonial Transitions in Europe: Contexts, Practices and Politics*. London: Rowman & Littlefield, 2015.
30. On the nexus between racial capitalism and surplus population on a global perspective see Thompson in this volume.
31. Miguel Mellino, *Governare la crisi dei rifugiati. Sovranismo, neoliberalismo, razzismo e accoglienza in italia e in Europa*. Rome: DeriveApprodi, 2019, p. 164 (my translation).
32. Michel Foucault, "The Confession of the Flesh (Interview)." In: *Power/Knowledge Selected Interviews and Other Writings*. New York: Pantheon Books, 1980, p. 195 (my italics).
33. Catherine Besteman, "Militarized Global Apartheid." *Current Anthropology* 60, 2019.

10

Abolish Frontex and end the EU border regime

Mark Akkerman

In the early morning of June 9, 2021, activists in Brussels (Belgium) targeted the liaison office of the European Union (EU) border guard agency Frontex, leaving fake blood on its doorsteps. In addition, two banners were dropped from the balcony with the text "Abolish Frontex." Later that day, actions took place in seven other countries across Europe and Northern Africa.[1] In an alarmist internal email sent to Frontex staff that same day, the then Executive Director Fabrice Leggeri – who later had to resign because of his role in (covering up) the agency's involvement in violent pushbacks – labeled *Abolish Frontex* as a "hate campaign" and expressed that he was "deeply shocked [by] these incidents."[2]

In its less than 20 years of existence, Warsaw-based Frontex has grown from a small agency coordinating border security efforts by EU member states, into the highest-funded EU agency, responsible for military border security operations at the EU external borders and increasingly also in non-EU countries. Frontex has built its own 10,000-person strong-armed border police force, coordinating joint deportations and fostering relations with the military and security industry. Frontex is regularly involved in violence, pushbacks, and other human rights violations at borders.

The campaign's demands

Abolish Frontex is a grassroots action-based network of over 130 groups and organizations.[3] The previously mentioned action day was accompanied by an open letter from the network to EU authorities and member states' governments, stating the context and objectives of the campaign:

> We oppose a world increasingly divided by fortified borders to protect the wealth of the rich from the desperation and righteous anger of the poor and oppressed. We believe in freedom of movement for all; in providing support and shelter for people on the move, and in working towards a world where people are no longer forced to flee their homes and can live where they choose to.[4]

This is further detailed in an extensive document that serves as the base of the campaign, listing nine main demands: "Abolish Frontex," "Regularise migrants," "Stop all deportations," "End detention," "Stop the militarisation of borders (and the military-industrial complex)," "Stop the surveillance of people on the move," "Empower solidarity," "Stop the EU's role in forcing people to move," and "Freedom of movement for all – end the EU border regime." The document concludes that "[t]he EU's border policies are inherently racist and reinforce colonial and capitalist power structures. It's time to abolish Frontex and the system it represents."[5]

The demands show that the campaign has several layers. While, as the name suggests, Frontex is the main target, as the spearhead of EU border and migration policies, the campaign is aimed at changing these policies as a whole: "End the EU border regime." Change does not mean reform, but abolition, as "[m]odern borders are colonial and racist constructs, and the EU's border policies institutionalise this violence, injustice and inequality. The EU has no right to stop people at its borders and no-one should be illegal."[6]

The colonial nature of EU borders can be seen in the way they are an essential part of a structure that permits the rich EU countries to exploit the Global South – in terms of labor, other (natural) resources and the environment – while keeping people exploited by this system out of Fortress Europe. As such, they build on old colonial relations, which are perpetuated to this day and in themselves serve as the base of power imbalances the EU uses to expand its current neo-colonial policies of border externalization. This allows the EU and its member states to enforce the cooperation of non-EU countries for their anti-immigration purposes, thereby ignoring the voices and interests of the people living in these countries.

Apart from the direct violence that the EU and its member states are committing against people on the move at and beyond their borders, the borders themselves are expressions of violence. They are used to keep people on the move out, exploit those who arrive as precarious labor or incarcerate them, and deport people to unsafety, poverty, repression, war, consequences of climate change and so on. Moreover, these borders keep a system of structural violence, as characterized by its colonial nature, afloat and expanding and are an essential part of the Global North's imperialist grip on the rest of the world.

In this context, border abolition is not something that can happen in a vacuum, it needs to be embedded in a strategy for fundamental change on other issues as well, including the EU's military, trade and foreign policies. Hence, the demand to "Stop the EU's role in forcing people to move" includes concrete points such as "end arms exports," "stop military operations in third countries," "abolish NATO," "end unequal trade relations," "stop extracting wealth and resources from third countries," and "prevent further climate change," by "work[ing] on climate justice, not green capitalism." Most fundamental is the final point in this list: "Take responsibility for the effects of centuries of colonialism, imperialism, violence, slavery, exploitation, oppression and exclusion. Make reparations and dismantle the current neo-colonialist order and infrastructure."[7]

Abolition, not reform

During its establishment and the formulating of its demands, *Abolish Frontex* took a lot of inspiration from other movements, expressing "respect for all the work that comes before and continues to be done at local, national and international levels in the struggle against borders, deportation, detention and structural racism."[8] In particular, the (US) Abolish Police movement has seen growing support after the killing of George Floyd in 2020. In that context, the issue of abolition versus reform was raised many times. Moderate groups argue that abolition is a step too far and there is merely a need for better regulations, training, transparency, accountability mechanisms and so on.

For more radical movements working on border and migration issues in Europe this liberal stance reflected the fundamental problem with many reformist organizations and groups, in particular large NGOs, who refuse to challenge the notion of border security and control, let alone the existence of borders themselves. While the moderate approach keeps these liberal groups on speaking terms with EU authorities and could potentially lead to some small improvements, it keeps the escalating course of the EU's migration policies and will never lead to the much-needed structural change. *Abolish Frontex* distinguishes itself from these reformist positions by constantly emphasizing the need for abolition and fundamental change.

While the campaign's main focus is on Frontex, this is seen as a means for challenging the EU border regime as a whole, which is a complex of police, military, prisons, borders and industry that needs to be abolished. As such, *Abolish Frontex* considers itself to be part of a broader global abolitionist movement.

In practice

Abolish Frontex is a completely horizontal, non-hierarchical network, made up of non-parliamentary groups and organizations. The groups involved are predominantly focused on challenging migration policies – from working in direct solidarity at borders to doing research or engaging in direct action – but the campaign also involves organizations with broader goals regarding militarism, arms trade, racism, international solidarity, and human and civil rights. As a network, *Abolish Frontex* does not organize around a central address or secretariat, but instead relies on the cooperation, commitment and priorities of participating groups across different countries and struggles.

All network decisions are taken on the basis of consent, in regular online meetings. Apart from trying to organize at least two international action days a year, the network serves as a platform for amplifying each other's actions, releasing statements, exchanging information, doing research, public speaking, and so on. *Abolish Frontex* regularly cooperates with and supports other groups and networks, such as those in solidarity with refugees in Libya, as well as national campaigns, such as the campaign for a referendum on Switzerland's participation in Frontex. While concrete actions and campaigns focus on certain issues with Frontex or specific aspects of EU or national policies, they are always placed in the context of border abolition and structural change, rather than reforms within the current system.

The international action day of December 18, 2021 (International Migrants Day), with over 30 actions in 13 countries in Europe and Africa, serves as an example of the diversity of mobilizations and other activities contained under the umbrella of the *Abolish Frontex* campaign.[9] The action day started with a blockade of the gates of the Border Security Training Centre near Schiphol Airport in The Netherlands, a Frontex training location at a military police base. Ten people were arrested. During the day there were demonstrations, banner actions and manifestations in Austria, Belgium, Bosnia-Herzegovina, Finland, France, Germany, Greece, Italy, The Netherlands, Spain and Switzerland, some with the general "Abolish Frontex" message, others focusing on specific issues, such as pushbacks or the situation in Libya. In Morocco, Italy and Togo groups organized commemoration activities and solidarity statements for people on the move who died during their journeys. In Paris activists dyed the Seine red, while adbusting and postering took place in Berlin, Brussels, Vienna, and several cities in Italy. Another blockade happened in Berlin, at the Europäische Haus, the location of the European Commission in Germany. In Turin, there was a protest against the Polytechnic University's contract with Frontex for creating maps. Film screenings, public meetings and spray painting were among the other actions taken.

The social media and press working groups of *Abolish Frontex* reported updates of the actions during the day and sent out press releases to announce and sum up the action day. These working groups are also active in between action days, to publish joint statements and give social media support to relevant actions and activities of member groups and others.

In the two years since the launch of the network there have been several such action days, with differing numbers of activities. They have shown that it amplifies our voice when we work together and support each other's actions, as it does when cooperating on joint statements and info exchanges. On the other hand, it is sometimes difficult to align priorities, when groups are working in different national contexts and face different challenges. It can be hard to make time to keep a network running when you're up to your ears in your own daily activities. And it can be equally challenging to continuously connect these day-to-day struggles to the overarching push for systematic change on a deeper level – especially in national contexts further removed from the EU's external borders and their ongoing violence. In general, the *Abolish Frontex* network and its participating groups have managed to do so though.

Meanwhile, the EU is firmly holding on to its course of repressive border and migration policies, expanding and refining its infrastructure of border security and control, increasing budgets, extending (enforced) cooperation with third countries, and growing increasingly closer with the military and security industry. This defines a political context where it is extremely hard to see wins and positive outcomes. Even developments that in the beginning work as a wake-up call for a wider public, can in the longer term lead to adverse outcomes. The horrific media reports on violent, illegal pushbacks at several EU borders from 2021 are a depressing example of this. After the initial public and political reactions of shock, EU policymakers and practitioners, led by Frontex, have gradually moved to a strategy of legitimizing such pushbacks instead of ending them. It doesn't help that more moderate and liberal political groups and NGOs often are more focused on scoring media points with their soundbite responses, refusing to work for systematic change, and being satisfied with weak, cosmetic compromises and greenwashing language.

However, in a time where (far) right parties keep hammering on ever more restrictive policies, it is of utmost importance not to submit to this shift to the right or to relent to moderation and centrism, but to keep the radical vision of abolition and a more free, humane and just world alive. *Abolish Frontex* has set out to do so.

NOTES

1. Abolish Frontex, "With Actions in 8 Countries a New International Movement Rises to 'Abolish Frontex.'" *Abolish Frontex*, June 10, 2021, https://abolishfrontex.org/wp-content/uploads/2021/06/PR-10June2021-2.pdf
2. Ludek Stavinoha, "Frontex: An EU Agency Gone Rogue?" *EUobserver*, June 19, 2021. https://euobserver.com/opinion/153256
3. Abolish Frontex, "Who We Are." *Abolish Frontex*. Accessed August 4, 2023. https://abolishfrontex.org/about-us/
4. Abolish Frontex, "Abolish Frontex, End the EU Border Regime." *Abolish Frontex*, June 9, 2021. https://abolishfrontex.org/blog/2021/06/09/abolish-frontex-open-letter/

5. Abolish Frontex, "Abolish Frontex. End the EU Border Regime." *Abolish Frontex*, June 2021. https://abolishfrontex.org/wp-content/uploads/2021/06/ENG_Abolish-Frontex-demands.pdf

6   Ibid.

7   Ibid.

8   Abolish Frontex, "It Is Time to Abolish Frontex and the System It Represents." *Abolish Frontex*. Accessed August 4, 2023, https://abolishfrontex.org/how/

9. Abolish Frontex, "Over 40 Actions to Abolish Frontex and End the EU Border Regime on International Migrants Day." *Abolish Frontex*, December 19, 2021. https://abolishfrontex.org/blog/2021/12/19/over-40-actions-to-abolish-frontex-and-end-the-eu-border-regime-on-international-migrants-day/

CONSTELLATION III

Political Horizons of
Border Abolitionism

11

"Shut them down"

Non-reformist reforms in anti-detention organizing

Helen Brewer, Tom Kemp, Bobby Phe Amis, and Joel White

INTRODUCTION

In the fight against borders, we dig where we stand. But where we stand is never certain. It is an undulating landscape, shifting in character, feeling, opportunity, and violence. The border is always becoming, and migration policy remains a moving target. The role of detention in the British state's deportation regime is always evolving. UK immigration detention in 2023 is a resurgent beast, this time accompanied by new additions: the plan to deport people seeking asylum to Rwanda, quasi-detention spaces in hotels, barges and barracks, and new short-term holding facilities. Yet, there was a period in 2019 when it felt like our movements had succeeded in substantially reducing the use of detention in Britain, when Immigration Removal Centres like Yarl's Wood, Campsfield, Morton Hall, and Dungavel were signaled to be closing and the population of detention dwindled to under 400 people.[1] As the border industrial complex shifts once more, it is critical that we learn from past struggles and recent histories to inform our present and future organizing.

This chapter seeks to learn from two interrelated anti-detention campaigns in Scotland during the 2010s: *We Will Rise*, a campaign to shut down Dungavel Immigration Removal Centre near Glasgow; and *Stop Detention Scotland*, a subsequent campaign to prevent the construction of a short-term holding facility (STHF) in nearby Paisley. Joel and Bobby were involved in these campaigns, while Helen and Tom were active in adjacent anti-detention and anti-deportation campaigns and groups in England. Together, the four of us think through these two campaigns, and assess the value of "non-reformist reforms" to the movement to abolish borders.

The concept of non-reformist reforms, initially detailed in the 1960s by New Left theorist André Gorz, was used to describe transformative anti-capitalist demands that could advance working-class interests by moving away from the binary impasse of "revolution" and "reform."[2] Our impetus here to inquire about non-reformist reforms in anti-border struggles comes through the theorizing and activism of prison abolitionists. In this, we draw predominantly on Black feminist writing and organizing from the US, along with more recent efforts to "make abolition speakable" in the context of the United Kingdom and its particular history.[3] Writing from the US context, Mariame Kaba et al. define non-reformist reforms as "measures that reduce the power of an oppressive system while illuminating the system's inability to solve the crises it creates."[4] In arguing that non-reformist reforms could form a basis for international prison oversight bodies, S Lamble writes: "A key question to consider is not only whether a proposed reform will reduce harm and suffering, but whether it simultaneously works to reduce the size, scope, and power of the system?"[5] In the prison abolition movement non-reformist reforms include: advocating a moratorium on prison building; responding to overcrowding through releasing certain categories of prisoners; measures that subject prisons to robust, public, independent scrutiny, and oversight that empowers prisoners; repealing laws that target oppressed groups such as those that criminalize drugs, sex work, immigration, protest, and property offenses; and diverting funds toward effective non-punitive, community responses to social harm that undermine the perceived necessity for prisons. *Critical Resistance* and *Abolitionist Futures* have, in the US and UK contexts, respectively, brought the concept of non-reformist reforms to bear on policing.[6]

As the "no-borders" movement has begun to organize around ideas of "border abolition," invocations of non-reformist reforms in anti-border struggles have become more common. Gracie Mae

Bradley and Luke de Noronha, for example, forefront non-reform-ist reforms as a key strategy for abolishing borders, identifying the repeal of recent "hostile environment" immigration legislation as examples of non-reformist reforms.[7] Similarly, scholar-activists such as Fiona Jeffries and Jennifer Ridgley from the *Ottawa Sanc-tuary City Network* have mooted "Sanctuary Cities" – municipal "safe zones" that refuse to comply with national and federal border regimes – as a possible site of non-reformist reforms, offering "unconditional access" to services such as healthcare, education, and housing.[8] Here, we join in these nascent attempts to test out how non-reformist reforms can contribute to formulating strate-gies for border abolition, but with a focus on two campaigns that did not explicitly use such language. For us this is a way of inter-rogating the theory we are drawn to, and hungry for, within the messy reality of some campaigns on the ground, in the hope that it will inspire further discussions on the possibilities of non-reform-ist reforms in border abolitionist struggles.

Such analysis is also implicitly a critique of reformist approaches to the violence of borders. There are clear examples of the pitfalls of organizing around reformist principles. For example, in the UK, coalitions of NGOs have campaigned for "28-day time limits on detention," the development of "alternatives to detention" such as electronic tagging (see Cape-Davenhill in this volume), and for certain categories of people who are recognized as vulnerable to be given certain safeguards against detention. Such measures legit-imize the border regime, even where they marginally diminish aspects of it, and usually work to create a hierarchy of "good" and "bad" migrants. These are shifting and deeply racialized categories, which often map onto adjacent binaries of "skilled"/"unskilled" workers or "illegal"/"legal" forms of movement, but in this case would practically mean that people in detention who had come through prison, "worked illegally," or had limited legal recourse in their immigration cases, were often excluded by the limits of such campaigns. These reforms also misinterpret detention as an analogous form of prison to be reformed as such, rather than as a component of a wider system of racialized "exploitation, expro-priation and expulsion."[9] Thus, having a concept of non-reformist reforms helps us consider how reforms that look like they challenge a system might in fact be working within the ideological confines of that border system. Not only this, organizing around reformist reforms gives rise to professionalized movements that may adopt a managerial states' view, and, crucially, do not involve people who are targeted by border controls.[10]

However, while holding to these critiques, we in no way aim to construct a prescriptive formula for non-reformist reforms in border abolitionist work. There is no perfect abolitionist strategy. Abolition is not an abstract thing to be discussed in abstract terms. We are not trying here to police a distinction between "good" or "authentic" non-reformist reforms on the one hand, and "bad" or "secretly reformist" non-reformist reforms on the other hand. Instead, we are sitting down to write this together in order to spend some time with the patterns, questions, and tensions that have come up for each of us in our experiences of anti-detention organizing in the recent past. In this chapter, we ask how the concept of non-reformist reforms can support our movement-building. But we also ask how that same concept can sometimes trouble and muddle our attempts to imagine, and actively summon, a world without borders. We are interested in non-reformist reforms for how they help us reflect on our ways of working together and being together and in how the imperfect putting into practice of non-reformist reforms can speak to the messy and deeply differentiated realities of resisting border violence day-to-day.

As such, any analysis of non-reformist reforms in the context of border abolition must attend to the historical and geographic specificity of the system we fight, and the constant ways in which people face this system day-to-day. In a world shaped by Empire's enduring redistribution of wealth, migration has emerged as a key strategy of working-class survival, a strategy undermined and criminalized by border controls, as Aviah Sarah Day and Shanice Octavia McBean point out.[11] People move defiantly every single day, despite the seeming totality of border controls. The task of abolitionists is to make the seemingly impossible possible, and every act of defiance against the border can help contribute to this task. Migration is a worldmaking project that makes life and lives possible, which is not to say that it is not heavily criminalized, and crisscrossed with violence and death. The promise of abolition is not merely to oppose institutions of state violence, it is to create new networks, modes of relating and infrastructures that support flourishing lives: "abolition is a presence," in Ruth Wilson Gilmore's terms.[12] One of our key claims through this piece is that, while most discussions of non-reformist reforms focus on the diversion of resources or the neutralization of specific laws, we should also be attuned to how they facilitate relation-building and interpersonal connections. How the non-reformist reform is plotted, articulated, and demanded is key here, and we should resist the temptation to engage with them in a mode of abstract political premeditation. Instead, by considering them within the messy reality of movement-building and organizing, we can make non-reformist reforms a part of our *means* as well as something that gets us toward desired *ends*. For us, this ultimately means that abolishing borders is a world-building project, because abolishing borders summons revolutionary anti-capitalist futures while building both community power and anti-oppressive infrastructures of care. It is from this understanding of abolition, in the here and now, that we evaluate the potential of non-reformist reforms throughout this chapter.

HISTORICAL CONTEXT FOR *WE WILL RISE*

Immigration detention is the administrative incarceration of people whose immigration status is contested by the state. According to Home Office figures, 24,443 people were detained in the UK in 2019, at the apex of the campaigns being analyzed in this chapter, with around 1,600–1,700 people in detention at any one point.[13] In the UK, detention takes place in a network of immigration removal centres (IRCs), short-term holding facilities, and often also within mainstream prisons. The only detention center in Scotland is Dungavel IRC, which opened in 2001 at the site of a former hunting lodge and prison, a one-hour drive south of Glasgow. In 2015, following years of different campaigns against Dungavel and detention more broadly, grassroots movements in Scotland coalesced into a new group called *We Will Rise*. Outlining the history and practices of the group can here inform our analysis of how non-reformist demands – though not framed explicitly as such – have functioned in border abolitionist work, and could be drawn on in future struggles.

We Will Rise emerged through conversations among migrant justice and antiracist organizers in Glasgow, many of them linked to the *Unity* Centre – a drop-in space for people in the asylum and immigration system in the city. Supporting people via phone that were being held across the UK's detention estate was a key part of the *Unity* Centre's day-to-day casework and key members of the *Unity Centre Organising Collective* and the emerging *We Will Rise* group had direct experience of detention themselves. By 2015 new peer-support groups such as *LGBT Unity*, *Unity Language Exchange*, and *Unity Sisters* had been formed, all drawing in different constituencies of people in the struggle for papers, many of whom were "appeal rights exhausted." This shaped the "abolitionist" ethos of the center, although it was more often referred to as "unconditional support." This distinguished the center from organizations and groups elsewhere in the city that accepted the existence of immigration controls, refusing support to people without clear legal recourse. People from *Unity*'s various peer-support groups were regularly involved in direct actions at the nearby Home Office reporting center, when friends of *Unity* had been detained there while on regular "signing" or "reporting" appointments with the Home Office. Such direct actions involved physically blockading the gates of the center and stretched back to the origins of *Unity* as a "signing support" stall in 2005 and 2006, linked to the *No Borders Network* emerging across Europe at that time.

The years between 2013 to 2015 had seen changes in *Unity*'s structure, with attempts to democratize decision-making and deal with the structural imbalance of having high numbers of people without experience of the immigration system in the *Unity Collective*. Such conversations and changes came alongside a flurry of work on "fast-track removal" flights, emergency appeals against imminent deportations, immigration raids, and concerted detention casework. Theresa May's "hostile environment" legislation in 2014 and 2016 proved a pivotal shift in such work. Although it is crucial to historicize these new pieces of legislation as part of a far longer attempt to diffuse the British border regime into public life, it is also important to recognize the considerable panic created by these particular policy changes among people in Glasgow around signing rules, educational access, bank account monitoring, and the (ultimately defeated) "Deport First, Appeal Later" policy. Early *We Will Rise* meetings stemmed from this disquiet and organizational upheaval, along with the generally high levels of people in detention, many of whom had direct contact with friends and family linked to *Unity*.

Initial meetings debated some kind of long-term protest camp at Dungavel IRC. But after questions were raised by people in the immigration system about how possible it would be for them to participate in such an action, *We Will Rise* focused on holding a series of large community meals to assess possible strategies and ideas. These events became key to *We Will Rise's* organizing model, as up to 100 people would join for food and social time. This was mixed with large consensus-decision-based discussions where people would decide on the *We Will Rise* strategy for the coming months and join working groups focused on things like media, childcare, and logistics. Key to this was fundraising – through a mixture of parties and applications to activist funders such as Lush and the Edge Fund – to provide bus pass money, childcare, and delicious meals at all *We Will Rise* events. Food was key here, with meals always including halal meat options alongside vegan ones, in response to initial complaints about the exclusion of meat and halal options that reflected the diets of those most affected. Such measures were key, as people surviving on meager asylum support amounts (£35 or less) were able to travel to the venue, get involved in making and eating the meals, and build relationships while there.

The decision to organize a big day of action at Dungavel IRC was an important start for building community power. This drew heavily on experiences of participating in the 2015 Shut Down Yarlswood mobilizations in Bedfordshire and London, with a large *LGBT Unity* and *Unity Sisters* contingent hiring minibuses down to the demos that year. Connections formed through these trips and subsequent organizing were often profound and joyous: people learned about different organizing models and ways of doing politics, formed long-term friendships, and fell in and sometimes out of love. This linked to wider forms of being together embedded in the communities around *We Will Rise*, and into the group's culture, including: collective attendance at asylum appeal hearings, reading groups, informal sports sessions, and large fundraising parties, which created space to dance, cook, sing, and share music together. Such activities helped constitute dense social bonds, many of which continued way beyond the lifespan of the group itself.

Everyday demands – such as redistributing fundraised money toward bus passes for those who need it or never having meetings and events without adequate childcare – were combined with ones to "End Detention" and "Shut Down Dungavel." The framing of these demands in an unconditional and non-reformist way – transitionally looking to diminish the border regime, without legitimizing it – worked to include those who had been left out of more bounded reformist campaigns. The focus on detention, as a technique of border control that hovers over the lives of almost everyone in the immigration system, also created a space to critique divisions of "good/bad" migrant, and "citizen/non-citizen." This mirrored the practical attempts to address "who is in the room" by providing bus fare and childcare, allowing for friendships and ways of being together that exceeded such state categories. This was, of course, always limited, as structures of white supremacy and activist saviorism continued to operate through the group, and within it. At best, the non-reformist promises of the group – *shut down all detention* and *papers for all, or no papers at all* – illuminated rather than hid these oppressive dynamics, allowing for discussions and attempts at organizing that addressed them, rather than burying them or starting from a reformist NGO position focused on "good" migrants and predetermined small wins.

TRANSNATIONAL DAY OF ACTION

This first concerted *We Will Rise*-led protest was planned for May 7, 2016, to coincide with a "transnational day of solidarity with detained people and protest against detention centres," and protests at detention centers across Europe. Interestingly, despite this being sometime before the language of "border abolition" entered wider activist and academic parlance, the *We Will Rise* statement for this event was as follows:

> *We Will Rise* is a group of migrants, refugees, asylum seekers and their allies who have come together to organise and take direct action against the systems, institutions, and corporations who contribute to our oppression. We are the movement we want to see. We aim to take on all forms of oppression, including between ourselves. We aim to empower those most affected by migration barriers – to lead a movement for change and for allies to work effectively with them … Reform is not the answer, we want abolition. We expect our allies to respect our politics and work with us towards these ends.

Such a statement can be seen as emerging from, articulating in the present, and creating the future conditions for non-reformist reforms and abolitionist practices. Reflecting on the words now, however, we note (with some unease around what it means to unpack such rhetoric from a position of academic hindsight) how such statements necessarily fail to reflect the messiness of trying to enact such principles, especially around centering people in the asylum and immigration system. The *Surround Dungavel* demo involved people who had been through detention and the immigration system themselves in both key organizational roles and as speakers on the day. But this placed a considerable burden on the three or four core organizers with direct experience in the group, creating tensions about what constituted being an ally, or an accomplice, as well as a friend. These tensions percolated through into future campaigns. Efforts were made to involve more people with experience on the day, but these rarely brought people into the regular organizing processes of what coalesced into a "core group."

Following the example of the *Shut Down Yarlswood* mobilizations, the *We Will Rise* demo on the day physically surrounded Dungavel IRC and installed a portable speaker system on a hill overlooking the main IRC yard. A large banner showed a phone number that people on the inside could phone – many of whom then spoke to the crowd, in various languages, or joined in with chants over the speakers. This overcame attempts by the IRC administration to ignore or demonize the protest. For instance, IRC management had chosen to mow all the lawns on the grounds inside Dungavel at the start of the day in order to try and drown out the sound of the protest, while several people detained inside informed *Unity* that IRC staff had told the detainees that this was a far-right gathering protesting against the people held inside.

Beyond the day itself, the *Surround Dungavel* demo and subsequent *We Will Rise* actions around it helped renew a focus on campaigning and community-building within migrant justice activism in Glasgow, which many felt had dropped off through the pressures of casework and everyday battling of the hostile environment at individual and legal levels (often framed as "firefighting"). *We Will Rise* events made room to collectively educate each other about immigration law, support people with both their immigration cases and the daily struggle of living with "no recourse to public funds," and signpost to other groups. Crucially though, this was always paired with campaigning, an active critique of the border regime, and an invitation to consider the structures preventing people from accessing material needs.

STOP DETENTION SCOTLAND AND THE PAISLEY CAMPAIGN

The demand to "Shut Down Dungavel" was not uncontroversial. Many NGOs operating in the Glasgow area and those linked to them were often keen to reassert that a closure of Dungavel would mean that people would be moved down south to England, advocating instead for a "time limit" to indefinite detention. *We Will Rise* were very aware of this, particularly as members who had been inside the IRC pointed out that Dungavel was widely considered "nicer" than other IRCs, and closure could mean being cut off from lawyers, friends and family. However, members with experience of IRC detention were also deeply angry at the system and the prospect of piecemeal reformist changes, so were energized by the emergence of groups that explicitly called for the shutdown of all detention centers. The tensions of this non-reformist demand – "Shut Down Dungavel" – were not avoided or buried in *We Will Rise*'s work, but made central as a problem to be unpacked together in ways that could challenge the logic of reform. This meant having to articulate a position such as: "We think it is false to use the threat of people moved down south as a reason to continue the violence of Dungavel – release everyone inside back to their families and communities," using a similar logic to prison abolition campaigns. Regularly having to have this discussion meant attempting to build practical arguments for abolition in the day-to-day, and although this was challenging, it involved bringing in people who had in effect been necessarily excluded by reformist demands, along with those who were already convinced by more non-reformist approaches.

As far as a non-reformist demand goes, "Shut Down Dungavel," was in a sense, successful. Following the campaign and widespread media scrutiny of the IRC, the British Home Office announced in September 2016 that Dungavel would be closing, with the private contract to run it also ending. This was greeted by *We Will Rise* with a muted celebration, a group statement from September 8, 2016, reads:

> On hearing that Dungavel will close, we extend our deepest respect for the courage of those struggling for papers who have led this movement to shut down this brutal facility. This is a major achievement for our community and a testament to the power of collective action. The Home Office have bowed to the power of this movement. We also wish to acknowledge the effort of fifteen years of activism to close Dungavel. [One spokesperson] Sally Martinez said: *"Tonight we celebrate, tomorrow we escalate the fight to end detention."*

But the Home Office decision to shut Dungavel was accompanied by a plan to open a 51-bed short-term holding facility in the nearby town of Paisley, next to Glasgow Airport, in order to facilitate quicker deportations and removals. People linked to *We Will Rise* mobilized quickly against this, under a new campaign group named *Stop Detention in Scotland*. This group brought in local politicians and used planning objections in a remarkably quick and extremely effective campaign. The separate name of the new campaign also indicated its shift away from *We Will Rise*'s emphasis on large community meals, open meetings and attempts to center and amplify the lived experience of people in the struggle for papers.

This change in tactic and framing caused some friction, as did *Stop Detention Scotland*'s more explicitly Scotland-focused framing. What was the tradeoff between quick, effective mobilization that drew on key expertise in areas like planning law, and a longer-term project of sharing of skills and building capacity? Did a Scottish framing imply that detention was OK elsewhere, or simply a pragmatic focus on destroying a key pillar of the British detention estate? All reforms, even non-reformist ones, imply a scale and some form of state entity to act upon or against – and it was in the shift from the Dungavel to Paisley campaigns that this became most illuminated in this case. The key context here was the long historic movement for Scottish independence, and the fact that the Scottish government in Edinburgh did not have devolved powers over immigration and asylum issues. As such, the ruling Scottish National Party (SNP) has often presented itself, and Scotland, as a "welcoming" alternative to the British state, but was not able to influence border controls, beyond voting as a minority party in the British Parliament. The 2014 Scottish Independence Referendum had left the SNP keen to assert local opposition to the British Parliament at Westminster, with immigration detention offering one such issue on which to take a stance. Here it is important to note that the referendum had galvanized a huge range of people, including migrant and refugee groups, with many Commonwealth Citizens voting in Scotland for the first time and going on to become active in SNP and Green Party politics. *Stop Detention Scotland* played strategically on these political shifts to great effect, but this exposed tensions around strategy that pivoted on questions of engagement with the state, processes of movement-building and the importance of "lived experience" leadership. Ultimately, this was a question of whether such campaigns built toward a broader project of border abolition.

REFLECTIONS FOR FUTURE CAMPAIGNS

Future non-reformist reform strategies for border abolition could benefit from considering how people within the asylum and immigration system are often cut out of quick mobilizations at the level of planning law and local politics. Often these kinds of mobilizations come with short timeframes and seem to need particular kinds of "expert" knowledge to anticipate and disrupt the official processes and procedures. This is in no way to suggest that these kinds of quick planning law-targeted campaigns are "bad" strategies, but instead to suggest we start to build-in training about planning law and working with local government into the kinds of large community meals, parties, trips, and protests through which community power can be strengthened.

The discussion of non-reformist reforms should not only be about the content of a particular demand, but also about the process by which that demand is constructed, and the form it takes in terms of action. The *Stop Detention in Scotland* Paisley mobilization was clearly non-reformist – "no new detention centres" and "no detention centres" at all – but did not build community power among the people most affected by immigration detention in the same way that the *We Will Rise* community meetings did. This all then felt compounded by the success of the campaign: the new Paisley facility was rejected by the planning committee of the local Renfrewshire Council in November 2016, but the Home Office announced that this would mean Dungavel would remain open, as it still is today.

Though in a sense the argument about detention was won by both *We Will Rise* and *Stop Detention Scotland*, this was not ultimately converted into a long-term abolitionist win at Dungavel. A new site was stopped, which was a key victory. But as we have seen with the use of budget hotels as proxy-detention centers, the Home Office is very malleable in adapting infrastructure for the border regime. Indeed, one such budget hotel in Erskine, is – as of March 2023 – housing more than 200 people in the immigration system, just 5 miles from the former proposed site at Paisley. Though these are very different types of border infrastructure, and we should not underestimate how powerful it was to defeat the building of a new detention facility in Paisley, it is also important to see how the border regime will adapt and mold its carceral infrastructure to continue holding people in the system.

Future attempts to mobilize around non-reformist reforms need to contend with these problems, of what a "win" really is, if, as the *We Will Rise* statement quoted above argues, "one site of trauma, maltreatment and violence will be replaced by another." Transitional abolitionist demands need to consider timeframes and possible state reactions, along with the geographic scales at which a demand and campaign can operate. The long-term, community-building tactics of *We Will Rise* created the grounds for the quick and effective political mobilization of *Stop Detention Scotland*, but the success of the latter had an arguably opposite effect in the longer term. The regular praxis of *We Will Rise* – community meals, stalls, banner making, and protests at Dungavel, the Home Office and in Glasgow city center – built upon but also helped to strengthen a community of people willing to actively challenge the detention system, and to take leads from those within it. Such vital "world-building" does not always align with more decisive, time-limited campaigns, and the tensions therein require constant attention and discussion.

We Will Rise emerged from abolitionist lifeworlds way beyond Glasgow: Crossroads Women's Centre, who had provided the model for the *LGBT Unity* and *Unity Sisters* peer-support groups, *Sisters Uncut*, who had quickly mobilized when a key *LGBT Unity* organizer had been detained in England, *SOAS Detainee Support, Coventry Peace House, Critical Resistance, No One Is Illegal,* and too many more to mention. The practices of such groups, beyond the temporality of "demand" and "win" or "loss," has sustained campaigns and people for many years since, in all kinds of diffuse, relational ways. Alongside these many groups and campaigns, *We Will Rise* created a political imaginary and a prefigurative space in opposition to detention both at its most clear physical manifestation – the IRC – and in the IRC's long shadow across communities in Glasgow. This was animated by the key non-reformist reform of ending detention in Scotland, in all the messy forms that might take, and a deeper abolitionist ethos, "we will not stop until they are all free." Here, we see glimpses of Gilmore's abolitionist "presence," where the violence of the border is not allowed to fully condition the struggle against it.

CONCLUSION

This chapter has discussed the utility of non-reformist reforms in movements for border abolition, drawing on our experiences of two linked campaigns opposing immigration detention in Scotland. We have tried to show how a concept of non-reformist reforms can support both strategic interventions against the state and movement-building within the already vibrant abolitionist lifeworlds of "unconditional support" in the UK. In doing so, we have emphasized the messy tensions and power dynamics arising from our attempts to build community power and our struggles to redefine community beyond the reach of the state's legal categories or its reification. We have argued that non-reformist reforms can be an important tool in the struggle for border abolition, involving people that are excluded by more reformist NGO approaches that tweak and legitimize the border regime and are often focused on the narrowly constructed notion of "good" migrants. We tried to avoid a binary critique of "non-reformist" and "reformist" measures instead showing, through detailed analysis of two campaigns, how the former involves political tensions, interpersonal conflict, and difficult strategic decisions – all of which are worth scrutiny and careful appraisal.

Such analysis is only as useful as the impact it can have on actual struggle, and we hope this piece has been valuable in some way for those fighting detention and the border in all its forms today. Beyond this, we hope it encourages others to share their experiences and strategies in this struggle, beyond the immediate activist debrief and the tectonic pace of academic and archival historicization. The history of grassroots and radical campaigns against detention, along with resistance and protest by "detainable" people themselves is vital to understand when building abolitionist strategies for the future.

The key demand of these campaigns – "Shut Down Dungavel" and "End Detention" – worked as a non-reformist reform in two ways. First, the demand clearly made a case for a material reduction in the detention estate, rather than pushing for new carceral techniques in reformist programs of "alternatives to detention" or marginal "time limits." Second, "Shut Down Dungavel" worked as a movement-building tool to frame and galvanize a wide constituency of those affected by border violence, from whom the demand emerged. Non-reformist reforms can undermine the logic of the detention system and the mechanisms which prop it up. They work to build movements, as they encourage campaigns to look forward, up and out from their target campaign to embed a systemic political imaginary. Ultimately, we know that immigration detention is not just a particular form of imprisonment, but one tool of the UK's mass deportation system. Similarly, the process of criminalization has to be understood as part and parcel with the violent dispossession imposed on racialized communities, wherein criminalization and punishment are offered as the only solutions to social problems rooted in exploitation and expropriation. As abolitionists, we need to understand these systems of power and use non-reformist reforms to dream up, to map, and to plan the interventions required to undo more and more of it: to undo it all.

NOTES

1. Jerome Phelps, "How the UK Turned Away from Immigration Detention." *Detention Forum* (blog), September 2, 2020. https://detentionforum.org.uk/2020/09/02/how-the-uk-turned-away-from-immigration-detention/
2. André Gorz, *Strategy for Labor: A Radical Proposal.* Boston: Beacon Press, 1967.
3. Gargi Bhattacharyya, Adam Elliott-Cooper, and Sita Balani, *Empire's Endgame: Racism and the British State.* London: Pluto Press, 2021, p. 198.
4. Mariame Kaba, Berger Dan, and Stein David, "What Abolitionists Do." *Jacobin*, August 24, 2017. https://jacobin.com/2017/08/prison-abolition-reform-mass-incarceration; see also Thomas Mathiesen, *The Politics of Abolition Revisited*, 1st edition. Abingdon, Oxon: Routledge, 2014.
5. S. Lamble, "Bridging the Gap between Reformists and Abolitionists: Can Non-Reformist Reforms Guide the Work of Prison Inspectorates?" *Institute for Criminal Policy Research* (blog), 2022. www.icpr.org.uk/news-events/2022/bridging-gap-between-reformists-and-abolitionists-can-non-reformist-reforms-guide
6. Abolitionist Futures, "Defund the Police," *Abolitionist Futures.* Accessed June 13, 2023. https://abolitionistfutures.com/defund-the-police
7. Gracie Mae Bradley and Luke de Noronha, *Against Borders: The Case for Abolition*, 1st edition. London; New York: Verso, 2022.
8. Fiona Jeffries and Jennifer Ridgley, "Building the Sanctuary City from the Ground Up: Abolitionist Solidarity and Transformative Reform."

Citizenship Studies 24(4), May 18, 2020: 548–567. doi: 10.1080/
13621025.2020.1755177

9. Gargi Bhattacharyya. *Rethinking Racial Capitalism: Questions of Repro-
    duction and Survival.* Maryland: Rowman & Littlefield International,
    2018, p. 182

10. Azfar Shafi and Ilyas Nagdee, *Race to the Bottom: Reclaiming Antiracism,*
    1st edition. London: Pluto Press, 2022.

11. Aviah Sarah Day and Shanice Octavia McBean, *Abolition Revolution.*
    London; Las Vegas: Pluto Press, 2022, p. 150.

12. Ruth Gilmore Wilson, n.d. quoted in, Adrienne Maree Brown, *We Will
    Not Cancel Us: And Other Dreams of Transformative Justice.* London: AK
    Press, 2020.

13. "How Many People Are Detained or Returned?," *GOV.UK.* Accessed June
    13, 2023. www.gov.uk/government/statistics/immigration-statistics-year-
    ending-december-2019/how-many-people-are-detained-or-returned

12

Abolitionist potential and ambivalence in daily struggles against the border regime

Watch the Med – Alarm Phone

Deanna, Rubi, Lolo, and Camille: We are a working group within Watch the Med – Alarm Phone *(from now on just Alarm Phone), but we are not the representative voice of Alarm Phone. Within Alarm Phone there are heterogenous viewpoints and perspectives, and these debates are ongoing. For us this is a platform to articulate our ideas and our position in relation to existing debates, but this is not a positioning of Alarm Phone on these issues.*

Watch The Med – Alarm Phone is a network of activists in Europe and North Africa, running a self-organized hotline for people in distress in the Mediterranean Sea. The project provides a practical and political intervention in the struggle for freedom of movement, fighting not only to end border violence but also to abolish the border regime. This goal is grounded in the acknowledgment that violence is not contingent, but an inextricable condition of borders.

To respond to the multi-layered forms of border violence at the European borders, *Alarm Phone* generates resistance on multiple levels. On a practical level, it amplifies calls for assistance, provides Safety at Sea information, relays distress calls, and pushes for rescue in real time. When receiving calls from or alerts to people in distress at sea or in border zones, *Alarm Phone* relays the information to the competent authorities and different actors from civil society. In addition, distress information is made public mainly on social media, as well as through journalists, to put pressure on authorities. On the one hand, this contributes to counteracting deaths at sea and attacks against people on the move by mobilizing interventions, amplifying calls for assistance and making them visible. On the other hand, the *Alarm Phone* infrastructure – through its 24/7 hotline and permanent presence along different migration routes – creates a point of contact for people on the move in crucial moments of their journeys. An example of this practical infrastructure is the way Safety at Sea information is produced and distributed in digital and physical formats by communities on the move, activists on the ground and via social networks.

On a political level, *Alarm Phone* counter-maps the reactions of authorities to the presence of boats in distress, reactions which include illegal pushbacks as well as inaction through non-assistance. *Alarm Phone* documents border violence by collecting testimonies of people who call the hotline. These are reconstructions and counter-narratives produced by the people on the move themselves about the violence they experience, materials which *Alarm Phone* amplifies to hold authorities accountable. Friends, partners, and families of missing people also regularly call *Alarm Phone*, searching for information on their loved ones, revealing the complete absence of infrastructures for tracing people's fates. This systematic neglect shows that while some forms of violence can be documented, others are rendered invisible, or "invisibilized," producing new and often under-discussed forms of border violence.

In this conversation, we would like to unpack the abolitionist potential and ambivalences of our work, the tensions between short-term intervention and long-term political trajectories, between practical politics and theoretical frameworks, and the relationship between solidarity and abolition.

We would like to talk about the relation between the work of *Alarm Phone* and its abolitionist perspective, including its complexities and contradictions (for example, the fact that we call coast guard authorities on a daily basis). There are often some frictions between short-term interventions and our abolitionist political framework. One example of those frictions might be the cases of criminalization of people on the move. In those cases, our interventions happen in the frame of the criminal justice system. To support people who have been criminalized, we often have to use a legal strategy that is not directly in accordance with our political beliefs (i.e., legal arguments such as self-defense, state of necessity, etc.), but it becomes a necessary tool in court. Nonetheless, frictions between daily organizing practices and broader abolitionist aims do not necessarily emerge as contradictions in our work. Short-term actions and long-term demands can support each other in order to pave a path to a radical political change and toward a real freedom of movement for everyone.

Deanna: Within *Alarm Phone*, there are several ongoing conversations about border abolition and prison abolition. Several activist groups and networks are organized separately on these issues, and rarely do the conversations around prisons and borders go together. Often we speak of border abolition, but when we do so we do not think about the punitive and carceral aspects of borders. Sometimes we speak about border abolition and we call for freedom of movement, but then the notion of abolition is decontextualized from its political and historical roots. In our struggle for freedom of movement it is important to highlight the carcerality of borders, how they operate by confining and punishing people, and the necessity for the abolition – rather than reform – of all systems of oppression which are carceral and punitive in their language and practice. Several political and humanitarian responses to border violence go in the direction of creating less violent borders, or somehow better borders, but they do not go in the direction of abolition. For me it is very important to link these conversations around prisons, punishment, control and against borders as a form of control and confinement. They are interrelated and as much as borders need and create prisons, prisons need and create borders.

Rubi: For me these are very linked and abolition does not mean to only abolish something, but also to create an environment where people can leave and travel, and live where they want to live as well as where they are able to. This needs the support of society and allies. *Alarm Phone* is one attempt in this direction, because we facilitate movement, which is very important. In regard to the criminalization of the freedom of movement, we try to counter the narrative defined by punitive institutions, we try to find new words and new narratives to define what is happening.

Lolo: One thing is to create counter-narratives that are strong and that show that there is an alternative, but with this comes a need to create not only counter-narratives but also real spaces that propose an alternative. Here I see important connections to the work of *Alarm Phone* where there are different efforts not only trying to abolish something and to fight against something, but also creating something new. This is not limited to counter-discourse, but also to practical steps such as building networks, connecting with projects and communities that are related to the wider space of *Alarm Phone*. We create physical connections, friendships, and build new alternative communities. This way we can actually create something that is not only an idea, but something that is practically existing. This for me is an important part of an abolitionist practice, be this against the border regime, or against the prison system. These oppressive systems are overlapping, but there is a whole system of alternatives that are constantly being built in antagonism to them.

Camille: This will to create new spaces is also illustrated in how we relate to the *Alarm Phone* and in how members of the *Alarm Phone* are all part of different struggles and movements. This is not only in relation to the Mediterranean Sea, the Channel, and the Atlantic Ocean, but also in relation to what happens for people in different countries, the different ways people are detained, how they are subjected to violence not only before going into a migration journey but also when they arrive, and the violence people experience in non-welcoming regimes that are in place. This really impacts our narratives and how we relate to different projects, how we try to connect them to create bigger networks and new solidarities. These kinds of activist engagements are not just about border or prison abolition but also about building different societies in the places we live in. I really like the idea that you all mentioned about creating new spaces, but also creating new ideas and new dreams that are not "idealistic," but real political projects that go into the direction of the abolition of prisons, borders, and all the tools used by states to reinforce their punitive regimes.

Deanna: Starting from these points we can also think about the criminalization of all the attempts to create alternative communities and friendships, alternative forms of "passage" and of solidarities by relating in a non-hierarchical manner with people on the move and creating communities across the North and South of the Mediterranean Sea. These alternatives are criminalized because they are not following humanitarian or carceral logics, and defy racialized hierarchies of white-to-Black or North-to-South solidarity. Building these bridges and friendships, facilitating freedom of movement, as you all said is an abolitionist practice against the carceral and punitive logic of borders: and because these practices show that an alternative to carcerality exists, they are criminalized. As a result of potential criminalization, these practices have to happen underground, to remain hidden, or in silence as we cannot openly speak about it. Fighting against the criminalization of people on the move and against the violence of borders by bringing positive alternatives becomes a crime in itself. We are punished when we try to, and *because* we try to bring abolitionist alternatives to punitiveness, we become again completely entangled into the circle of repression, action, reaction and defensiveness that often closes the space for the creation of radical alternatives.

Lolo: This gives a reference to the close interrelation between the prison system and the so-called criminal justice system and the border regime. Because in the end the same means are used to enforce control: means of surveillance, control and incarceration, as well as escalating processes of militarization. To enforce control in that way also means to criminalize and repress the possibility of creating attractive alternatives. And this is something that we witness with an increasing brutality in the border regime, with processes of criminalization, the whole process of border policing, not only at the border but also to enforce migration control in a broader sense. This development shows the lack of recipes that the state or state authorities have to enforce control – done so by using armed force, imprisonment, and encampment in different ways. And in doing so authorities do not only seek to control the movement of people but also to disrupt the building and emergence of strong relationships and alternative visions that reject the status quo.

Camille: This makes me think about the work we do to make visible what is going on at sea and at the different borders, which means the violence but also the criminalization. The core of our activism is, I think, also to fight the invisibilization that states would like to maintain on their actions and their consequences on people. This aim to make the violence visible, to actively witness it, is present in all our actions: in the daily support we try to provide with the hotline, in the reports we write, in the support to different campaigns and commemorActions. For example, the commemorActions are moments of commemoration of the people who were killed by the border regime, raising political demands of the families and loved ones of the missing, as well as for our networks. The use of social media, the documentation and the archives are also really central to what we do. It helps to create and support new narratives to counter the dominant ones of states. With the criminalization of people crossing borders, as well as people trying to support them or raising other narratives, states try to silence them and make alternative ways of living in this world invisible. Creating spaces to speak and hear alternative voices and ideas is also an important part of our abolitionist struggle.

Rubi: With the last shipwreck off Libya, I thought about what would have happened if the boat had not been in touch with the *Alarm Phone*: everyone would have drowned very secretly, nobody would have known. We made a lot of effort to make it visible and to scandalize what happened, not expecting much change at all, but at least to make visible the daily violence of the border regime. I recently also ran again into a case from 2019, and I realized that it was just a few years ago, but even then the situation was somehow different, less threatening, because, for example, Frontex had no air surveillance to spot boats moving to Europe and it was only one year since the Libyan Search and Rescue zone was established, so the so-called Libyan coast guards were much less effective in forcing people back to Libya. In a few years so much has changed. I was shocked again, because when we fight against something we easily get used to the fact that all this violence is the norm, that it is the usual situation. But it is good to remember that it is not normal, and it is getting more and more violent. We have to really be prepared. It is hard to enlarge our space as increasingly, we are focused on defending our space, which is becoming harder and harder. Also, with the climate crisis with more people wanting to leave, and with Fortress Europe becoming more and more violent, somehow I have the feeling we do not have much more time. I feel increasingly under pressure to have in mind this postcolonial situation where exploitation is getting harder and harder, and where keeping our space is one of the main tasks for me at the moment.

Deanna: You mention the shipwreck and increasing violence, as well as accountability through our counter-surveillance, counter-monitoring, reporting, and archiving. This points to many questions and discussions we are currently addressing within *Alarm Phone*. Especially after the shipwreck in Crotone and the following shipwreck off Libya involving merchant vessels, several civil society organizations mobilized to produce criminal complaints against the state, so as to bring the coastguards and states to account for these deaths. We all referred back to the October 3, 2013, shipwreck off Lampedusa, where the coast guard was on trial and eventually accused of manslaughter – although they were not punished because the case fell in prescription. Within our networks we asked ourselves: how to respond to this violence, how can our counter-monitoring and counter-surveillance contribute to accountability and justice, but also, first of all, what kind of justice are we seeking?

What is important, for me, is to reconstruct the events in order to show where responsibility lies. This helps inform the political discussion, because the mainstream discussion is really centered around blaming the smugglers, blaming people for their own deaths as well as framing shipwrecks as accidents or exceptions to the norm. With our work we contextualize what happened within a broader political framework. We show that it is not the sea that is killing people, but the border regime. We make visible how this violence is historical as well as political, and not the unexpected result of an emergency. We try to show this violence is the result of colonial legacies, racist laws and global inequalities. We try to show that this violence is chosen politically, every day, and as such is preventable: it is not an unintended consequence of the border regime. This is key for changing the narrative and eventually how we fight against the border regime. In my view, all this does not need to lead to a formal trial for manslaughter.

One of the discussions in our network is where do we stop, where is our boundary? We try to change the narrative, changing the perspective and making visible the political context in which these things happen. This, for me, does not exclude, but also does not require, so-called "criminal justice" forms of accountability. In a way we point the finger at the context but then do we take that extra step and formally accuse coast guard officers for killing people, do we need to ask a judge to punish people with imprisonment for murder and manslaughter? What alternative forms of justice can we imagine and prefigure?

Lolo: For me this is the key point. I think one does not exclude the other. The strength of being part of a diverse network as *Alarm Phone* is to choose different strategies of resistance – to do so with an abolitionist vision does not exclude putting pressure via legal procedures. For me it is very clear that there are different ways to push against the border regime and its consequences. In some situations one possible way is to choose an institutional path, for example by filing a criminal complaint. This means to follow this very institutional and formalized road within a framework that we generally and explicitly reject and that we want to abolish. When doing that we need to ensure in parallel to not forget where we come from and what our political commitments are. We should embed those practical steps into a wider political context in order to have a combination of abolitionist demands while filing a complaint or doing strategic litigation. Strategic litigation is a good example in this case, as it seems to me inherent to its very concept that you don't only use legal arguments but try to push forward political narratives, counter-narratives.

Camille: To go back to the point on strategic litigation and the use of law: it is important to try to have an overview about all the legal tools we can use. There is of course criminal law, and maybe those cases are the most visible and spectacular, the ones that can have the most emotional impact, because then the charges are raising strong carceral wordings such as manslaughter or murder. But there are other strategic litigations that we can elaborate based on administrative law, civil law or human rights law, especially in front of the European Court of Human Rights or the African Court for Human and People's Rights. There are different levels of courts that we can address: from domestic courts to international bodies such as the UN committees, even if their decisions are not binding for states. All those legal tools are way less visible in the media, because, maybe, they're more complicated to explain, more technical, but can also address a specific case in a different way. This conversation about which types of law and procedures we want to use is very interesting because depending on which legal tool we use, we address the same issue in different manners. For example, working with administrative law, we can make the state, and not a particular person, be condemned for not doing something it is bound to do, such as providing minimal services such as access to asylum procedures, water, food and shelter. This was used in Calais in Northern France for example, forcing the French authorities to provide minimal services such as access to water to the people stuck there.

In all those cases, people are in critical situations and legal tools are used as short-term remedies to address an urgent matter: law is then used to stop the state from endangering people in a particular and immediate harmful situation. These interventions do not address the substance of the matter. One example is the demand for immediate and urgent measures, based on Article 39, in front of the European Court of Human Rights concerning people being stranded on islands on the Evros River. However, such legal remedies can also be used to amplify a different political narrative and to force states to act – such as in Calais or at the Greek Evros border – or at least to address the situation in front of the courts.

There is, for me, a difference between those cases, and the criminal cases. The accountability does not target the same "body": an institution/a system or a person. Having in mind the different legal tools can perhaps sometimes, within the very strict framework of the law, open the discussion on the manner we would like to address a specific case: what are our aims, what are the routes we want to take to achieve them, and the methods that we prefer to exclude?

Rubi: People going to prison creates a lot of additional harm, and everybody knows that this won't change anything and it does not bring back the losses of, e.g., drowned people in a shipwreck.

We often start from the assumption that one person would be punished, e.g., the coast guard officer or whoever is considered responsible, but of course we can't really imagine that an officer of a state institution is going to go to prison. We know that a lot of people go into prisons because they take their freedom of movement, but we don't often experience that those responsible within institutions go to prison.

Apart from this, it is difficult to imagine alternatives because in this current system we don't have many tools. In this punitive system this is the only existing practice, formulated not from our side but from the state's side or the courts' side: to hold individuals responsible and to punish them. Also, families and survivors often look for individual responsibilities and this form of accountability.

However, with the experiences we have with families of missing people or in the case of invisible shipwrecks, it is clear that states and institutions really neglect that they are somehow involved or responsible. Many people are demanding that state institutions at least acknowledge and apologize for what happened. Somehow what is necessary for families of the missing is this acknowledgment, and the confirmation that the event happened as it happened. At the moment, if authorities refuse responsibility and claim shipwrecks are accidents, they are just refusing to acknowledge that it happened the way it happened. This is the task of the *Alarm Phone*: we describe and reconstruct what happened, and we address who is responsible.

But sometimes, families or survivors search for state recognition of state violence. In the struggles against police violence and police murder in Germany, while some refuse to search for justice within the same state institutions that perpetrated violence against them, some families or survivors place much hope in these trials, despite their daily experience of institutional racist violence by the state, the police, the juridical system. Only at the end do they realize that it was not helpful at all and that there is still no state recognition, and that they are still alone. It is hard for them to realize that this kind of approach: that the "criminal justice," did not help them. So they continue searching, but it soon becomes clear that the support they need can be found only in the community and among those who experience similar murders. This is the real support, this is where people support each other and understand what happened, the only way to recognize the pain inflicted by this institutional violence. But it is a very long struggle.

I can compare this with what we are doing as *Alarm Phone* in supporting relatives in search for the missing, as well as reconstructing shipwrecks. We are in solidarity, we stand very clearly on their side. Sometimes we are in contact over years. When I remember the parents of missing people speaking at a gathering we organized in Palermo, even when they saw a picture of their dead child they could not accept that this was true. It is very clear that there is a huge need for recognition of these crimes.

Deanna: What you say about the role of communities makes me think of the slogan "there is no justice, there is just us," placing communities of care at the center of our thinking about the meaning of "justice," and creating alternatives to so-called "criminal justice."

If accountability and recognition is not achievable through criminal law or criminal procedures, there is a difference between accountability that leads to *punishment* and broader accountability that leads to wider *consequences*, not necessarily punitive ones. If we see punishment as the only tool to create justice, we limit our imagination and our capacity to act outside this framework. I know that these trials are part of a broader struggle for social and political change, and are not only oriented toward punishment. But the logic of these trials is based on the production of evidence to prove that a law has been violated, which often brings results either based on technicalities or on lack of convincing evidence. When we go down this route, we become entangled in a toxic dynamic dictated by criminal law where one accuses and one defends, one accuses and the other defends. The state will keep defending itself rather than recognizing its violence, and it will always be stronger than us in defending itself and in producing or removing evidence. Moreover, it is being judged against laws the state itself has created.

This way, we initiate these harmful processes where there is us against the state, or communities on the move against the racist criminal justice system, namely communities of racialized non-citizens against the state who made the laws that they are judging themselves against. We really need to highlight the lived experience of many families and survivors who went through the criminal justice system to obtain justice, and just face more racist violence and other forms of victimization, by being questioned and interrogated by a racist court, by being dropped into these very horrible white supremacists spaces while trying to bring justice for the loved ones they lost.

We can fight a lot to change these laws, but this is not necessarily done through the criminal justice system.

Therefore, to answer the question "is there justice or is there just us?" we need to reflect and rethink what we mean by justice and by accountability, by consequences rather than punishments, and on how we can bring all these issues together to create more social and racial justice.

Camille: Criminal law is really constrained: as the state is the one judging the accused person. It is not the victim or the family. What is on trial, is the breach of the state law and state-defined order. As a result, the political decisions and the border regime will never be on trial. The freedom of movement, the right for everyone to use a plane or a ferry to travel to Europe, and to settle where they want, this can all be raised as political arguments by the lawyers of civil parties, but the states' policies are not on trial and they are not being judged. In criminal proceedings, we associate our demands to the ones of the state, and it is asked to the judge to decide if the coastguards or an employee of the state did something wrong and breached the "state-defined order." If the person is found "guilty," judges are asked to impose a sanction or a punishment which, depending on the crime the person is accused of, can be imprisonment. As no-border activists, the question is then how do we address it: we can approach trials by bringing a strong political discourse and counter-narratives showing the violence of the border regime, and using the courtroom as a public space to amplify political demands. This can happen, but in the end, the judges will not address that, or if they do, this will remain just a marginal aspect.

There is also an essential difference between, on the one hand, engaging with criminal law because we are asking the prosecutors to initiate a case, and on the other because we decide to provide support to a person being criminalized by the state (e.g., the cases where a person is criminalized as "captain/boat driver"). In the latter, we engage in these spaces because we are committed to supporting a person facing another kind of violence of the border regime, namely, the use of criminal law to criminalize people who use their freedom of movement to cross borders.

Deanna: These points are all related to the hypocrisy of the state and of the courts – which are somehow separate but not entirely – when they accuse a state official of murder or of having committed an illegal action. Within *Alarm Phone* we had several discussions around the conviction of the captain of the merchant vessel *Asso Ventotto*. He was sentenced to one year of prison, accused of illegally pushing people back to Libya after rescuing them. For us it was difficult to agree on whether we should celebrate this as a political victory, or if instead we should send letters of solidarity to the captain in prison, as we do with other captains that exercise freedom of movement and that facilitate other people in exercising their freedom of movement. I would controversially be in favor of sending solidarity letters to this merchant vessel captain although his actions prevented freedom of movement and led to a pushback to a place people were escaping from. For me, his conviction is a symbol of the hypocrisy of the Italian state which with one hand gives money, resources and trainings to the so-called Libyan coast-guard to facilitate illegal pushbacks to Libya every single day; while with the other hand convicts a merchant vessel captain for doing exactly the same thing. This is counterproductive because it masks how these violent practices happen every day and how, every day, they are enforced by the state. It is also counterproductive because it brings up the language of "exceptionality" as if "the norm" was breached by a rotten apple. For this case, as well as for shipwrecks, the main narrative is that these are exceptions, accidents, mistakes, or that crimes were committed rather than acknowledging that this violence is the norm and it is imposed by state laws who, for instance, criminalize merchant vessel captains and civil actors who rescue people at sea and bring them to Europe. By bringing merchant vessel captains, as well as coast guard officers, to prison we do not fix the problem, we just legitimize this hypocrisy and we mask the actual responsibilities.

Lolo: On this example, I would agree, and I think it is quite an exceptional example. I agree with pretty much all of what has been said. I think the question on what is the alternative and why there is such a strong desire to file criminal complaints and to go down this road, although people already know that it will be very hurtful and that the chances for justice through this road will be very small or nearly non-existing, is key. I think part of the answer is that the debate of alternative visions is not strong enough yet, which is something that needs to be acknowledged. And maybe also existing alternatives seem not strong enough, in practice. For people seeking for something called justice to come to the point where justice means "just us," is a long journey. It has to be built upon collective memory and acknowledgment that seeking justice through institutionalized ways often does not lead to anything. So maybe deconstructing trials and institutional forms of justice in the long term means to go through them again and again? It means to keep filing complaints if people have the desire to do so. To document this, to build a strong narrative of how else to do it in the future, showing alternative ways of mutual struggles for justice outside the hostile framework of the criminal justice system. This counts especially for trials against the state or state actors, as we know that they almost never lead to anything. We know this for trials against police officers, for trials against any coast guard officer or state institution: it is almost impossible to win against them in legal procedures. If we experience this collectively and we have exchanges about it, we may realize that the state does not go against itself, which seems quite a logical conclusion. But also, looking at it more practically, yes, they may convict an individual merchant vessel captain, but they will never convict their own institution for systematically doing the same. To still file these complaints, therefore, means to collect experience on these practices and on these limitations. On the other hand, these can also become important moments for networking, or for building strong bonds among different people who are affected by different forms of border violence or struggles against it. Overall, I think these trials can become important moments of exchange to build momentum around a wider perspective, which is outside or beyond these institutionalized ways of seeking justice.

Rubi: I would like to add that we often also have the problem that there is not much evidence that we can collect to file these complaints. And in cases where there is evidence, such as, for example, Frontex crimes, there is a question of what can be done with it. There is a lot of public knowledge about Frontex crimes, a lot of media reports, a lot of evidence but nothing is happening and there are no consequences. And of course the lack of consequences is a political decision in itself. We put in a lot of effort but nothing is changing. We are planning to prepare a workshop on Frontex crimes to collect evidence, but we know that there will not be consequences even if evidence of their violence is widely shared and known. So, I wonder what could be a good way, how can we bring accountability not in a punitive sense, and what could be our approach and our demands beyond accusing and scandalizing.

Lolo: I do not have a solution, obviously, but maybe this is a good example to show the dilemmas we face in the work we do. Frontex was more and more in the spotlight in the last years and there was a lot of pressure on it from different sides. People on the move started to identify Frontex as a violator of their rights to move and to report in detail about the violence they suffered at its hands. This has added important evidence against the EU agency. Then there was a wide constellation of activists and journalists who started to put pressure on the agency and still do – sometimes in a more coordinated way and sometimes in a less coordinated way. This led to aggregated pressure that forced the director Fabrice Leggeri to step back – to the point that he was forced to resign. But the question remains: what did this materially change? The resignation of Leggeri was received as a political victory, because he was, with others, responsible for what was happening. But the violence of this agency continued, in a very similar way to what it was before. This is why we need to ask, which strategies we can think of to further push against the agency and stop the way it is working. This is for me the central question. However, it is quite difficult to practically address it.

Camille: This brings us back to what we said earlier, that with our abolitionist methods we try to create new solidarities and new spaces. We try to create broader and broader networks on diverse topics, to engage with each other on a transnational point of view and to connect these struggles together: this is already bringing change. They are slow, too slow, yes, but we keep creating new solidarities that build on one another. We keep learning from previous attempts and initiatives. For instance, on the criminalization of migration, many networks of solidarity were created, in different regions, and are now trying to connect with each other. I think those relations, and the counter-narratives that come from them, are at the core of our struggle; they fight against the state narrative that presents itself as the unique way to "order the world." We are trying to show that we can connect to each other differently: through friendships, the creation of moments to meet, but also on a daily basis, by exchanging information and direct support. Sometimes, it can be tiring but when I look at the existing networks I am impressed by all the bridges that are created daily and all the connections that are reinforced. By acting, we also fight for those alternative realities, because state repression is targeting them in order to make them disappear. Our struggles are often also about how to continue to exist. Maybe it is "just us," but "just us" is really big.

Deanna: You are all saying really beautifully how abolitionism is about creating something rather than just destroying something. It is about creating something beautiful as opposed to the ugliness of the states and their borders. This makes me reflect again on the continuum of criminalization of abolitionist alternatives to punishment and control. What criminalization does in that context, is not to just put people in prison. The criminalization of these alternative and abolitionist practices tries to repress their productive and creative potential, to reduce the possibility of creating communities, putting us in "defense" mode, in a modality of reaction to state narrative and practice, of "keeping our space," rather than of creation of alternatives and amplification of our spaces. What criminalization is doing is not so much about locking us up, but trying to lock our imaginaries. And to lock our capacity of thinking differently or outside of a certain logic, as when we get stuck in the criminal justice system as a reaction to violence. So much energy goes into defending ourselves, reacting to and engaging with the state logic and narratives, that sometimes we risk not having the energy to build something different, or forget that something else is possible.

What this legal system is doing is confining and bordering our imaginaries and our capacities to create bridges with our friends in the South, our capacities to say that we are in relationships of friendships and alliance, not just of charity. For instance, when we are criminalized for rescuing people, we do not argue that we are doing so in our struggle for defying the border regime and as part of our vision to abolish borders and create freedom of movement. We will say that we are innocent, as we were just saving the lives of suffering and desperate people. This, for me, really kills the political imaginary of our movement and our struggle, as it creates a narrative of white saviorism which is very colonial and often with racist tones. It reproduces a representation of our practices as white, as humanitarian and as charity-oriented, which are innocent rather as opposed to those who are then portrayed as guilty, evil, smugglers. This for me is rejecting any possibility of alliances and friendships and it kills the political elements of our struggle against borders. The criminalization of abolitionist alternatives is doing exactly this. It is confining our imagination and is depoliticizing the creation of these alternative communities, imposing on us a language and a practice that often contributes to dehumanizing or subjugating people on the move.

With this, we have to keep in mind that as much as state actors do not go to prison, also white European activists rarely go to prison, although they might be targeted by criminalization. The

190

people who actually end up in prison for envisioning and practicing alternatives to the state are racialized non-citizens, who might be accused of trafficking rather than of solidarity, who cannot use the "humanitarian" clause to Article 12 on Facilitation, and who do not have a strong civil society solidarity and legal support.

Rubi: I agree that white solidarity is not so much affected by punishment, but it still is from time to time. It depends, of course, on the kind of actions and activities that have been targeted by states in those proceedings. I think that, in our area, which is publicly called Search and Rescue, we can quite easily refer to those actions as humanitarian. For several reasons this is the wording we use in our public statements and reports.

Still it is quite contested in our internal discussions. Indeed, we don't act because of this humanitarian approach. It is quite clear that what we do is not humanitarian. But, as you said, states try to destroy ideas that could build different societies and systems. And if we do not label our actions as Search and Rescue, it could endanger our fight. If the state defines your action as violent, then the punishment can be very harsh. It is based on the idea that there are different types of violence: the state violence that is always perfect, and the activist violence that is not and should be criminalized. In this case, the state and the justice system somehow dehumanize you, or at least, exclude you from this humanitarian system. It then brings new obstacles to the solidarity we can receive from other actors or the public, as it could maybe create more distance between our actions and a part of the civil society.

Camille: I think this is important to address, the fact that state violence is also present in the framing of more radical or subversive actions as violent, how states are using those wordings to undermine different actions that go against their own narrative and interests. The border and punitive regimes stigmatize any action that would undermine what they are building as the only "true and possible way" to interact with one another. This narrative targeting activists as "dangerous" is used to legitimate the state's actions and repression is stronger every day. How do we claim the place to have counter-action in this context? How do we protect ourselves collectively without losing our radical voice? How to protect state-free spaces so all networks can exist, even in the most repressive states? This is something we fight for as well with the "sensibilization" work we do, trying to reach a broader public to explain why we exist and why we do what we do, as well as to make strong and radical ideas accessible.

Lolo: I think this whole debate raises many important points. When I was listening, it came to my mind that we quite often and increasingly go into very technical discussions and choose very technical roads to explain certain developments. I see this, for example, when we try to find the right narratives or also when we accuse somebody of wrongdoing. One example is how we address all the technicalities concerning the Search and Rescue zones, who is responsible for reacting to a distress case, how they react, etc. Sometimes, I think we do not put enough effort into pushing the very strong and connecting narratives that do exist in our networks. Maybe it is only an impression, but there are, for example, very strong claims from our friends in the South, in non-European countries. I remember being in meetings where, while working on common argumentation, they often focused more on what we actually want and why we want it. They put at the center freedom of movement as a fundamental right, they draw migration as a human and historically constantly present phenomenon, and describe the Mediterranean as a common and not a divided space. These narratives are very strong and many people can relate to them. Those claims are often abolitionist in nature. I think that in our debates and in the claims we use, such important reference points are often a bit put aside. They are not completely invisibilized, but I think other arguments became much more dominant. This is a crucial point. The question is not only where we put the focus on in practice, but also in the discussion. When there was an attempt in Greece to criminalize *Alarm Phone*, we stood up and said: whatever they do, we will continue doing it, because it's the only alternative we see. We said: this is what we have been doing and will continue to do with determination.

13

Capitalism, mobility, and racialization

Abolitionisms at the border

Brian Whitener

A fundamental insight of abolitionist thought is that carceral systems, no matter how hellish their aspect, are not broken, but working as intended.[1] This prison work is multifarious; housing surplus populations, tearing individuals from their families and communities, disciplining bodies, and repurposing financial surpluses for warfare are just a few outlined in the carceral abolitionist literature. The same insight applies when we turn our attention to that hand-maid of carcerality, the police, and even more so if our object of study is the dense carceral and policing apparatus of the global border regime. Although perhaps at first difficult to believe, a system that features forced migration, deportation and detention, death and depravation, and resurgent nativism is not broken. One of the open questions of border abolition is what then is the work, of course always multiple, that this system accomplishes? This is one of the questions this piece seeks to answer. At the same time, in the face of such inhumanity, it is easy to allow stasis and sadness to overtake us, but as abolitionist thought teaches us these systems were made by human hands and, as such, can be undone by them. Where there is militant struggle there is also growth, or as Joy James says "new bones,"[2] and space for political experiment and creativity both political and theoretical, which is the spirit in which this piece is offered.

Much recent work on border abolition focuses on the carceral and policing apparatus that attend global bordering and migration. In this piece I explore a different set of connections between abolitionisms, mobility, and capitalism. First, I make an argument for the importance of control of mobility as a historical, and necessary, feature of capitalism, which I do by examining how much contemporary discourse on migration has a "hydraulic" imaginary. Forced mobility and immobility is a central concern of the best work on border abolition[3] – what I draw out here is that these dynamics are definitory to capitalism as a social system. Second, I demonstrate how the control of mobility has served as a material support for multiple processes of racialization.[4] While much anti-capitalist work on migration locates racializing processes at the boundary between formally free and coerced labor, I argue that the fixing or forced circulation of populations has historically served as a critical site where the racializing work of linking beliefs and practices takes place. Following from this, I argue for thinking of bordering devices as complex techno-juridical infrastructures which underpin capitalist control of mobility and as devices for fixing bodies in space and inciting them into movement. Finally, this piece closes with a set of reflections on the abolitionist political horizons this chain of concepts opens for us.

SURGES AND SURPLUSES: CAPITALISM AND MOBILITY

At some point after the 2008 Global Financial Crisis, though it is difficult to say with certainty exactly when, migration, a concern of conservative pundits and radical theorists since the beginning of globalization, came to be represented through the language of surges and crises. Not just so in the United States, but also in Europe and slowly globally, where borders were becoming increasingly carceral, militarized, and externalized. This language figures migrants as collective physical entities which move by surging and swarming, and which, in their sudden, rapid movement, produce crises in the carceral and other infrastructures of borders. Surging – to my ear – is a hydraulic language; hydraulic in that migrants here are presented as a dehumanized, viscous solution. If squeezed on one end by climate catastrophe, state violence, or economic collapse, migrants emerge on the other end. Most often in surge-language, migrant "waves" are painted as responding to conditions in "home" geographies, which cause them to break against the imaginary and real walls constraining movement.

One finds this language of surging and swarming in publications in liberal, conservative, and far-right media. A version exists within critical academic work where, in discussions of migrants as a surplus population, one sometimes also finds a hydraulic imaginary. I should be clear that I use and agree, in general, with the idea that many migrants form part of what Karl Marx and other thinkers have called a "surplus population." Many, myself included, have written about how contemporary global capitalism has produced twin crises of surplus capital and surplus populations. Surplus capital being all the financial and fictitious "wealth" that needs to be profitably invested and has led capitalists, financial and otherwise, into riskier and crisis-prone ventures. Surplus populations are those masses of individuals only indirectly integrated into circuits of capitalist accumulation and consumption. Much current work on prison abolition and on changing forms of racial domination centers on prisons as a response to rising surplus populations and a turn from welfare to warfare, as Ruth Wilson Gilmore puts it. I think surplus population is a very useful, in fact, essential concept for the present. What I'm interested in drawing out is how sometimes, though not always, when migrants are figured as a surplus population we find there a hydraulic imaginary.

To give one example, following Raúl Delgado Wise and Humberto Márquez Covarrubias, "capitalist restructuring" in neoliberal Mexico resulted in an enormous surplus population who were forced into migration.[5] In the account of Sara Farris, the migration of global surplus populations helps reduce wage costs in countries of the historic global core and reinforces wage differentials.[6] Here the pressures are accurately rendered changes in capitalist political economy or value formation, but in each case, whether migrants are seen as being pushed out of their homes or pulled into new territories, their movement as movement or as a feature of capitalism is strangely undertheorized. Migrants, pushed or pulled, move like any liquid, whose surplus spills out into new areas following "natural" principles like gravity. This obscures how important, both historically and in the present, the control of mobility has been to capitalists. Of course, (forced) mobility and (forced) immobility or what I call fixing and incitement, have long been a concern of no-borders organizers and authors, as well as border abolitionists;[7] my contribution here is to argue for control of mobility or fixing in place and incitement to move, as a *constitutive feature of capitalism*, as a requirement of capitalist social relations and one whose centrality to capitalism as such has been overlooked. I think we need to have a better, more thorough, and more serious account of why mobility and immobility matters to capitalism as a social and economic system and how mobility and immobility tie into racialization, and I will make my case by returning to Marx's original work on surplus populations and migration.

Discussing how surplus populations arise from the process of accumulation of capital, Marx in *Capital Volume 1* explains how machines are employed to make labor redundant, leading to the expulsion of workers and the creation of a surplus population that sit on the fringes of capitalism. Interestingly, in this same set of passages, Marx touches on how surplus populations become migrating ones:

In the centres of modern industry – factories, workshops, ironworks, mines, etc. – the workers are sometimes repelled, sometimes attracted again in greater masses, so that the number of those employed increases on the whole, although in a constantly decreasing proportion to the scale of production. Here the surplus population exists in the floating form.

Both in the factories proper, and in the large workshops, where machinery enters as one factor, or even where no more than a division of labour of a modern type has been put into operation, large numbers of male workers are employed up to the age of maturity, but not beyond. Once they reach maturity, only a very small number continue to find employment in the same branches of industry, while the majority are regularly dismissed. This majority forms an element of the floating surplus population, which grows with the extension of those branches of industry. Some of these workers emigrate; in fact they are merely following capital, which has itself emigrated.[8]

So much of Marx's language, which is a language we have inherited for discussing surplus populations, uses hydraulic imaginaries, such as "floating," where workers flow to and from as if according to a hidden natural principle. The mention of emigration here is typical of much of Marx's writing where the movement of workers and bodies is also, and often, presented as hydraulic in nature. Hydraulic in that workers are pushed and pulled; pushed by their increasing numbers as surplus overflows the limits of available supports for life and pulled as they "merely" follow capital on its opportunistic journeys across the planet.

Marx wrote an entire volume of *Capital* on circulation, but pick up this volume and there is almost no mention of the circulation of labor, surprising given how keen capitalists have been to control it across history. We can explain Marx's inattention to mobility at a theoretical level as a result of his method. Marx's method in his critical account of capitalism is to hold variables constant in order to better reveal the internal dynamics of his object of study. Unfortunately, one of those variables that Marx held constant – and which has yet to be taken up in a serious way – is the mobility of labor, as *Capital* assumes labor is already found where it is needed; pushed and pulled by unseen hydraulic forces. However, in the historical moments of the text, we can see how preoccupied, particularly in the colonies, capitalists were with finding, securing, and temporarily fixing in place workers. For example, Marx discusses the writing of the English colonist Wakefield, "who discovered that, in the colonies, property in money, means of subsistence, machines and other means of production does not as yet stamp a man as a capitalist if the essential complement to these things is missing: the wage-labourer" and the case of the English-founded Swan River Settlement, "where a great mass of capital, of seeds, implements, and cattle, has perished for want of labourers to use it."[9] A quick glance into any book of colonial history will show how much the mobility of workers was a concern for early capitalists and the vast logistical systems they built to both incite and control mobility. For Marx, the creation of labor power as a commodity was what made capitalism different from other systems of social organization. However, just as important to, and definitory of, capitalism has been the control of mobility, meaning the ability to incite movement or to fix bodies into place (which, again, does not mean giving up the language of surplus population), and, further, the control of mobility has been a dense site where early, and durable, forms of racialization were produced, particularly in the Western hemisphere.

FIXING, INCITEMENT, AND CAPITALIST RACIALIZATION

Marxist treatments of migration have tended to see race as tied to or emerging from a distinction between free and unfree labor. Both Nicholas De Genova and Yann Moulier-Boutang start from the free/unfree labor distinction and describe racialization as proceeding from it. For Moulier Boutang, the labor contract emerges as a way of immobilizing the body of the proletarian and mobility then becomes a weapon, a means of resistance to the contract and labor discipline. There is a direct line between the struggles of slaves to reappropriate their bodily autonomy and migrants exercising their right to flight.[10] Starting from Marx's insight that "labor in a white skin can never emancipate itself," de Genova argues that slavery was necessary for the production of "abstract labor" or "the figure of labor literally shorn of its humanity and stripped of all qualitative specificities."[11] On his account, degraded forms of migrant labor – structured by the racialized difference of national bordering – result from a similar process of "sociopolitical branding."[12]

I start from a different, though related, matrix – namely, how mobility, meaning the means by which bodies and labor power appear as proximate to or are disappeared from sites of production, and the control of mobility, meaning the direct or indirect fixing in place and inciting into movement, are a critical, structural concern of capitalism. The question authors like de Genova and Moulier Boutang answer is "How do we get different kinds of workers and how are current migration and migrant dynamics an outgrowth of prior histories?" while the question I want to answer is: "How do workers appear (or not appear) where they are needed (or not needed) and how is difference, in part, constituted by the group-differentiated exposure to being incited to move or fixed in place?" Without laborers in sufficient numbers, there is no accumulation; conversely, too many laborers without employment also constitutes a problem for capital, and in each case, fixing and incitement are the mechanisms for securing capital's coveted ends. I see these inquiries as complementary, but they imply, as we will see by the end of this chapter, certain political differences, as both de Genova and Moulier Boutang see mobility as a site of resistance. I agree that mobility can be a site of resistance to global capitalist fixing and incitement, but it is also a dense site where racialization, subordination, and value are joined in a complicated site of potential unfreedom.

Perspectives, regardless of their political affiliation, that overlook the need of capital to have workers appear at the sites of production are hydraulic, because they tend to assume there are invisible or unremarkable mechanisms that push and pull workers from one place to another and which serve to distribute them in the ways that capital requires. We live in times of surplus population and, perhaps, in moments of labor scarcity it is easier to see capital's need for and work to incite and fix. However, this need and its infrastructures are clearly visible in the present. We can find particularly direct cases if we look at the juridical regimes controlling Chinese internal labor migration, the worker visa systems of Gulf countries like Qatar, moments of regional concern over a lack of agricultural or other laborers after the passing of anti-migrant legislation, and, perhaps most recently, the way workers were forced back to work at the beginning of the COVID-19 pandemic.[13] Understanding fixing and incitement as central to capitalist accumulation rests on the argument that without a sufficient supply of the right kind of bodies in the correct quantity in determined locations, there is no value production. I think this dynamic has been as important in the history of capitalism as – while also being a key part of – the creation of labor power as commodity, processes of formal and real subsumption, and the production of feminized and unwaged reproductive labor. Seeing it as a historical requirement of accumulation allows us to grasp the root of a linked series of historical processes of inciting and fixing bodies in service to capitalism – such as the transatlantic slave trade, the *congregaciones* of colonial Spanish empire, the rise of "coolie labor," and juridical regimes of exclusion – which form the historical background of the complex array of contemporary means for the control of mobility.[14]

That the control of mobility is a concern of capitalism will not be news to anyone involved in migration or border organizing. The demands of the *freedom to move* and the *freedom to stay* reflect an acknowledgment of mobility as a contemporary site of unfreedom. What is perhaps new here is the deep historical background of this unfreedom *and* its centrality for capitalism as a system of social organization, and the durable, yet changing, articulations with processes of racialization.[15] While a detailed historical account is not yet possible, hopefully we can begin to see how fixing and incitement is a critical site for the production of racialized difference. When Ruth Wilson Gilmore writes that "racism is the state-sanctioned and/or extra-legal production and exploitation of group-differentiated vulnerabilities to premature death, in distinct yet densely interconnected political geographies,"[16] one component of this exposure is the control of mobility. In contemporary work in US-based critical race and ethnic studies, one finds an archive of these threaded dynamics of unfreedom and examples of how controls over mobility were deployed in amalgamated forms to produce racial hierarchies and material processes of racialization.

For example, Simone Browne's work reveals the degree to which current technologies of mobility control are rooted in histories of anti-Blackness and her work outlines how central the control of mobility was to US slave society. She writes:

> In the plantation system, the restriction of the mobility and literacy of the enslaved served as an exercise of power. The racializing surveillance of the slave pass system was a violent regulation of black mobilities. On and off the plantation, black mobility needed to be tightly regulated in order for slave owners to maintain control, so, as ex-slave Anderson Furr put it, one had to "git a pass for dis and a pass for dat."[17]

Katherine McKittrick provides another window into how mobility and Blackness twine together across histories of US slavery:

The forced planting of blacks in the Americas is coupled with an awareness of how the land and nourishment can sustain alternative worldviews and challenge practices of dehumanization … It is through the violence of slavery, then, that the plantation produces black rootedness in place precisely because the land becomes the key provision through which black peoples could both survive and be forced to fuel the plantation machine.[18]

While Browne traces the long-standing anti-Blackness of mobility controls, with McKittrick we can see how fixing was deployed, and resignified by Black resistance, as one piece of a broader tapestry of material processes of racialization.

We can see a set of similar concerns reflected in recent work in critical Indigenous studies. Robert Nichols' *Theft is Property!* details how colonialism required Indigenous communities to be invested with limited property rights so that they could then be dispossessed of those rights and land. Nichols' point is that a propertied relation to the land had to be produced and was a result of colonialism.[19] However, as Nichols' work also shows Indigenous groups in the United States, once saddled with a propertied, instead of a self-determined relation to land, were targets of dispossession, which resulted in forced displacement. Nichols' work can help us see the play of fixing and forced movement as a condition of the history of native–settler relations in the United States.

Taking together Nichols' point that a relation to the land has to be produced, Browne's attention to mobility controls, and McKittrick's notion of fixing and its resignification, we have a set of diverse racializing processes distributed along a continuum of mobility. Drawing from this expanded archive – which includes Harney and Moten writing on the transatlantic slave trade as the birth of modern logistics and the "science of whiteness" – we can also see the diverse ends to which the control of mobility has been put.[20] These are histories that run deep and from this archive we can begin to glimpse at least a few narratives that crisscross hemispheric, and global, history, including how from early in the colonization process, both Indigenous and enslaved labor were submitted to a shifting array of controls that fixed and incited movement. In colonial Latin America where Indigenous labor was widely used, Indigenous groups were placed into *congregaciones* in order to facilitate their availability for work. Once Indigenous labor had become too depleted for the needs of capital in certain parts of the new colonies – particularly the Caribbean and Brazil – early capitalists turned to enslaved African labor, creating the first transnational logistical infrastructure for the mass movement of workers. However, exposure to incitement or fixity was then, as now, profoundly racialized, turning as it does on the "exploitation of group-differentiated vulnerability to premature death."[21]

These examples help us see the forced sedimentation or concatenation of control of mobility, racialization, and capitalist accumulation. They are isolated examples, and a full history, including how fixing and incitement have changed over time, remains to be developed. Yet how difficult it often is to make visible all the work, both direct and indirect, both centralized and decentralized, that goes into moving bodies around the globe so that they can appear where needed or be disappeared from where they are not. Much like Marxist feminists have demonstrated the importance of invisibilized, gendered labor in the home, which is required for the reproduction of labor power, we have to make visible all the work that goes into directly moving labor or in producing the conditions for its movement, fixing, and disappearance.

Moreover, it is critical that we see the incitement to movement and fixing of bodies as definitory to capitalism as labor power as a commodity – a historical constant of capitalism is the construction of powerful infrastructures and systems for the mass movement of bodies and their containment. When we combine the abolitionist insight that the border/migration system isn't broken, with capitalism's structural need to control mobility, we have a provisionally new perspective on what the work is that the global border regime is doing. Rather than a hydraulic over-spilling of surplus populations, we have complicated, centralized and decentralized logistical infrastructures marked by profound historical continuities with prior iterations of mechanisms for inciting and fixing the movement of bodies through space and time. Such a perspective could help us view borders as complex techno-juridical infrastructures that incite and fix – a complex infrastructure like the *congregación* or transatlantic slave trade. Here juridical refers to all of the legal and institutional frameworks and articulations that produce, backup, and articulate out of the border complex, while techno- refers to all of the carceral, physical, and material/immaterial extensions of the border complex across space and time. Clearly, one of the primary ways mobility is fixed, controlled, and incited today is through the mechanisms of the border complex – which if we expand our idea of "bordering" to include any incitement to movement or coercion to immobility, we could extend to prisons and the after-effects and contemporary instantiations of segregation, apartheid, or other racialized divisions. Provisionally, we might argue that any techno-juridical infrastructure which fixes or incites would be a mechanism for, either directly or indirectly, solving the distribution of bodies and labor power problem for capitalist production or making sure the right kinds of bodies appear in the appropriate places in the appropriate number so accumulation can continue.

ABOLITIONISMS AT AND AGAINST THE BORDER

If capitalism requires the ability to fix or incite or to move bodies to and away from production; if racialization, in part, emerges from this control of mobility; and if capitalist accumulation, racialization, and control of mobility are forcibly sedimented together across history, what might this mean for abolitionist organizing in the present?

Like no-borders work, border abolition work has centered control of mobility as a key dynamic of contemporary social formations. As Andrew Burridge writes, "[A] challenge that a no-borders politics of mobility puts forth is to contest the existence, purpose, and outcomes of borders, controls, detention centers, and other processes that lead to both coercive mobility and immobility."[22] The early border abolitionist work of Jenna M. Loyd, Matt Mitchelson, and Andrew Burridge amplifies the no-borders analytic outlined above by showing how walls and cages structure and produce coercive forms of mobility and immobility. Their work helpfully develops what they call a "key abolitionist tool": "the analytic ability to understand how seemingly disconnected institutions of state violence – walls and cages – are interconnected, and how they produce and police social difference."[23] In their work, these interconnections between border and prison abolition are routed back through mobility: "Because mass incarceration is a form of 'coercive mobility,' prison abolition is a clear extension of radical commitments to the freedom of movement."[24] Their work also pushes back on the criminalization of migrants by arguing that "mobility is a human condition." However, in this move, there is a risk of naturalizing mobility and obscuring how profoundly capitalism has intervened in fixing and inciting. A theoretical perspective that centers capitalism's deep historical control over mobility might lead us to de-emphasize mobility as a position of naturalized resistance often found in autonomous and no-borders organizing and spur us to think about how to attack at the root of the forced sedimentation of accumulation, racialization, and control of mobility and their manifestation in bordering infrastructures.

At the same time, a perspective that focuses on the historical concatenation of race and mobility under capitalism can allow us to expand the important cross-institutional analysis of Loyd et al. In this essay, we have already sketched a few historically significant moments and sites of durable racialization containing a dialectics of mobility and immobility. If we think of the production of the category "Indian" in what becomes Mexico between the sixteenth and seventeenth centuries, we can see both a movement of bodies to new spaces (*congregaciones*) where they are then fixed into place to make possible accumulation.[25] In the aftermath of the war of 1812, native groups in the American southeast were forced into movement in a process of involuntary removal and then confined into new geo-spatial territories. The emergence of mass incarceration, in a US or any other context such as Brazil, requires both the forced mobility of individuals out of communities and then their fixing. Three of the most important contemporary US social movements have centered demands of "Abolish ICE," "land back," and "defund the police," which are all demands that involve mobility or an end to constraint or incitement, even if they are not *solely* demands about mobility. What the perspective developed in this chapter can help us see is how mobility and immobility, fixing in place and incitement into movement, cut across contemporary, as well as historical, social dynamics.

Moreover, I believe that control of mobility as constitutive of capitalist power and fixing and incitement as a dense node of racialization commits us to a politics of the abolition of race as a structuring principle of social order.[26] Abolishing racialized hierarchies and replacing them with new forms of sociality is central to abolitionist political thought. We can see it in Gilmore's insistence that a common "failure of imagination rests in missing the fact that abolition isn't just absence ... Abolition is a fleshly and material presence of social life lived differently"; Angela Davis and Gina Dent's emphasis that "[t]here are those who put undue emphasis on the process of destroying or abolishing or dismantling, and we point out that abolition is about rebuilding"; and Fred Moten and Stefano Harney's claim that abolition would mean not just the abolition of the police, prisons, and courts, but the "founding of a new society."[27] Each of these authors, in different ways, frame abolitionist politics not just as the abolition of police, prisons, slavery, or borders, but rather as the creation of a new world or production of new social relations. A demand like "Abolish Race as a Structuring Principle" might not draw millions to the streets but, as an analytic, forced sedimentation can focus our attention on the profound and concrete ways current rebellions are rebellions precisely against the social relations of capitalist racial and colonial ordering.

Finally, centering the concatenation and forced sedimentation of these relations can lead us to a revaluation of the role of marginalized political forms, such as uprisings, riots, and rebellions, in our anti-capitalist, anti-state abolitionist politics. In the US, the George Floyd uprising, where millions took to the streets and many confronted the police in unprecedented ways, mainstreamed a version of abolitionism which called for the police to be "defunded." Reckoning with the limits of the Floyd uprising and where defund campaigns have ended up has sparked a renewed discussion around the political orientation of abolitionist movements. Dean Spade has worked to show other abolitionists why they should also be anti-statist.[28] Jarrod Shanahan and Zhandarka Kurti have argued that "[t]he strengths of abolitionism are also its weaknesses; the emphasis abolitionists place on practical activity in the here and now has led to an underdeveloped conception of what a revolutionary transformation of society along abolitionist lines would actually look like."[29] Joy James, whose work I hope border abolitionists will engage more deeply with in the future, has also levied several important critiques of abolitionism. First, she distinguishes between a Black revolutionary tradition and its struggles and abolitionism, arguing there are important differences in terms of political strategies, targets and lineages.[30] Second, she makes the point that academic abolitionism is often divorced from the poor, lumpen, and/or working-class subjects who engage in the most risky forms of response to state and capitalist violence and whose exposure leads them to become targets for the full force of state repression.[31] These are productive, useful critiques which, for me, do not require relinquishing the term abolition but rather ask us to continue to discuss what politics it names.

My line through these conversations starts from the forced sedimentation of accumulation, racialization, and control of mobility. This forced sedimentation, due to its long historical trajectories, also positions us, again politically, within longer traditions of Indigenous, Black and anti-colonial struggle. In André Gorz's *Strategy for Labor*, where he makes the case for differentiating non-reformist reforms from reformist ones, he argues that this is our only path forward because "seizure of power by insurrection is out of the question, and the waiting game leads the workers' movement to disintegration."[32] Pursuing the strategy of non-reformist reforms is, for Gorz, necessary given the relative weakness of the workers movement (i.e., its inability to carry through an insurrection). Gorz's distinction underpins a fair amount of the strategy and tactics within many abolitionist groups. From my perspective, however, Abolish ICE, Standing Rock, and George Floyd – these were uprisings and attacks, at least partially, on the forced sedimentation of racial order, capitalist accumulation, and control of mobility and territory that have typified social relations in this hemisphere for over four centuries. What these moments show is that, in the US context, and a Hemispheric one I would argue, the once marginalized political forms of the uprising, rebellion, and insurrection are not a distant fantasy any longer – they are a part of the contemporary political vocabulary, and forced sedimentation can help us see the duress the current racial order has been placed under. As well, centering the historical process of these relations' production can help us see the durability of these racial orderings and raise the question of what would be required to finally overcome them. While a mere focus on the forced sedimentation of mobility, racialization, and capitalism might not directly translate into a political strategy, where it can be useful is in giving us a different set of genealogies to work out of and, perhaps, indicating a way through contemporary impasses. If we share the belief that the presuppositions behind Gorz's famous non-reformist reforms strategy are, without being fully superseded, no longer as salient as they once were, then there is a longer set of historical struggles – marked both by painstaking organizing and sudden uprising – in which we can position and develop the meaning of our current abolitionisms at, and against, the border.

NOTES

1. Many thanks for feedback on and citations for this piece go to: the *Border Abolition Now* editorial collective, Amelia Frank-Vitale, Daniel Nemser, Amy De'Ath, and Christopher Chen.
2. "'New bones' grow out of the political cultures of material struggles." Joy James, "'New Bones' Abolitionism, Communism, and Captive Maternals," *Verso* (blog), June 4, 2021. www.versobooks.com/blogs/5095-new-bones-abolitionism-communism-and-captive-maternals
3. See, for example, Jenna M. Loyd, Matt Michelson, and Andrew Burridge, "Introduction: Borders, Prisons, and Abolitionist Visions." In: *Beyond Walls and Cage: Prisons, Borders, and Global Crisis*. Athens: University of Georgia Press, 2012; Gracie Mae Bradley and Luke De Noronha, *Against Borders: The Case for Abolition*. London: Verso, 2022.
4. When I use racialization throughout this chapter I mean it to carry the echo of Patrick Wolfe's "race is colonialism speaking." Racialization does not exist without colonization, and my usage does not imply a politics of inclusion into the state.
5. Raúl Delgado Wise and Humberto Márquez Covarrubias, "Capitalist Restructuring, Development and Labour Migration: The Mexico–US case." *Third World Quarterly*, 29(7), 2008: 1361.
6. Sara Farris, "Social Reproduction and Racialized Surplus Populations." In: Peter Osborne, Éric Alliez, and Eric-John Russell (Eds), *Capitalism: Concept, Idea, Image – Aspects of Marx's Capital Today*. Kingston upon Thames: CRMEP Books, pp. 121–134.

7. See, for example, Bridget Anderson, Nandita Sharma, and Cynthia Wright, "Editorial: Why No Borders?" *Refuge* 26(2), 2011: 5–18.

8. Karl Marx, *Capital Volume 1*. Ben Fowkes (Trans.). New York: Vintage, 1976, p. 794.

9. Marx, *Capital*, 932, 934.

10. Yann Moulier-Boutang, *De la esclavitud al trabajo asalariado. Economía histórica del trabajo asalariado embridado*. Madrid: AKAL, 2006, pp. 23–49.

11. Nicholas De Genova, "Migration and the Mobility of Labor." In: Matt Vidal, Tony Smith, Tomás Rotta, and Paul Prew (Eds), *The Oxford Handbook of Karl Marx*. New York; London: Oxford University Press, p. 8.

12. De Genova, "Migration," 6. For another account see Nandita Sharma, "States and Human Immobilization: Bridging the Conceptual Separation of Slavery, Immigration Controls, and Mass Incarceration." *Citizenship Studies* 25(2), 2021: 166–187.

13. See, for example, Adam Hanieh, *Money, Markets, and Monarchies: The Gulf Cooperation Council and the Political Economy of the Contemporary Middle East*. Cambridge: Cambridge University Press, 2018; Eli Friedman, *The Urbanization of People: The Politics of Development, Labor Markets, and Schooling in the Chinese City*. New York: Columbia University Press, 2022.

14. On exclusion and movement or mobility, see Christopher Chen and Sarika Chandra, "Remapping the Race/Class Problematic." In: Kevin Floyd et al. (Eds), *Totality Inside Out*. New York: Fordham University Press, 2022.

15. This background includes, as well, some of the early South African discussions of racial capitalism and its control of worker mobility. See Zachary Levenson and Marcel Paret, "The Three Dialectics of Racial Capitalism: From South Africa to the U.S. and Back Again." *Du Bois Review: Social Science Research on Race* 20(2), 2022, pp. 1–19.

16. Ruth Wilson Gilmore, "Race and Globalization." In: R. J. Johnston, Peter J. Taylor, and Michael J. Watts (Eds), *Geographies of Global Change: Remapping the World*, 2nd edition. Malden: Blackwell, 2002, p. 261.

17. Simone Browne, *Dark Matters: On the Surveillance of Blackness*. Durham: Duke University Press, 2015, p. 59.

18. Katherine McKittrick, "Plantation Futures." *Small Axe* 17(3), 2013: 11.

19. Robert Nichols *Theft is Property!* Durham: Duke University Press, 2020, p. 115.

20. Stefano Harney and Fred Moten, *All Incomplete*. New York: Minor Compositions, 2021, pp. 15–19. See also Susan Zieger; "Back on the Chain Gang: Logistics, Labor, and the Threat of Infrastructure." *Social Text*, 40(4), 2022: 43–68.

21. Gilmore, "Race and Globalization," 261.

22. Andrew Burridge, "'No Borders' as a Critical Politics of Mobility and Migration." *ACME: An International E-Journal for Critical Geographies* 13(3), 2014: 465.
23. Loyd et al., "Introduction," 3.
24. Loyd et al., "Introduction," 11.
25. Daniel Nemser, *Infrastructures of Race: Concentration and Biopolitics in Colonial Mexico*. Austin: University of Texas Press, 2017, Chapter 1.
26. Chris Chen, "The Limit Point of Capitalist Equality." *Endnotes 3*. https://endnotes.org.uk/translations/chris-chen-the-limit-point-of-capitalist-equality
27. Clément Petitjean, "Prisons and Class Warfare: An Interview with Ruth Wilson Gilmore." *Verso* (blog), August 2, 2018. www.versobooks.com/blogs/news/3954-prisons-and-class-warfare-an-interview-with-ruth-wilson-gilmore; Hanna Phifer, "For Angela Davis and Gina Dent, Abolition Is the Only Way." *Harper's Bazaar*, January 14, 2022. www.harpersbazaar.com/culture/art-books-music/a38746835/angela-davis-gina-dent-abolition-feminism-now-interview/; Fred Moten and Stefano Harney, *The Undercommons*. New York: Minor Compositions, 2013, p. 42.
28. Dean Spade, *No Prisons, No Borders, No Cops, No State?* Paper presented at the 29th Annual Rose Sheinberg Lecture, NYU Law, March 30, 2023. www.youtube.com/watch?v=SdZ6Rr878rk
29. Jarrod Shanahan and Zhandarka Kurti, *States of Incarceration: Rebellion, Reform, and America's Punishment System*. London: Reaktion Books, 2022, p. 143.
30. Joy James, "Airbrushing Revolution for the Sake of Abolition." *Black Perspectives*, July 20, 2020. www.aaihs.org/airbrushing-revolution-for-the-sake-of-abolition/
31. Joy James, "The Plurality of Abolition." *Groundlings* (podcast), January 1, 2021. https://groundings.simplecast.com/episodes/joy-james
32. André Gorz, *Strategy for Labour: A Radical Proposal*. Martin A. Nicolaus and Victoria Ortiz (Trans.). Boston: Beacon Press, 1967, p. 8.

14

Rising waters from New York City to Pakistan

Abolitionist organizing at the intersection of immigration justice and the climate crisis

Vignesh Ramachandran and Akash Singh

INTRODUCTION

Nobody was prepared for the hours of torrential rain and resulting waters that would sweep through the streets and flood the subways when the remnants of Hurricane Ida passed through New York City on the night of September 1, 2021. At least eleven New Yorkers living in mostly unregulated basement apartments in Queens drowned in their homes as a result of the overwhelming flooding. Rising costs of rent across the city have forced many poor, and often undocumented immigrants to live in illegal basement apartments. These unregulated apartment units usually lack windows and adequate secondary exits in cases of fires or floods. People reported water rising from 2 feet to nearly ceiling level and shared stories about their struggle to escape from their flooded apartments. Tenants lost valuable belongings and were forced to throw out flood-soaked furniture. Immigration status paired with the affordability crisis hitting working people has created an acute climate vulnerability, particularly for undocumented New Yorkers who fear retaliation from landlords and the state.

There is a sick irony to the images of Hurricane Ida's impact in New York City: immigrants from countries experiencing the immediate impacts of the climate crisis, like Bangladesh, standing in rising waters in the Bronx, Queens, and Brooklyn. Migrants whose homelands are experiencing droughts, flooding, and fires are facing similar catastrophes in working-class poor communities in the US. In this chapter, we consider how the border and climate crisis impact the everyday lives of working-class immigrants in New York City. We ask: how does the US border facilitate extra vulnerability to the climate crisis and environmental injustice? What might the experiences of working-class immigrants tell us about the transnational components of border-induced climate change vulnerability? And lastly, how might we, as abolitionists, understand working-class, immigrant organizing in NYC for a robust social safety net and life-affirming institutions in the context of the climate crisis?

In response to the regimes of state-sanctioned, group-differentiated vulnerability[1] to the climate crisis and environmental injustice, we look to the history and contemporary organizing of *Desis Rising Up and Moving* (DRUM). DRUM is a membership-led organization of low-wage South Asian and Indo-Caribbean immigrants, workers and youth in New York City. DRUM members make up some of the working-class immigrant communities impacted by the compound effects of the border and climate crises that we describe above. They are impacted by increasingly severe storms and environmental injustices in their home countries in South Asia and the Caribbean, while also experiencing uneven exposure to the adverse effects of the climate crisis and environmental racism in New York City. By describing DRUM's history of organizing against immigration enforcement and policing in New York City, we outline DRUM's working-class abolitionist framework and how it might apply to organizing at the intersections of immigration reform and climate justice organizing. To do so, we walk through examples of abolitionist organizing from DRUM members' transnational experiences of climate change impacts and environmental injustice, traversing stories from Punjab, Bangladesh, Pakistan, and New York City.

SITUATING DRUM'S ANALYSIS
OF ABOLITIONIST ORGANIZING

DRUM's organizing makes abolition praxis; DRUM centers both immediate socio-economic needs on the ground and the longer-term shifts in social relations necessary for abolition. We, as a member of DRUM's staff and a researcher who has closely collaborated with the organization, do not speak authoritatively for DRUM, but rather want to pose questions that will help the organization to develop a sharper vision of the relationship between the climate crisis and border abolition. For us and DRUM, abolition means connecting our ongoing struggles to the broader horizon of social transformation – organizing for a world without cages, police, or borders; caring reciprocally; and as Ruth Wilson Gilmore eloquently puts it, making freedom a place.[2]

But in practice, it can be difficult to envision what abolition looks like in our world, particularly when conditions of unfreedom are perpetuated all around us. These conditions of unfreedom encompass the widespread disinvestment in public resources and welfare instituted by neoliberal capitalism, as well as the expanding of the role of the police and carceral systems in managing surplus populations.[3] In particular, the police are increasingly present in the lives and neighborhoods of working-class communities, instituting novel modes of social control to compensate for the disinvestment of neoliberal austerity.[4] Moreover, borders and immigration enforcement are integral to social control and produce immigrants as surplus, exploitable labor. Borders distinguish the type of work you can do and your wage based on your immigration status and by maintaining the threat of detention and deportation. The violence of the border extends far beyond the barriers and demarcations of the border itself. Through border externalization, the United States outsources migration policing to other countries like Mexico, making nation-state boundaries the last, not first, place of contact with immigration authorities.[5] Border externalization is supplemented by migration deterrence – the fortification of nation-state boundaries through physical walls, and the expansion of migrant detention, surveillance, and policing internally in the United States, especially in major cities like New York City.[6]

These expanding carceral geographies and material conditions of neoliberalism produce material and spatial reorganizations of working-class communities by the state and ruling class to solve social problems.[7] These conditions have limited working people's skills and abilities to analyze the contradictions of capitalism that impact their everyday lives. In response to these conditions Ruth Wilson Gilmore advocates for organizing for abolition through a politics of recognition: developing both an understanding of the complex, sometimes contradictory, subject positions that people are coming from, and building "the [popular] recognition that [abolition] is something we *can* do."[8] By organizing for basic needs and rights, our movements bring together diverse groups of people and develop the consciousness that another world is possible. A politics of recognition builds the skills, abilities, and enthusiasm that animates people to organize for change. At DRUM, organizers work to develop members' understanding that as people who intimately know the conditions of the working class both in their homeland and in the US, immigrants hold unique insights on how to challenge global border regimes. Building this understanding might involve organizing for non-reformist reforms, while collectively developing an abolitionist horizon. André Gorz describes "non-reformist reforms" as reforms that erode the power and violence of carceral institutions through situated, site-based organizing for alternatives to violence.[9] In organizing for these non-reformist reforms, we build the popular consciousness of what meeting everyday social needs, building community safety, and making life outside of routine discipline and violence can look like. As Charmaine Chua reminds us, organizing for a world without cages, police, and borders cannot happen overnight; abolition is not an event.[10] Abolitionist organizing requires meeting people where they are at and building up their capacities to imagine and organize for alternatives to violence. It requires thinking with working-class people about alternatives to punishment and accountability, without relying on what we have been taught our entire lives about police and their role in so-called justice. Abolitionists don't have ready-made solutions to the innumerable instances of violence and harm that exist in the world. Rather we build a commitment to a process which combats mass alienation and disconnection from the social and political activities which shape people's lives.

We see DRUM's approach to abolition as situated in a radical tradition that continues to find alternatives amidst the seeming impossibility of change. It draws on W. E. B. Du Bois's understanding of abolition democracy in the post-Reconstruction South, the revolutionary organizing of Stokely Carmichael and Ella Baker of SNCC, the anti-colonial independence movements of the Global South, among others. However, DRUM's approach to abolition also emerges organically out of the particular conditions of South Asian and Indo-Caribbean immigrant working-class communities in New York City. As we begin to describe above, DRUM's praxis is rooted in its members' experiences of migration and the border, immigration enforcement, policing, and incarceration. As the climate crisis intensifies, DRUM members' experiences of floods, droughts, and other climate change impacts need to be incorporated as part of the material conditions from which DRUM organizes. In the following sections, we draw on these histories and stories to articulate how DRUM's climate justice organizing both meets material needs on the ground while moving toward an abolitionist horizon of a world without borders, police, and prisons.

THE "WAR ON TERROR" AND THE CONDITIONS OF UNFREEDOM IN IMMIGRANT COMMUNITIES

DRUM was founded in 2000 as an effort to build consciousness about how the deteriorating socio-economic conditions in working-class South Asian and Indo-Caribbean communities were tied to the racial targeting of immigrants by the New York Police Department (NYPD) and Immigration and Naturalization Services (INS). This not only included police harassment of street vendors and immigrants in the streets of New York City, but also the conditions of immigration itself – namely the austerity-induced defunding of social services in countries across the Caribbean and South Asia and the resulting political unrest which threatened the lives of minorities and leftist groups.

Following the terrorist attacks on September 11, 2001, existing apparatuses of criminalization impacting working-class immigrants intensified, particularly for South Asian, Arab and Muslim immigrants. The US government used the "war on terror" to institute a form of racial capitalist governance that explicitly criminalized "surplus" immigrant labor by detaining and deporting undocumented working-class immigrants, expanding the use of the Immigration Reform and Control Act of 1986, Immigration Reform and Immigrant Responsibility Act of 1996 (IIRIRA), and Antiterrorism and Effective Death Penalty Act of 1996 (AEDPA).[11] It also expanded the surveillance and policing capabilities of state agents in working-class communities through the establishment of the Department of Homeland Security and the institution of the PATRIOT ACT.[12]

This massive expansion in policing infrastructure came at the cost of social welfare and life-affirming institutions. Ruth Wilson Gilmore details how with the growth of the anti-state state and the defunding of social welfare institutions, comes the expansion in the size, legitimacy, and scope of practice of the police, prisons, and military-industrial complex.[13] As a result, policing and carceral institutions are called upon to carry out two functions in society: on one hand, they are required by the state to exercise social control; on the other hand, they also become the default responses to crises caused by the dismantling of public social services in working-class communities.

In response, DRUM's organizing combated the criminalization of working-class immigrant communities *and* extended mutual aid infrastructures to support detainees, undocumented workers, and families impacted by policing, immigration enforcement, and detention. DRUM organized mutual aid and legal support for immigrants inside detention centers and communities across New York City. Alongside these immediate needs, DRUM developed a public campaign to stop the disappearances of immigrants, targeting the Immigration and Naturalization Service (and later Immigration and Customs Enforcement or ICE), the FBI, and the NYPD. Freeing immigrants from detention and preventing their deportation was explicitly tied to meeting the material needs of immigrants facing state-sanctioned violence and developing their capacities to organize, support each other through solidarity and mutual aid, and imagine everyday life without the threat of surveillance, detention, and deportation. DRUM's organizing addressed immediate, socio-economic needs of working-class communities during the "war on terror" while developing a broader horizon that centered on the abolition of policing and immigration enforcement alongside the restoration of socialized care in working-class,

immigrant communities. This analysis is central to DRUM's organizing around climate justice in the contemporary moment.

Following these campaigns in the immediate wake of 9/11, DRUM
shifted its strategy to center coalition and solidarity building with
other immigrant and racialized groups. Connecting disappearances of community members in New York City during the War on
Terror with the detention, expulsion, and deaths of immigrants at
the border, DRUM contested the increasingly violent immigration
enforcement apparatus through solidarity, relationship-building,
and political education on the increasing importance of the border
to policing and racializing immigrants. For DRUM and allies, the
deaths and violence at the border were the result of policies of
militarization at the border influenced by the post-9/11 environment of tightening national security and general anti-immigrant
sentiment across the US. As a result, DRUM's membership developed a practice of evaluating immigration proposals and reforms
based on how they would impact communities living alongside the
border. DRUM members committed to not throwing border communities under the bus and refused to support reforms that would
increase enforcement and further criminalize crossing the border.

Both the transnational and exceptionally local effects of the
border and immigration enforcement became central to DRUM's
organizing in the decades after 9/11. Moreover, contestational
movements to push the horizon of abolition (e.g., Abolish ICE),
were always accompanied by efforts to expand the capacities of
working-class immigrants to build solidarity and meet material
needs on the ground. With this materialist abolitionist approach in
mind, DRUM led and won campaigns at the local and state levels
to grant driver's licenses for undocumented immigrants in New
York State; to limit NYPD's ability to conduct unconstitutional
searches; to prevent Amazon from building a new headquarters in
Queens; to protect funds for free metrocards for NYC students; and
to secure $2.1 billion in unemployment relief for undocumented
workers who lost their jobs in 2020. At the federal level, DRUM
members formed a key sector of South Asian and Indo-Caribbean
youth who alongside other national groups won Deferred Action
for Childhood Arrivals (DACA), a program which at its peak
provided work permits and protection from deportations for

over 800,000 young people. Following the election of Trump in 2016, DRUM launched the Hate Free Zones Community Defense campaign, a broad coalition of community that organized to fight against workplace raids, deportations, and mass criminalization by conducting "Know Your Rights" workshops, coordinating rapid response teams to stop deportations, and affirming neighborhood commitments to "love and protect each other."

ABOLITIONIST ORGANIZING IN THE WAKE OF THE CLIMATE CRISIS

This history of organizing lays the ground for DRUM's emerging climate justice work. We understand countries in the Global North as responsible for the level of production and consumption that are necessary to continue the current extractive system of racial capitalism. Rather than cope with the externalities of this system as they manifest in pollution, trash, rising sea levels, etc., Global North countries both offload the repercussions to countries in the Global South (including the origin countries of many DRUM members like Bangladesh, Guyana, Pakistan) and sequester these negative impacts within their own borders in environmental justice communities, often populated by working-class immigrants. The border as an essential regulatory tool for the state nominally defines who is and who is not a victim of climate and environmental injustice by hardening borders and regulations to limit movement between nation-states. At another level, the border continues to do what it has always done as a central feature of racial capitalism – differentiate a population internal to the US through documentation and targeted policing. For working-class immigrants, the border designates peoples' citizenship status, the jobs they can have, the neighborhoods where they can live, and more.

In what follows, we share working-class immigrant experiences that articulate the need for abolitionist organizing that addresses border violence and environmental injustices. Border abolition and climate justice must be internationalist and begin from the experiences of people on the frontlines. We turn to stories of DRUM members from Punjab, Bangladesh, and Pakistan for lessons and learnings about what abolitionist organizing can look like. In particular, amidst a world simultaneously on fire and under water, how might organizing for climate justice intersect with border abolitionist thinking? Where does border abolitionist thinking push climate justice frameworks and offer new strategies for living in a world in crisis?

Austerity, the Green Revolution, and the farmers' protests

Our biggest take away has been like would you rather be broke in America or would you rather be broken in India? These are two very different things. I'd rather work at 7/11 and Subway and barely get by [in the US] than [work] something there [in India] and barely get by, right?

The main base of the economy [in India] is agriculture, but the people who are farmers don't control their own resources.

(Puneet)

When Puneet immigrated to the US from India, she was around 11 years old. She and her younger brother had traveled to California with her mother to look after her aunt who was about to give birth. Puneet now lives in New York City and has organized with DRUM for over a year alongside South Asian and Indo-Caribbean communities, and more specifically with Punjabi Sikhs in Queens.

Puneet and her family, like many other migrants, saw opportunities in the US that weren't available to them back home. In recent years, large numbers of Punjabi youth have migrated out of the region citing a lack of jobs. Moreover, neoliberal austerity reforms have defunded and privatized formerly public services like education and healthcare exacerbating financial stressors in the region. For Puneet, the reality of this situation can be summarized as: "Where would you rather be broke?" With the promise of work abroad and respite from familiar violence in Punjab, Puneet's answer was overwhelmingly the US.

For Puneet, the plight of small farmers in Punjab exemplifies the social conditions that proliferate across Punjab, but also gestures to the possibilities of organizing for a future that contests the conditions of austerity and the climate crisis. The neoliberal shift that devastated small farmers began in the mid-1960s when the Green Revolution took root in India, promoting a shift away from subsistence farming toward commercial farming linked to the market.[14] In a state like Punjab where many farmers are small landholders as opposed to large, commercial farms, this had a particularly devastating effect. Farmers were forced to borrow funds in order to afford technologies required by capital-intensive farming – tractors, fertilizers, genetically modified seeds, and more. The expensive farm inputs and restricted government subsidies pushed small farmers into a debt trap, intensified by the emerging neoliberal consensus in India that privatized social services like education and healthcare.[15] The regime of debt and privatization has resulted in tens of thousands of farmer suicides. This organized abandonment was reinforced by organized violence.[16] Neoliberal disinvestment and economic unevenness as a result of the Green Revolution in Punjab was accompanied by the intense securitization of the state by Indian armed forces, most notably in 1984 with Operation Blue Star. As Puneet so eloquently said to us, when faced with the market reality question of "am I going to grow something that's maybe going to bring me the most money ... or am I going to grow something that's going to [be] better for the environment ... for the soil," farmers are going to do what is best for their families, not the environment.

In 2020, the Indian government passed legislation which would further empower corporations and deregulate the purchase, production, and storage of agricultural commodities.[17] The reforms threatened to intensify the already precarious social conditions of farmers also facing the ramifications of the COVID-19 pandemic and climate change impacts like drought, rising temperatures and resulting crop failures.[18] In response, India's farmers unions launched massive demonstrations opposing the legislation. The movement began in 2020 in Punjab, but quickly spread across small farmers in India, and in solidarity, members of the Punjabi diaspora organized protests across the United States, Canada, and the United Kingdom, and major US farmers' groups and unions issued a statement of solidarity with the protests.[19] In addition to international solidarity, the farmers' protests were a site of cross-religious and cross-community solidarity and mutual aid. Farmers organized communal shelters; collectively took care of social reproduction needs like laundry, cooking, and healthcare; and developed community safety networks.[20]

As Puneet's story shows us, the "choice" to migrate leaves many migrants between a rock and a hard place – life in disinvested regions of the Global South or life in the disinvested working-class neighborhoods of the US. For many Punjabi farmers, the conditions of neoliberalism and austerity brought forth by the Green Revolution and capital-intensive agriculture are intensified by the climate crisis, more droughts, extreme weather, and crop failures. But for us and Puneet, the farmers' protests depict the abolitionist world-building potential of organizing in the midst of the climate crisis; they gesture to the international, cross-community solidarities and social movements necessary to contest the cascading disasters of neoliberal reforms and the climate crisis. These are the conditions that shape the political consciousness of many of DRUM's Punjabi members. The crises of capitalism and climate will not be stopped at the US border; DRUM members face similar problems in the US. Working-class New Yorkers feel the impacts of government officials who choose to divest from essential services and exclude undocumented workers from social programs. Puneet's experiences offer us a jumping-off point to consider the ways that DRUM members already carry and theorize the relationships between global capitalism, climate, and migration.

The social conditions before the protests also depict how the climate crisis is intensifying existing inequalities that working-class people face, particularly through debt regimes and the reliance on privatized social services. This is a global crisis and the protests show the need for internationalist abolitionist social movements to challenge the neoliberal power and states, while forging the relationships necessary for collective life and thriving.

Hurricanes, flooding, and housing justice

I had huge dreams, and expectations [about coming to the US]. It was my first journey by plane. I was excited to reunite with my daughter. I heard gossip about a lot of money and luxury ... Whatever dreams were in my eyes, I have not seen even a single bit of it. Once I'm here, I experienced the total opposite ... [In Bangladesh] it's good looking, organized, and there's space to breathe. But here [in NYC], it's like a slum. It's what the slums in Bangladesh might be like.

(Morsheda)

Morsheda, who has been a DRUM member since the beginning of the COVID-19 pandemic, lives with her children and grand-children in a tight two-bedroom apartment in Brooklyn. Before moving to Brooklyn, she lived in the Bronx for a decade after immigrating to the US from Bangladesh. Morsheda is a part of DRUM's housing justice committee and is engaged in a statewide fight to win basic tenant protections and build power among work-ing-class renters. For years she has dealt with housing insecurity, moving from apartment to apartment.

The picture that Morsheda paints of struggling to put down roots in the US is well-known to most working immigrant families in New York City. Morsheda came to the US after her husband passed away in Bangladesh. Before coming to the US, she also lived through the 1991 Bangladesh Cyclone, one of the deadliest tropical cyclones ever recorded, an experience which continues to haunt her. She was left with virtually nothing in her homeland and decided that her best option would be to reunite with her children already living in the US. Upon arriving in the US, she found that most of what she had been told was waiting for her in America would not be the reality for someone like her.

The cramped housing that Morsheda and her family now live in is a slight improvement on the one-bedroom in the Bronx that they previously all shared. But the reality is that it's still not sufficient. New York City's median rent currently hovers around $4,000.[21] Prices like this make it impossible for poor, immigrant families to easily move into adequate and spacious housing. Morshe-da's case reveals how people are forced to sacrifice space, privacy, and comfort for more affordable rent prices. These housing con-ditions are intensified by extreme weather and other impacts of the climate crisis, like we witnessed with the deaths of those living in basement apartments when Hurricane Ida swept through the city.[22] Housing issues have become a focal point of organizing for racial, immigrant and environmental justice organizations. Undocumented and documented immigrants fear speaking up about the lack of proper exits or windows that won't open because it could mean an eviction by their landlord or an order to vacate by NYC's Department of Housing Preservation and Development. DRUM's experience supporting members through housing issues has shown that landlords would often prefer to evict a tenant asking for repairs with the intention of finding a new renter who will tolerate subpar conditions.

The deplorable housing conditions Morsheda and other undocumented immigrants face gestures to how documentation status prevents people from speaking up to improve their conditions through public social services or fighting for the rights and dignity that everyone is deserving of. Importantly, it shows how immigration status is a key factor in climate change vulnerability and environmental racism, especially when drawing on Ruth Wilson Gilmore's conception of racism as "state-sanctioned or extralegal production and exploitation of group-differentiated vulnerability to premature death."[23] As a part of a statewide coalition fighting for housing rights in New York State, DRUM members like Morsheda have led fights to cancel rent in the early years of the pandemic, implement an emergency rent relief program, and pass basic tenant protections. Members engaged in housing fights understand the risks of speaking up due to their immigration status and class position, but in doing so build the recognition that we all deserve better. Morsheda's housing justice organizing is another example of how DRUM members' unique insights are central to advancing abolitionist struggle through non-reformist reforms.

As others have written, immigrant housing issues are environmental justice issues, whether discussing the conditions of housing at immigrant detention sites or in working-class urban neighborhoods.[24] As Braz and Gilmore argue, organizing for public goods like education, healthcare, and affordable housing offers pathways to organize for both the divestment from carceral infrastructures and the revitalization of communities threatened by the three P's – police, pollution, and prisons.[25] In the case of New York State's most recent budget controversy, New York Gov. Kathy Hochul refused to respond to statewide demands for housing relief and other social services unless she could also roll back bail reforms, a move which would increase the duration and number of incarcerations across the state. Morsheda's experiences of climate disaster in Bangladesh and housing injustice in New York City are not uncommon and shape the radical tenant organizing led by DRUM, CAAAV, and other working-class immigrant organizations in the city.[26] Importantly, it articulates how housing justice can be reframed as a climate justice reform and an abolitionist demand, expanding the horizon for what is possible and building the recognition that safe, affordable housing is a right despite immigration status.

Immigration justice after the 2022 Pakistan floods

> At least working class people in Pakistan can speak up for their rights because they are identified as being the people of Pakistan. But over here [in New York City], how can they speak up when their own country has disowned them? When you know this, this particular country that they are living in doesn't recognize them, and so they're living in a form of invisibility and that just brings a lot of fear with it.
>
> (Mohiba)

> I think if you're talking about people's lives, their sustenance, their survival, then you can at least … think about these people who run shops here, who drive your taxis, who do your grocery stores, who like, are sweepers here. Like at least you should think of them when their people back home are literally underwater as we speak, there are areas in Pakistan where water still hasn't dried out. It really shows the lack of empathy and the empathy that has come to define the global financial system.
>
> (Raza)

> After all this is a political issue for the United States.
>
> (Raza)

The transnational effects of the US's post-9/11 border regime are most apparent in Mohiba and Raza's stories about organizing for Temporary Protective Status (TPS) and Special Student Relief (SSR) in Brooklyn, designations which would grant undocumented immigrants access to work permits, the ability to send needed relief money to their loved ones back home, and protections from deportation. TPS and SSR functions as an important humanitarian protection for migrants in the US whose home countries have been impacted by climate disaster, war, or other extraordinary circumstances. In 2022, Pakistan was devastated by an unprecedented amount of rain during the monsoon season, resulting in a series of storms that killed more than 1,700 people and floods impacting one in seven Pakistanis. The floods predominantly affected agricultural land in rural areas of Pakistan, displacing people in those regions and impacting others across the entire country. This climate catastrophe also comes at a time of steep inflation and interest rates of 20 percent, the highest they have been in decades in Pakistan. At the time of writing, approximately six months after the devastation, millions still struggle to purchase basic necessities, thousands live in shelters, and nationwide financial disaster looms.

Mohiba and Raza are international students from Lahore pursuing master's degrees in New York City. Because of their involvement in the left student politics and increased securitization in public universities, Mohiba and Raza were left with few higher educational opportunities in Pakistan. They applied to programs overseas and immigrated to the US.

After the floods hit Pakistan, Mohiba and Raza found themselves trapped by rising costs back home and in the US. They sent whatever money they could to their families struggling in Pakistan while also having to take out loans to pay for housing and basic needs in Brooklyn. Somehow, they managed all this while working the limited hours their student visas allotted them and completing their coursework.

Through their connections with other Pakistani leftist activists in NYC, they got connected with DRUM and the campaign for TPS and SSR designation. They themselves would benefit from SSR (and TPS post-graduation) which would grant them off-campus employment eligibility and the option to take on fewer courses. The two have actively been connecting with other potential SSR recipients, as well as supporting the grassroots work of connecting with undocumented Pakistanis in Brooklyn who would potentially benefit from TPS. Currently, DRUM and the coalition fighting for TPS and SSR estimates that more than 50,000 undocumented

Pakistanis would benefit from Temporary Protected Status and Special Student Relief.

Organizing for TPS and SSR is complicated by the history of police surveillance and immigration enforcement in Brooklyn's Little Pakistan which has created an atmosphere of distrust and anxiety that poses additional challenges to organizing and exercising local power. How do we expect people to come together and fight for mutual benefit when they've been taught to keep an eye out for potential informants in their restaurants and places of worship? These experiences of living and organizing in Little Pakistan highlight how border abolition encompasses the abolition of the entire US security apparatus that surveils, detains, and deports immigrants. While not a perfect solution, TPS and SSR can be understood as a non-reformist reform. They offer immediate respite to the conditions of austerity and climate disaster faced by millions of Pakistanis. Moreover, organizing for TPS and SSR offers a pathway to build recognition that things *can* change, both in Brooklyn and in Pakistan. TPS and SSR meet immediate needs on the ground, and expand how we might think about immigration rights amidst the climate crisis. This work also builds people's capacities to address the ongoing alienation and distrust in the community, developing the capacities and conditions where we can organize with each other to build life-affirming institutions in the place of the police, immigration enforcement, borders, and carceral system.

CONCLUSION: ORGANIZING FOR NON-REFORMIST REFORMS

DRUM launched its campaign for TPS and SSR in October 2022. Since then, members of the organization from Little Pakistan in Brooklyn and DRUM organizers have pressured both US and Pakistani officials from NYC to the COP27 UN Climate Summit to take swift action and designate TPS. For Mohiba, Raza, and DRUM, this prolonged fight for TPS is indicative of a lack of accountability on the part of the Global North. As Raza puts it: "This is part of the larger conversation about inequality in terms of the global economic contributions to the pollution of the world, and who gets most impacted by it. And yeah, and racism as well in terms of how you attempt to recover it." Pakistan accounts for less than 1 percent of global emissions of planet-warming gasses, but is the eighth most vulnerable nation due to the climate crisis. TPS designation is in no way an instant cure to the challenges facing Pakistanis both at home and abroad, but it is a straightforward program that would support the undocumented workers who quite literally underpin the American economy. Through this campaign for status and protections, movements for immigration justice can influence how the US and other Global North countries will respond to future climate disasters in other countries. But will we fight for TPS every time a country experiences a climate disaster?

The fight for TPS for Pakistan is a field of struggle that may open a path toward uniting movement forces to ensure protections for climate refugees globally. It is one clear example of how organizing at intersections between immigration justice and climate justice broadens the horizon for border abolition. In our broader fight for border and police abolition, as well as for the re-building of life-affirming institutions, we see organizing for TPS and SSR as a non-reformist reform. For millions like Mohiba and Raza, TPS and SSR meet material socio-economic needs in the US and their home countries – they allow migrants to stay and work legally and safely in the US, while sending much-needed remittances to their families in a country in crisis. In a world increasingly impacted by the climate crisis, organizing for TPS and SSR has the potential to bring together the climate and immigration justice movements to meet needs on the ground while at the same time broadening the vision for lives that are possible through political struggle. However, TPS and SSR are just one part of the transnational internationalist social movements that embody life-affirming politics and dismantle the institutions that uphold the conditions of unfreedom around us. The sites of struggle we describe above show how we might build the widespread recognition that we deserve care and safety regardless of where we are from. Moreover, starting from the life experiences and organizing efforts of working-class immigrants in the US shows how abolitionist organizing is a necessary response not only to border and police violence, but also to the systemic disinvestment in working-class life in the US. From the farmers' protests in Punjab to housing justice organizing in New York City, the movement for border abolition is growing. We do not have all the answers, but the three vignettes we share in this chapter offer examples of an abolitionist politics developing at the intersection of immigration justice and climate justice and how organizing for non-reformist reforms like TPS and SSR builds the recognition that abolitionist futures are possible.

NOTES

1. Ruth Wilson Gilmore, *Golden Gulag: Prisons, Surplus, Crisis, and Opposition in Globalizing California*. Berkeley: University of California Press, 2007.
2. Ruth Wilson Gilmore, "Scholar-Activists in the Mix." *Progress in Human Geography* 29(2), 2005: 177–182; Ruth Wilson Gilmore. "Abolition Geography and the Problem of Innocence." In Ruth Wilson Gilmore, Brenna Bhandar, and Alberto Toscano (Eds), *Abolition Geography: Essays towards Liberation* London; New York: Verso, 2022, pp. 471–495.
3. Ruth Wilson Gilmore, *Golden Gulag*; Loïc Wacquant, *Punishing the Poor: The Neoliberal Government of Social Insecurity*. Duke University Press, 2009; Neil Smith, "Global Social Cleansing: Postliberal Revanchism and the Export of Zero Tolerance." *Social Justice* 28(3), Fall 2001: 68–74.
4. Alex S. Vitale and Brian Jordan Jefferson, "The Emergence of Command and Control Policing in Neoliberal New York." In: Jordan T. Camp and Christina Heatherton (Eds.), *Policing the Planet: Why the Policing Crisis Led to Black Lives Matter*. New York: Verso, 2016; Ruth W. Gilmore, and Craig Gilmore, "Beyond Bratton." In: Jordan T. Camp and Christina Heatherton (Eds), *Policing the Planet: Why the Policing Crisis Led to Black Lives Matter*. New York: Verso, 2016.
5. Alison Mountz, *The Death of Asylum: Hidden Geographies of the Enforcement Archipelago*. Minneapolis: University of Minnesota Press, 2020.
6. Jenna M. Loyd, Matt Mitchelson, and Andrew Burridge (Eds), *Beyond Walls and Cages: Prisons, Borders, and Global Crisis*. Geographies of Justice and Social Transformation 14. Athens: University of Georgia Press, 2012.
7. Jenna Loyd, and Ruth Wilson Gilmore, "Race, Capitalist Crisis, and Abolitionist Organizing." In Ruth Wilson, Brenna Bhandar, and Alberto Toscano (Eds), *Abolition Geography: Essays Towards Liberation*. New York: Verso, 2022.
8. Loyd and Gilmore, "Race, Capitalist Crisis, and Abolitionist Organizing," 465.

9. André Gorz, "Reform and Revolution." *Socialist Register*, 5, March 17, 1968. https://socialistregister.com/index.php/srv/article/view/5272; Critical Resistance, "Reformist Reforms vs Abolitionist Steps in Policing," *Critical Resistance*. Accessed July 31, 2022. https://criticalresistance.org/resources/reformist-reforms-vs-abolitionist-steps-in-policing/

10. Charmaine Chua, "Abolition Is A Constant Struggle: Five Lessons from Minneapolis." *Theory & Event* 23(5), 2020: S-127.

11. Harsha Walia, *Border & Rule: Global Migration, Capitalism, and the Rise of Racist Nationalism*. Chicago: Haymarket Books, 2021; Nicole Nguyen, *Suspect Communities: Anti-Muslim Racism and the Domestic War on Terror*. Minneapolis: University of Minnesota Press, 2019; Alex Lubin, *Never-Ending War on Terror*. *Never-Ending War on Terror*. Berkeley: University of California Press, 2021.

12. Sunaina Marr Maira, *Missing: Youth, Citizenship, and Empire after 9/11*. Durham: Duke University Press, 2009; Junaid Rana, *Terrifying Muslims: Race and Labor in the South Asian Diaspora*. Durham: Duke University Press, 2011.

13. Ruth Wilson Gilmore, "In the Shadow of the Shadow State." *S&F Online* 13(1), Spring 2016. https://sfonline.barnard.edu/navigating-neoliberalism-in-the-academy-nonprofits-and-beyond/ruth-wilson-gilmore-in-the-shadow-of-the-shadow-state/

14. Sukhpal Singh, Manjeet Kaur, and H. S. Kingra. "Farmer Suicides in Punjab: Incidence, Causes, and Policy Suggestions." *Economic & Political Weekly* 57(25), 2022.

15. Singh et al., "Farmer Suicides in Punjab."

16. Ruth Wilson Gilmore, "1. Forgotten Places and the Seeds of Grassroots Planning." In: Charles R. Hale (Ed.), *Engaging Contradictions*. University of California Press, 2019, pp. 31–61.

17. Satendra Kumar, "New Farm Bills and Farmers' Resistance to Neoliberalism." *Sociological Bulletin* 71(4), October 1, 2022: 483–494.

18. Vivek Gupta. "Flood and Drought Are Ravaging India's Farmlands." *Quartz*, November 10, 2022. https://qz.com/flood-and-drought-are-ravaging-indias-farmlands-1849766266

19. Kusum Arora, "From Students and Dalits to the Punjabi Diaspora, Volunteers Made the Farmers' Protest a Success." *The Wire*. Accessed March 29, 2023. https://thewire.in/agriculture/from-students-and-dalits-to-the-punjabi-diaspora-volunteers-made-the-farmers-protest-a-success; The Tribune, "US Farmer Groups Deliver Solidarity Statement to Indian Farmers," *The Tribune India*. Accessed March 29, 2023. www.tribuneindia.com/news/nation/us-farmer-groups-deliver-solidarity-statement-to-indian-farmers-215225

20. Pranav Jeevan P., "Lessons from the Farmers' Protest: Mutual Aid, Decentralisation and Direct Democracy." *Catharsis Magazine*, 2022. www.catharsismagazine.com/post/lessons-from-the-farmers-protest-

mutual-aid-decentralisation-and-direct-democracy; Sarang Narasimhaiah, "Farmers against Fascism: How India's Farmers' Protests Cultivated Alternatives to Neoliberal Hindu Nationalist Dystopia." *Perspectives on Global Development and Technology* 20(5–6), February 11, 2022: 511–528.

21. Anna Bahney, "Manhattan Median Rents Hit Another High in March." *CNN Business*, April 13, 2023. www.cnn.com/2023/04/13/homes/manhattan-rentals-march/index.html

22. Rebecca Chowdhury, "Renters of Basement Apartments Fear Claiming Ida Aid." *Documented NY* (blog), October 20, 2021. https://documentedny.com/2021/10/20/basement-tenants-struggle-to-secure-funds-after-hurricane-devastation-illegal-basement-apartments/

23. Gilmore, *Golden Gulag*, 28.

24. David Pellow, and Jasmine Vazin, "The Intersection of Race, Immigration Status, and Environmental Justice." *Sustainability* 11(14), January 2019: 3942; Julie Sze, "Asian American Immigrant and Refugee Environmental Justice Activism under Neoliberal Urbanism." *Asian American Law Journal* 18, 2011: 5–24.

25. Rose Braz, and Craig Gilmore, "Joining Forces: Prisons and Environmental Justice in Recent California Organizing." *Radical History Review* 96, October 1, 2006: 95–111.

26. Morsheda herself is also a survivor of a climate related disaster in Bangladesh, the 1991 Bangladesh Cyclone, one of the deadliest tropical cyclones on record.

15

"We're about destroying the entire apparatus"

An interview with *Contra Viento y Marea, El Comedor Comunitario*

Can you explain to us what you do?

Devi Machete: We are *Contra Viento y Marea* [Against All Odds], *El Comedor Comunitario* [Community Dining Room], a community kitchen in the Zona Norte of Tijuana. We are known in this community simply as *el comedor*. We are a mutual aid project. Currently we're serving 1,000 hot meals with dignity every single week. (Prior to the COVID-19 pandemic, we served around 3,000 plates per week). But we do a lot more than just cooking and handing out prepared meals, we have a donation center; two bodegas on the rooftop of the kitchen we built ourselves to store essential goods we distribute out to folks in the community; we provide clothing, shoes, hygiene products, personal care items, diapers, sleeping bags, toys, and basic medicines; and we also have a small community garden on the rooftop. Additionally, we hold community events like a free acupuncture clinic once a month, and in a few weeks we're opening a free school here too! The *Escuela Libre y Laboratorio de Arte Tijuana* aims to provide "Free Education for Liberation" to young adults and adults who have been denied traditional educational opportunities due to their immigration status, poverty level, race, gender, sexual orientation, and other factors. We're currently holding workshops inside the dining area of the community kitchen and on the rooftop garden. All our meals, goods, services, workshops, and events are completely free for everyone!

Our collective is composed of Central American migrant/refugee youth who arrived in the November 2018 migrant caravan and anarchist organizers from Mexico, the US, and beyond. Through our mutual aid organizing model, we've succeeded in using a consensus/dialogue-based decision-making process that doesn't require creating hierarchies among ourselves as volunteers. We don't have an executive director or a board of trustees. Everyone who puts in time and labor gets to participate in the decisions. The people we serve, who live in our community, mostly originate from various parts of Mexico (Baja California, Guerrero, Matamoros, Veracruz), Central America (Honduras, El Salvador, Guatemala, Nicaragua), South America (Colombia, Venezuela, Brazil, Ecuador), and the Caribbean (Haiti, the Dominican Republic, Cuba, Jamaica), but also those who come from other far away countries like Cameroon, Ukraine, and Russia. We see the changes in migration patterns taking place on the ground even before they're reported in the news because we work directly with those who recently arrived at the border.

We are located 15 minutes away from the international port of entry El Chaparral, and a few blocks from the border wall in an area that is heavily militarized and overpoliced. We have the National Guard (*Guardia Nacional*), the Municipal Police (*Policía Municipal de Tijuana*), the Mexican Army (*Ejército Mexicano*) the Attorney General's Office (*Ministerio Público*), and all kinds of other federal, state, and local agencies patrol our neighborhood armed to the teeth. There's extreme corruption in all levels of Mexican security forces, and the Mexican government overall. Mexico is a narco-state where there's blatant impunity for all crimes. It is one of the deadliest countries in the world for journalists, and the fourth most hazardous country in the world for human rights defenders. The extraordinary amounts of violence are not just impacting migrants and human rights defenders, but the general population too. In addition, Tijuana is at the top of the list of the most dangerous cities in the world. It is a death trap for thousands of people, in particular for migrants/refugees/deportees and those from marginalized communities. Tijuana has a skyrocketing homicide rate, heinous femicides targeting young women in particular, mass graves, black sites, and deeply entrenched sex, drugs, and arms trafficking rings. Brutal cases of mutilation, torture, and forced disappearances are commonplace. It's under these circumstances that we have managed to carve out a space for folks to feel safe, welcomed, and in community.

AndreaM: Right now we serve a lot of people who have been deported from the United States. Those people are the most vulnerable because they're maybe Mexicans who lived a long time in the United States and they don't speak Spanish. But if you add all those who are deported from the US to the already complex situation we have in Tijuana – involving people arriving from every part of Latin America – we see all kinds of vulnerability.

Could you all say a little bit about how you think of abolition, within the context of the project or how an idea of abolition informs the project and talk about what border abolition looks like from where you all are?

DM: Border abolition for us means a framework we use to organize ourselves internally, but also for how we want to see society organized. We believe in abolition because it provides us with a framework from which to understand the context of violence we are seeing play out in real time. It also helps us come toward a new vision of what we want to see happen in our society, economic changes, political changes, social changes – abolition ties those together in a way that allows us to move forward thinking about the greater picture of what we need to do to reshape society.

Anarchists reject all authority that isn't justified, most notably, we repudiate the existence and legitimacy of the state. By definition, anarchists are aligned with abolition because abolition means we abolish the state and replace it with services people need to survive, that people need to thrive. Get rid of the borders, border patrol, the walls, the National Guard, Mexico's immigration enforcement arm, the Instituto Nacional de Migración (INM), then invest in free education for life: free public housing that is adequate, that is affordable in the sense that people have free access not just discounted access; free healthy food; free healthcare that is high quality given at the point of necessity; and services for folks that need preventive care such as free maternity and child care. All of these things come together in a vision of abolition because the money that's going to fund all the free programs and all the free projects that we need comes from stripping funds away from the police, away from militarization; away from the state. We have more than enough money to fund these things if we only stop funding the border wall, stop funding the detention centers, end the war on drugs, all of it. I'm talking about abolition not just in this context of Tijuana or Mexico, but I think it needs to happen everywhere, we need to abolish every state. We need to end US imperialism. We can't allow the US to continue being an empire because Latin America will never be free to turn to abolition.

A: I completely agree. I think one of the most important things to consider is the context. We are working in the *comedor*, and it is a great environment where people can become aware of all these dynamics. This is very important because in the experience of migrant people, sometimes you see organizations and civil associations that really have no interest in letting people be aware or act for themselves, in their interests and according to their will. In the "humanitarian" world, people are not treated as human beings, with dignity, and it's really important to have such spaces like the *comedor*, to show a different way of working and living with migrant people.

Border abolitionist organizing is different from a lot of the other kinds of organizing that people do at the US–Mexico border. Could you talk about some of the difficulties or complications in sustaining an abolitionist project in that context?

A: For many organizations, migration is a business. If you don't pay attention, people just become numbers, and reports are filled out with those numbers and the biggest worries are about how much funding I can get from such a large number of people, instead of prioritizing their dignity.

DM: The *comedor* is very different from nonprofits or large NGOs. We are organized through solidarity and mutual aid, meaning everyone who comes participates as a volunteer and does so because they want to, not because they're coerced. We measure our success by the quality of our relationships and we organize on the basis of friendship. There's no distinction between those that are doing the organizing and those that are receiving the services. They're the same community, the same group of friends, the same circle of volunteers.

Of course, there are distinctions in terms of economic privilege between some of us that have more economic stability and so we offer economic stipends to those who need them, mainly our migrant volunteers. We give them money for transportation and food. Not just the food we cook for meals, but staple food boxes with rice and stuff from the kitchen, like those we give out to people in the neighborhood with stoves. We also give them clothes that come in as donations. They have access to all the donations that come in actually. We don't say, "Oh you can only have like three things" or how a shelter would say, "Only pick a few things and that's it," they have access to whatever it is that comes in. There's a sense that we're not here to restrict the resources but to ensure that they get out to everyone who needs them. We have a horizontal internal organizing structure. That's one difference.

Another difference is that we rely on small donations, and the solidarity of the hundreds of accomplices, allies, and partners on both sides of the border, to run all our projects. We don't have large grant donors, meaning we don't allow donors of a foundation or nonprofit to decide how we do things. We care about the wellbeing of our volunteers, and our community above and beyond counting how many people we served. Our objective is to build up the community, not earn grants for the sake of promoting ourselves and boosting our own incomes.

By taking in small donations, the volunteers have the power to decide together, in conjunction with the people we serve, how we operate, what services we give, and all other major decisions. When organizations rely on large donors exclusively, they have to cater to the whims of the elite whose funding is running everything. They must have an executive director or a board of trustees that is responsible for overseeing the work of those on the ground. We believe the volunteers who work directly with the community and the people who receive the services know best what should be done, not anyone else, especially not wealthy donors. That's a major distinction between mutual aid projects versus the nonprofits.

Here's another difference. Nonprofits get funding, for example, to support Central American migrants. If there's a person who's deported, who comes from the US or is from Tijuana, they don't get this money, they don't get help. So, these elite funders unintentionally create artificial scarcity. This allows racism and other types of discrimination to flourish. In the way that we do our work, we don't care where you're from, if you come to our food program and you need food: we give you a plate. If you come and you need a backpack or you need shoes, we just give it to you. We don't ask you things like, "Let me see your documentation. Are you legal?" We don't ask anything, we just give the stuff and that's it.

A: A big difference between a project like the *comedor* and some civil associations, who have a different view, is that the donors decide how the volunteers will do their job. They often use a hierarchical structure to exercise power over people, and they keep feeding the divide between people and migrants, and between different classes of migrants. This doesn't happen at the *comedor*.

It sounds like to me one of the things you're saying is that border abolition would be the abolition of the business of the border. Or that border abolition involves the abolition of all the profit-making off of migrants and the set of social relations that it generates which produces hierarchies making borders between people or exercising power on or over people. And it sounds like in the context of the project another idea of abolition that's present is the production of new social relations that aren't structured in that way for you all.

DM: Absolutely. Border abolition is an umbrella term that covers a lot of different aspects of work that people are doing through mutual aid projects. For example, in the landscape of border abolition, there's several areas. Those that are focused on using the hammer to chip away or to smash down the state institutions that are physically extracting people from their countries via deportations, to incarcerate them in jails, prisons and detention centers (which are also jails and prisons by another name), to exploit them. There are organizations, groups, and collectives devoted specifically to using a diversity of tactics to attack those institutions to bring them down. So that's one area of the abolition landscape.

Then there's those groups working with people who are caught inside the belly of the beast, supporting prisoners trapped within carceral and punitive systems. That's also another piece of the landscape, organizations doing detention support, sending commissaries, writing letters, noise demos, and overall doing tons of work in that area.

Then there are organizations or groups or collectives like us that are modeling in real life what it would be like to have a world where there's free food, free care, and free resources for all. Our project is about implementing what we imagine it would be like to not have the state, but doing it now, not waiting for the state to collapse or be abolished. We are starting to build that beautiful world where we would all be supported, cared for and loved. I think that's the difference between the way we do this project and the way nonprofits do humanitarian aid. They don't want to challenge or abolish the state, they want to work with the state as partners. They don't want to completely stop the forced migration flows because they're making money off of every migrant/refugee that comes through, so they don't necessarily want to end the whole business of the border, they just want to play their role in it. We're about destroying the entire apparatus, the entire border business model. We're creating an alternative that showcases what it really means to have dignity and humanity-centered; what it truly means for us to achieve building a radically new world where we live in harmony. Honestly, it's a lot of fun because we get to imagine and build the world that we want to live in right here, right now, regardless of the lack of resources, the violence from the state and nonstate actors, the mass surveillance, the detentions, harassments and arrests of our volunteers by the police. Every abolitionist project at its core contains a seed of this new world too.

What are some of the contradictions or some of the difficulties that you feel abolition as a movement needs to address or overcome in the coming months or years?

DM: We have to take into consideration that we're living in a hyper-capitalist apocalyptic nightmare where we're teetering on the brink of environmental collapse from climate change. We have less than ten years to turn back the tide or else humanity and every other life form on this planet could cease to exist. We're seeing ever-increasing numbers of climate refugees coming to US, European, and Canadian borders fleeing from the Global South, trying to escape the consequences of climate change, but also imperialism and all the other forms of organized domination and the violences it produces. For example, the violence and corruption that happens from the mass extraction of natural resources from poor countries throws them into turmoil. As a result, the wealthy get richer and the poor get poorer. Poverty creates crime and criminals eventually get well organized and very rich. Then people have to flee the gangs and drug cartels. But those are not officially recognized categories or reasons to be granted US asylum. These gangs and cartels in Mexico, Colombia, Haiti, etc. are the direct result of US imperialism and the immense poverty produced through the systematic looting of Latin America and the Caribbean.

We're finding ourselves in a situation where if we're not able to take power away from the state, overthrow the late-stage capitalist economic world order, end US hegemony, reverse the warming effects of climate change, and resolve all of the most serious/urgent crises of our lifetimes in the next few years, then the whole planet, everyone and everything on it, is going to irreversibly collapse into an abyss. And so, we often find ourselves conflicted about how to best proceed with promoting our vision of the world and fighting back. Under these circumstances of duress, what's the best way to move forward with our goals? How do we bring people into the abolitionist movement? What do we do with those who will never accept an abolitionist agenda? Who can we partner with to support our agenda?

As a migrant organizer in Tijuana, I have come to the realization that migrants/refugees are the ultimate anarchists. They are mostly in favor of an abolitionist vision of the world. They just don't know or use the words "anarchism" and "abolition" to describe themselves and their political orientation, but they are practicing anarchism in their daily lives. Migrants and refugees dexterously deploy direct action and mutual aid tactics to effectively avoid persecution, survive inhumane conditions and overall fly under the radar. They're actively contesting the state's power over their lives by not waiting for permission or papers to cross international borders, often living without an ID or a bank account for months or years at a time. There's a saying one of my gay migrant youth organizer friends from Honduras says, "*Todxs en el piso o todxs en la cama*" (Either we all sleep on the bed or we all sleep on the floor), meaning nobody gets left behind. Migrants and refugees will largely share their resources and pass on essential information to others whom they just met on the road. Additionally, they travel hundreds of thousands of miles to pursue their dreams, or to escape from the most repressive governments. Whether that's train hopping, riding bikes, hitch-hiking, and traveling in small groups or large caravans, migrants and refugees traverse borders like they don't exist. Refugee youth will say: "F the police, we can't work with the police. We won't call the police, we won't deal with the authorities. The authorities only exist to harass, arrest, deport and exploit us." They already share our anarchist values, they just don't know that the word for "f the state" is anarchism.

Throughout the past 18+ years I've worked organizing migrants and I've come to the conclusion that if we find creative ways to expand alternative mutual aid or solidarity economies where power and ownership is collectivized, migrants would eagerly join abolitionist projects. What we really need to do is offer them a viable pathway to participate in a mutual aid economy, instead of the current capitalist economy. Migrants spend all their time and energy cycling back and forth between crushing dead-end jobs with terrible wages, like at a *maquiladora* or at a construction site, they don't have the bandwidth to participate in anything that's not paid work.

Our abolitionist movement needs to expand efforts to mass exit the capitalist economy and move toward a mutual aid or a solidarity economy. Every job is a dictatorship of the boss and of the company. It doesn't matter that we have a "democracy" as our government if each workplace, where we go to almost every day and spend most of our time, is a dictatorship. All of us need to break free from the current economic system where every job is a dictatorship of capitalist bosses and the evil companies/corporations they represent. It doesn't matter what the political system is if we have to spend most of our waking hours enduring a dictator boss in every workplace. If we generate meaningful, well-paid jobs that operate as worker cooperatives, our abolitionist movement will rapidly spread.

A: Even though it's messy, talking about the complexity doesn't minimize the work that we're doing. I think ultimately others are going to involve themselves in mutual aid at the border. I like telling them what to expect, rather than having them feel like this is the first time anyone's faced these problems and has no resources or clue how to face it. I would say one of the challenges of a space like this is to spread our practices. It's really hard for a group of people to try to do something different, because you are considered the "radical" one and shunned. I feel what happens with groups that are doing radical work is that they get isolated because they often face problems with authorities. It becomes difficult to spread abolition practices with no consequences. Other groups won't want to work with you or support you and if they do it's like "Here just come pick up these like sacks of rice and then you can go."

We have tried to do overtures with a group that manages one of the biggest migrant shelters. We used to work with them when they used to have staff that were more radical, but then they left. We would always say, "Hey, let's do something together" and they would say, "Yeah" and then a few weeks later, that staffer would end up leaving. That would happen again and again. The bigger organizations want to be in the position of not asking for help; they want to be the top group and get requests from other groups, like it's a competition to be the most well-connected and well-funded. It's a part of the border business and nonprofit model.

The other thing that I see that happens a lot with groups like ours that do radical work is that our tactics and/or strategies get co-opted by other mainstream groups. For example, we do something new and other groups are like "Wow, that's really cool." They start to do it too but they continue to work in these patterns of hierarchy. They're not gonna take the part that's most radical and implement it, they just take the part that is easiest to do from the work we're doing and replicate that: they'll take the tactic, but won't take the strategy of abolition.

DM: As abolitionists, we're up against the nonprofit industrial complex and so we need to constantly come up with new, more innovative strategies and tactics because we're not going to beat them in terms of having more funding or resources. We're also in competition with the state and all those forces who want to exploit migrants. We're going up against the border business model, that's profiting immensely off the suffering of migrants. We're not gonna beat them by having bigger guns, tanks, or drones, we need to have bigger ideas. We need to have a much more intelligent approach to outmaneuvering them to spread our abolitionist vision of the world. We're more than capable of abolishing the state and every state, but we need to have the majority of the people on our side. To do that, we need to strengthen the abolitionist movement and spread it to every corner of the globe. If we're all part of the problem, by giving legitimacy, revenue and resources to the state, then we are all part of the solution too. We can withhold those things simultaneously, all together. They cannot incarcerate or disappear all of us. But we must act quickly; we're running out of time. We believe we need a revolution because we know the state will not let us go without a fight. We have to begin to live free from the state. Be the revolution now. We cannot wait for the revolution to come knocking at our door. All of us must play a part in bringing about the abolitionist utopia we desperately need.

The hope of the future lies in you, in me, in all of us being able to work and play together to bring about a future without hunger, poverty, war, alienation, and all the other evils. We are already building this new world here and now, at *Contra Viento y Marea, El Comedor Comunitario*. We invite you to join us in our abolitionist project and experience for yourself what it's like to live freely in community with migrant youth and anarchists.

Afterword

This afterword begins in the midst of an unbearable, annihilatory escalation in Israeli state violence against the people of Gaza. This violence did not begin in October 2023, when Hamas and other groups killed over 1,000 Israelis and took dozens more people hostage.[1] Since the blockade of 2007, Palestinians in Gaza have endured within the unremitting, deadly mechanics of an almost-total border, under an apartheid administered by the Israeli government.[2] Almost two thirds of Palestinians in Gaza are refugees, whose families were, in the shadow of the atrocities of the Holocaust, forcibly displaced by Israeli forces in 1948.[3] And for years they have, in Gaza, in the West Bank, and in exile, rejected the systematic denial of their rights. From the Great March of Return in 2018,[4] to the international movement for boycott, divestment, and sanctions,[5] to direct action against the companies that manufacture weapons for sale to the Israeli government,[6] Palestinians and their allies have deployed brave and creative means to insist on their freedom. Despite attempts to characterize any criticism of the actions of Israel as inherently anti-Semitic – set aside for a moment that identifying Jewish people with the state of Israel is precisely that – so too have many Jewish people in Israel and the diaspora campaigned for an end to Israeli apartheid, and for a political path to a just peace.[7]

Struggles for border abolition, and for the Palestinian cause, cannot be untangled. As my dear friend Reem Abu-Hayyeh says: "One day we will return, and we'll distort whole concepts of nationhood and borders to get there."

Border abolition and Palestinian liberation are both concerned with technologies and tactics of forced displacement, enclosure, surveillance, and the imposition of differentiated rights on racialized people. The chapters in this collection provide a meticulous account of the myriad kinds of violence committed by states under the auspices of bordering: the *Black Alliance for Just Immigration*

(BAJI) writes of the Haitian people still dying in the Atlantic, and Lauren Cape-Davenhill explains how so-called alternatives to detention can strengthen and expand the reach of borders. Simon Campbell sets out the role of encampment as part of a deliberate strategy of EU border management, maintaining Fortress Europe, and Francesco Marchi details the rise of the reception-industrial complex in Italy, creating what he describes as a "political economy of waiting."

There is a second ground for this entanglement however: both border abolition and the Palestinian freedom struggle are concerned with visions and strategies toward societies where everyone who inhabits them can live flourishing and dignified lives. "Border abolition is a radical political project of centering life and working for everyone's freedom," write the co-authors of one of this volume's beautiful collective contributions: "Unfolding and flourishing: strategies of border abolition feminism." As Luke de Noronha and I set out in our book *Against Borders,* "abolition requires that we are guided by dreams of a borderless future." In this way, border abolition is not only concerned with the absence of harmful bordering practices, or even the simple realization of a universal right to free movement. In pushing us to identify and build toward those life-affirming services, structures and relations that would make immigration controls obsolete, border abolition requires, as Josue David Cisneros points out, a more fundamental reshaping of global society.

Luke and I recently recorded a podcast with a (sort of) left-wing British media pundit. He approached us with the familiar *what-abouts* of the chattering classes: What about the abolitionist tendency to tear things down rather than make the world better; what about the risks of, in a world without borders, too many people moving to the Global North, at once and threatening community cohesion? At one point, he asked us something along the lines of whether abolition is too fringe to bring together a broad range of actors from across the progressive spectrum; whether as a slogan others might find it too "off-putting." It was at that point that I did two things. First, I pointed him to Ruth Wilson Gilmore's account of *Critical Resistance*'s abolitionist organizing against prisons in California, and the diverse, coalitional approach there that bore fruit. Second, I emphasized something that this volume illustrates wonderfully: abolition is not an abstract framework of the ivory tower. It is not a simple set of rhetorical arguments that we deploy in order to shift opinion polls. To borrow a phrase from Sivanandan, abolition is thinking in order to do.

Many of us come to border abolition because we are people on the move, or acting in solidarity with people on the move. We come to border abolition because we experience and witness the violence of bordering, and the inadequacy of liberal incrementalist frameworks for ameliorating that violence. In this vein, *Border Abolition Now* contains many valuable reflections on a whole host of abolitionist practices and strategies. *Women in Exile* outline how they navigate the presence in their organizing spaces of people who are not subject to immigration controls, and how they welcome allies in a way that supports the strategic demands of the group. Vanessa Thompson details the campaigns of the undocumented *Gilets Noirs* in France, while also looking to transnational networks working for the rights of refugees in Libya as examples of abolitionist multitudes. The co-authors of "Shut Them Down" think together about the large collective meals run by the Glasgow-based group *We Will Rise*, and the conviviality and strategizing that these meals enabled. DRUM makes a powerful case for better access to quality housing for working-class immigrants, setting out how in a world "simultaneously on fire and under water," housing justice can also help protect people from climate breakdown. There is no unified abolitionist strategy that will hold in all times and places, but these practical insights are invaluable to each of us as we navigate our own specific terrains.

I am still, months after first reading them, reflecting on the theoretical contributions of *Border Abolition Now* Texts, campaigns, and spaces that convene abolitionist organizers and thinkers create exciting, generative opportunities for uncertainty, disagreement, and simply figuring things out together. Despite how we might be caricatured by some, border abolitionists, and abolitionists more broadly, are extremely diverse in our theory and practice, even if we depart from shared ground. It's in those spaces of uncertainty and disagreement that we sharpen our frameworks and our strategies. For me, *Against Borders* was never supposed to be a definitive text, and since its publication I have been fortunate to be in conversation with many border abolitionists about difficult, essential questions. *What do political communities look like in a world without borders? Does border abolition require the abolition of the state?* One person in the audience at the launch of our book at the Institute for Contemporary Arts asked what border abolition means for the national liberation struggles of colonized peoples – in Palestine, in Kashmir, in Western Sahara. Just over one year later, I think that this question has answers, but certainly not just one.

Several essays in this collection reflect on the framework of non-reformist reforms in ways that I find extremely useful, troubling the idea that they are a magical solution to the problem of borders, or to the tensions between abolitionists and reformists. The authors of "Shut them down" in this volume point out that how we campaign for and move toward non-reformist reforms is just as important as winning those campaigns. Jenna Loyd offers an account of how we can oppose imperial efforts to weaken the right to asylum – especially salient as the UK Government threatens to denounce the Refugee Convention – without accepting liberal human rights frameworks as the horizon of our abolitionist vision. Activists who are part of *Alarm Phone*, through an insightful and generous conversation, work through their ambivalence toward using the legal system to help people on the move avoid criminalization, while recognizing that the legal system stymies abolitionist strategies, and "locks our imaginaries." Finally, Brian Whitener's chapter throws down an interesting, illuminating challenge that had me squinting into the middle distance for days. Whitener describes the historical and geographical specificities of the moment in which Gorz developed his framework for non-reformist reforms, and pushes us to reflect on whether (in the US at least) our movements might be sufficiently strong and vibrant that we would be better guided by some strategic framework other, and potentially more ambitious, than non-reformist reforms.

The shared ground from which I believe abolitionists depart is well encapsulated in *Contra Viento y Marea*'s contribution: "*Todxs en el piso o todxs en la cama*" (Either we all sleep on the bed or we all sleep on the floor). I hope that *Border Abolition Now* moves more of us to nurture our dream-spaces and abolitionist visions, and to build toward a world without borders, where nobody is left behind. *Women in Exile* put it best: it's time to "raise our voices and get loud."

Gracie Mae Bradley
Glasgow, October 15, 2023

NOTES

1. https://edition.cnn.com/middleeast/live-news/israel-news-hamas-war-10-15-23/index.html
2. www.amnesty.org/en/latest/campaigns/2022/02/israels-system-of-apartheid/
3. www.map.org.uk/news/archive/post/1501-generation-palestine-babies-born-under-blockade-and-airstrikes-in-gaza
4. www.amnesty.org/en/latest/campaigns/2018/10/gaza-great-march-of-return/
5. https://bdsmovement.net/
6. https://freedomnews.org.uk/2023/10/06/activist-who-targeted-factory-in-solidarity-with-grenfell-and-palestine-found-not-guilty/
7. www.jewishvoiceforpeace.org/

Notes on contributors

Mark Akkerman (they/them) is a researcher at *Stop Wapenhandel* (Dutch campaign against arms trade) and for the Transnational Institute (TNI) and has published extensively on the militarization and externalization of (EU) borders and the role of the arms industry. They hold a MSc in Public Administration and have long been involved in peace, no border, and anarchist movements, including the *Abolish Frontex* network since its start in 2021.

Helen Brewer, Tom Kemp, Bobby Phe Amis, and Joel White work together in a not-yet-named writing collective. Their shared writing and thinking has grown out of friendships built through organizing together and alongside each other in various configurations of abolitionist no-borders anti-detention organizing in the British mainland, including *Detained Voices, Unity Centre, We Will Rise*, and *End Deportations*. Together they draw on their different backgrounds in law, architecture, visual cultures, anthropology, and history to offer a militant approach to thinking with movement-building, and to writing about the connections, solidarities, affinities and complicities that push and pull them, us, states, and mobilizations together and apart.

Simon Campbell is an activist-researcher focusing on border infrastructures, state violence, and abolitionist struggles against the border regime. In recent years, Simon has been part of a number of solidarity groups engaged in documenting pushbacks at European borders, including the *Border Violence Monitoring Network*, and has studied a joint MA in South Eastern European Studies at the University of Belgrade and the University of Graz.

Lauren Cape-Davenhill is an ESRC-funded PhD candidate in the School of Geography at the University of Leeds. Her research interests include the intersections between the criminal justice and immigration systems, bordering, securitization, and the racialized dynamics of immigration controls. She takes an interdisciplinary approach, drawing on work from carceral geography, critical migration studies and criminology. Her research is informed by previous experience working and campaigning with migrant support and advocacy organizations in the UK and Europe.

Josue David Cisneros is an Associate Professor in the Department of Communication at the University of Illinois Urbana-Champaign. His research and teaching focus on rhetorics of resistance and social movement, especially as they concern issues of race and immigration. He is the author of *"The Border Crossed Us": Rhetorics of Borders, Citizenship, and Latina/o Identity* (2014) and numerous essays and chapters. He teaches classes on cultural studies and activist rhetoric, and is involved in labor organizing and anti-prison and anti-border movements.

Leah Cowan is a writer and editor on race, gender and state violence. They currently work at Project 17, an advice center that supports families with No Recourse to Public Funds who are experiencing poverty and homelessness, and have been involved in anti-detention and anti-deportation organizing in London.

Deanna Dadusc, Rubi, Lolo Naegeli, and Camille Gendrot are a working group within *Watch the Med – Alarm Phone* (from now on just *Alarm Phone*), but we are not the representative voice of *Alarm Phone*. Within *Alarm Phone* there are heterogenous points of view and perspectives, and these debates are ongoing. For us this is a platform to articulate our ideas and our position also in relation to existing ongoing debates. But this is not a positioning of *Alarm Phone* on these issues.

Doris Dede is an activist and an active member of *Women in Exile*, who has embarked on her career as a sociology student. She works as an empowerment trainer in the field of flight and asylum with a focus on women*'s specific topics, strengthening and networking for women* with refugee history.

Francesca Esposito is an activist scholar and community psychologist/organizer who has worked for the last 15 years supporting survivors of border and gendered violence. Her research focuses on the intersectional mechanisms of power and violence constituting detention sites and the role of psychologists in the border-industrial complex. Along with Aminata, she co-founded the *Unchained Collective* and is currently working on a short animated video illuminating the gender-racist violence of the detention regime. She defines herself as a border abolition feminist.

Sarah Hopwood is an intersectional feminist, anti-capitalist, abolitionist. She very recently completed her PhD at Teesside University, UK, researching access to refuge for migrant survivors of domestic abuse. She has been involved in multiple no-borders campaigns to close immigration detention centers and end other punitive forms of immigration control. Currently she works on the frontline supporting survivors of sexual violence.

Aminata Kalokoh is an advocate and coordinator at AVID – Association of Visitors to Immigration Detainees – and her role involves coordinating groups who visit UK immigration detention centers and advocating toward the closure of these carceral facilities. She is engaged in several scholarly-activist projects and has written and given public speeches on the multiple harms of detention and the role of psychologists in the border-industrial complex. She is also a co-founder of the *Unchained Collective*, a collective made up of people with and without lived experiences of detention who use creative means to work toward the abolition of oppressive border and detention regimes. In particular, they are currently working on a short animated video illuminating the gender-racist violence of the detention regime.

Jenna M. Loyd is an Associate Professor in the Department of Geography at the University of Wisconsin-Madison whose work focuses on health politics, carceral and abolition geographies, and the politics of asylum, refugee resettlement, and deterrence in US migration policy. She is the author of *Health Rights Are Civil Rights: Peace and Justice Activism in Los Angeles, 1963-1978*; co-author with Alison Mountz of *Boats, Borders, and Bases: Race, the Cold War, and the Rise of Migration Detention in the United States*; and co-editor with Matt Mitchelson and Andrew Burridge of *Beyond Walls and Cages: Prisons, Borders, and Global Crisis*.

AndreaM is Italian. Although he studied as a biologist, in Italy he participated as an activist in several projects to defend the rights of migrants and citizens in a community center in the city of Bologna, Italy, part of the association *Ya Basta Bologna*, which has been carrying out solidarity and mutualism projects in the city for years. For the past two years he has been in Tijuana, where he collaborates with various associations and civil organizations for the protection of the rights of asylum seekers and migrants. During this period he joined the *Comedor Comunitario Contra Viento y Marea* and became actively involved in the collective's projects in favor of the marginalized population in the Zona Norte of Tijuana. Since January 2023 Andrea coordinates the *Border Line Crisis Center*, a shelter and community center focused on the autonomy and empowerment of migrants.

Devi Machete is a renegade. They're a queer, anarke-feministe, antifasciste, and migrant/refugee/deportee organizer active in the ancestral territories of the Kumeyaay people (Tijuana, Mexico). Alongside Central American migrant youth from the November 2018 migrant caravan and accomplice anarchists, Machete is a member and co-founder of the mutual aid collective, *Contra Viento y Marea, El Comedor Comunitario* (CVM). Since February of 2019, *El Comedor Comunitario* has operated a community kitchen, frontline resource distribution center, and a rooftop garden. Last year, CVM initiated a street cat/animal support project and this past summer, a new community free school, *la Escuela Libre y Laboratorio de Arte* (ELLA). Prior to CVM, Machete co-launched the *Hecate Society*: a queer femme-led, art and media collective focused on cross-border solidarity work. Their expertise ranges widely from Participatory Action Research or PAR, to international relations, Republican Party fascism, revolutionary women/femmes, as well as mutual aid and direct action training, herbalism, and kitty doula. In addition to grassroots community organizing and these proficiencies, Machete, AKA Fat Drip, is an indie photographer, troubadour poet, experimental artiste, and novice tattoo artist.

They utilize their skills, crafts, and knowledge in transnational solidarity with all oppressed peoples fighting for liberation.

Francesco Marchi is a PhD candidate in International Studies at the University of Naples "L'Orientale." His current research project looks at the connections between humanitarianism, race and the political economy in Italy and Germany. Francesco's research interests mainly concern processes of racialization and postcoloniality in the European context.

Vania Martins is an abolitionist feminist and a community organizer. She works in the field of gender-based violence particularly with survivors with No Recourse to Public Funds. She has been involved in the transnational feminist movement for the last 15 years and has worked with refugees leading to her involvement in anti-detention and border abolition struggles.

Kathryn Medien is a lecturer in Sociology at The Open University. Her research draws on feminist and anti-colonial social theory to explore the colonial and imperial politics of state violence and resistance to it. She has been published in the *Sociological Review, Theory, Culture and Society, Current Sociology,* and the *International Feminist Journal of Politics.*

Elizabeth Ngari is an activist and one of the founders of *Women in Exile,* involved in different fields of *Women in Exile*'s work such as coordination of projects, facilitating different empowerment workshops for refugee women and people working with refugees, on flight reasons and how to open solidarity structures to refugee women.

Abraham Paulos is a seasoned communications expert, journalist, and movement leader who has advocated for human rights for over a decade. Abraham is the Deputy Director of Communications and Policy of the *Black Alliance for Just Immigration* (BAJI). He develops and implements BAJI's overall strategy nationwide with BAJI members and staff. Before joining BAJI, Abraham was the Executive Director of *Families for Freedom* (FFF), a position he held after facing immigration detention at Rikers Island and becoming a member of FFF. Earlier in his career, Abraham was a *Human Rights First* researcher focused on immigration detention. He also served as Program Director at *Life of Hope*, a community-based organization in Brooklyn that provides services to low-income immigrants, and as the communications coordinator for *WHY Hunger*, a global NGO tackling hunger and poverty issues. As a journalist, Abraham reported on urban policy and human rights for *City Limits*, the NYC civic affairs magazine, and the *Foreign Policy Association*, writing about foreign policy and global issues. Abraham is a Stateless Eritrean refugee, born in Sudan and raised in Chicago. He is a graduate of George Washington University with a degree in International Affairs and is finishing a Master's at the New School University.

Vignesh Ramachandran is a graduate student in Geography at the University of Wisconsin-Madison. His research focuses on economic geography, platform labor, policing, and the history of management. He has also been organizing in climate justice spaces since 2018.

Sara Riva is a Marie Skłodowska-Curie Research Fellow at the Spanish National Research Council and the University of Queensland. She is a feminist whose research looks at the intersections of neoliberalism, migration, humanitarianism and the border. Her work has been published in the *Journal of Citizenship Studies*, *Journal of Immigrant and Refugee Studies*, *Geopolitics*, and *Journal of Refugee Studies*.

Akash Singh is a member of *Desis Rising Up and Moving* (DRUM) and leads DRUM's communications work, as well as the organization's LGBTQI+ and arts & cultural organizing projects. Prior to working on staff, Akash joined DRUM as a member in 2015.

Vanessa E. Thompson is an Assistant Professor and Distinguished Professor in Black Studies and Social Justice in the Department of Gender Studies at Queen's University, Canada. Before she moved to Ontario, she was a lecturer at the Institute of Sociology at Goethe University Frankfurt and at the Faculty of Social and Cultural Sciences at European University Viadrina, Germany. Her scholarship and teaching focus on Black studies (especially Black social movements and Black feminism), anti-colonialism, racial capitalism and state violence, abolition and abolitionist internationalism, and critical ethnographies. She has co-edited *Abolitionismus. Ein Reader* (Suhrkamp, 2022) together with Daniel Loick, a special issue on Black feminisms with *Femina Politica* (2021) and her book *Black Socialities. Black Urban Activism and the Struggle beyond Recognition in Paris* is forthcoming with Manchester University Press. Vanessa organizes with abolitionist feminist movements in Europe and internationally, and is a member of the International Independent Commission on the Death of Oury Jalloh.

Brian Whitener is an Associate Professor of Spanish at the University at Buffalo and author of *Crisis Cultures: The Rise of Finance in Mexico and Brazil*. Other recent projects include *Raquel Gutiérrez: In Defense of Common Life* (Common Notions, 2024); *The 90s*; *De gente común: Prácticas estéticas y rebeldía social*, co-edited with Lorena Méndez and Fernando Fuentes; and the translation of Grupo de Arte Callejero's *Thoughts, Practices, and Actions* with the *Mareada Translation Collective*.

Elahe Zivardar is an award-winning Iranian artist, architectural designer, journalist, and documentary film-maker, who currently lives in Arizona, United States, where she obtained refugee status in 2019. After fleeing Iran, Elahe Zivardar was detained on the remote island of the Republic of Nauru for attempting to seek asylum in Australia from 2013 to 2019. During her detention in Nauru, she was highly active in using photos and video to document the horrific treatment and conditions endured by people seeking asylum and imprisoned offshore. An artist using diverse techniques including painting, photography, and documentary film-making, Elahe Zivardar seeks to depict and raise awareness on how refugee, stateless and migrant minorities are treated throughout the migration process, especially at borders. In addition to her artwork, she is active as an adviser to international refugee rights campaigns and organizations in Australia, the UK and the US.

Index

9/11 (11th September 2001) 84–5, 86, 117, 214, 216

Abolish Frontex campaign 7, 36, 54–5, 56, 59, 61, 63, 64, 147–52
Abolish Police movement (US) 149
Abolish Reporting campaign 125
AbolishCBP (Customs and Border Protection) 55
#AbolishICE (Immigration and Customs Enforcement) 54–5, 59–60, 63, 64, 204, 206, 216
abolition praxis 62–4, 101
abolitionism 50, 57–64, 107, 116, 205, 243
Abolitionist Futures (activist group) 158
Abolitionist University Studies [Abbie Boggs et al.] 62
Abu-Hayyeh, Reem 241
Action Against Detention and Deportation 30
Afghan refugees 79–81, 90
Afghanistan, US invasion of 79–80, 85, 86
Africa, borders in 72
African Court for Human and People's Rights 182
African liberation movements 72
African Union 72
Ahmed, Leila 86
Akkerman, Mark 7, 61

Alarm Phone network 8, 174–92, 244
  Search and Rescue service 179, 191–2
Albahari, Maurizio *Crimes of Peace* 130
Albanian migrants 132
Alternatives to Detention (ATD) 115–27
American Civil War 85
Amos, Valerie 86
anarchism 232, 237
Anderson, Bridget 21, 56
anti-Blackness 200–1
Anti-Terrorism and Effective Death Penalty Act (US, 1996) 215
Arab Spring (2011) 130, 133
Arendt, Hannah 82
Asso Ventotto (ship) 186
Asylum and Immigration (Treatment of Claimants) Act (UK, 2004) 120
asylum seekers 79, 81, 91, 133, 135–7, 142
Australia 27–8, 90
Aviram, Hadar 121

Baker, Ella 214
Balibar, Étienne 58
Balkans migration route 103, 106, 110, 133
Bangladesh 220–3
Berlin Conference (1884) 72
Berlusconi, Silvio 134

Beznec, Barbara 105
Black Alliance for Just Immigration (BAJI) 7, 69–71, 241–2
Black Lives Matter 98
Black Panthers 84
Black Vests movement 37, 44–5, 48, 50, 243
body as a border 29
Book of Negroes 39
Border Abolition Conference (2021) 2, 19
border controls 7, 21
Border Security Training Centre (Netherlands) 151
border studies 55–61
border-industrial complex 60–1
borders 1, 38–9, 58, 72–3, 212, 217
　non-reformist reforms of 63–4, 158–61, 1689, 171–2, 206–7, 213, 244
Boutang, Yann Moulier 198–9
Bradley, Gracie May 8, 158–9
Brankamp, Hanno 101
Braz, Rose 229
Breaking Borders to Build Bridges Conference (2023) 12
Brewer, Helen 7–8
Britain
　Alternatives to Detention in 115–20
　detention in 161–2
　"hostile environment" policy 24, 118, 162
Browne, Simone 200–1
Buddi Company 121
Buen Vivir movement 31
Burridge, Andrew 107, 203
Bush, George W. 86

Calais detention camp 182

California
　economic crisis (1970s) 131, 138
　prison system in 131
camp-watch groups 109
Campbell, Simon 7, 242
Campsfield detention centre 157
Cape-Davenhill, Lauren 7, 242
capitalism 21, 30, 42, 82–3, 195–6, 204
　see also racial capitalism
carceral feminism 25–6
carceral system 5, 23, 40, 57–8, 116, 193, 213
carceral racism 42–3
care work 29, 46–7
Carmichael, Stokely 214
Ceuta 103
Charles de Gaulle Airport, occupation of 45
children 80
Chimni, B.S. 89
Chua, Charmaine 213
Cisneros, Josue David 7, 242
Civil Rights movement 69
climate crisis 210–1
colonialism 3, 21, 44, 47, 56, 72
　and property rights 201
commemorActions 179
Contra Viento y Marea (Against All Odds) organization 8, 230–8, 244
Covarrubias, Humberto Márquez 195
Coventry Peace House 170
COVID-19 pandemic 79, 199, 219
Cowan, Leah 7
Critical Resistance (organization) 20, 158, 170, 242
Crossroads Women's Centre 170
Crotone shipwreck 180

Davis, Angela 19, 84, 85, 205
Day, Aviah and Shanice Octavia
    McBean 160
Deferred Action for Childhood
    Arrivals (DACA) 216–7
Defund the Police movement 204
Dent, Gina 19, 205
deportation 23, 122
    resistance to 30–1
Desis Rising Up and Moving
    (DRUM) 211–25, 243
detention 22, 71, 117–9, 122, 157,
    161
    resistance to 30–1
Detention Watch Network 59, 63,
    64
Dines, Nick 142
Du Bois, W.E.B. 213–4
    Black Reconstruction in America
    85
Duggan, Mark 41
Dungavel Immigration Removal
    Centre 157, 161, 163, 165–8

electronic monitoring (EM)
    119–24
Emirates Humanitarian City
    (EHC) 79–81, 88–9, 90–1, 92
encampment 105
European Court of Human Rights
    (ECHR) 182
European Union 54, 59, 61, 90,
    98–9, 102–3, 111, 242
    see also Frontex
externalization 102–3, 106, 212

Fanon, Frantz 47
Farris, Sara 195
Federal Bureau of Investigation
    (FBI) 215

feminism 3, 19, 22–4, 29–32,
    46–7, 86–8, 108
    Marxist feminists 202
Floyd, George 149, 205, 206
Fordism 40
"Fortress Europe" 59, 180, 242
Foucault, Michel and the
    "dispositif" 143
France 44–6
Freiburg refugee camp 98, 104,
    108–9
Frontex (EU Agency) 54, 147–52,
    179, 188–9

G4S Company 120–1
Gaza/Israel conflict 241
gendered violence 7, 22, 23–6
Genova, Nicolas de 84, 198–9
Germany 11–13, 98, 108
    Nazi era 100
Gilbert, David 84
Gilmore, Ruth Wilson 1, 5, 32,
    39–40, 42, 46, 58, 62, 83, 85,
    111, 116, 130, 138–90, 161,
    195, 200, 205, 213, 215, 242
    Golden Gulag 137
Glasgow 162–3
Global Financial Crisis (2008) 131,
    133, 194
Gorz, André 116, 158, 207, 213,
    244
    Strategy for Labor 206
GPS tagging 115, 120, 123–4, 126
Greece 37, 102

Haiti 44, 75–6, 242
Hall, Stuart 40, 48
    Policing the Crisis 83
Hameršak, Marijana 106
Hardt, Michael and Antonio Negri
    50

Harney, Stefano 1, 201, 205
Harvey, David 82
Hate Free Zones Community
    Defense Campaign (DRUM)
    217
Hess, Sabina 106
heteronormativity 28
Hobson, J.A. 82
Hochul, Kathy 222
housing depravation 58
Human Rights Watch 90
humanitarianism 81, 92, 100, 101,
    102
Hurricane Ida (2021) 210–1, 221

Immigration Act (US, 1965)
    69–70
Immigration and Customs
    Enforcement (US) 215
Immigration and Naturalization
    Services (US) 214, 215
Immigration Reform and Control
    Act (US, 1986) 215
Immigration Reform and Immi-
    gration Responsibility Act
    (US, 1996) 70, 215
Immigration Removal Centres
    (IRCs) 157, 161
immigration-industrial complex
    58, 63, 115, 120–2, 126
imperialism 82–7
    and the state 82–3, 87–8
incarceration 71, 116, 137–8, 204
    impact of economic change on
    135–9
INCITE! Women of Color Against
    Violence (organization) 85–6
India, Green Revolution in 218–20
International Migrants Day (2021)
    151

International Organization Migra-
    tion (IOM) 81, 98
intersectionality 21, 31
Iraq, US invasion of 85
Iraqi refugees 80
Israel/Palestine 241–2
    Great March of Return (2018)
    241
Italy 130–7, 133–5, 186

James, Joy 193, 206
Jeffries, Fiona 159
Jineology 31

Kaba, Marianne 158
Kalili, Laleh 83, 89
Keynesianism 83
Kurdish women 31
Kurnik, Andrej 105
Kurti, Zhandarka 205–6

labor 39, 198–9
    circulation and mobility of 194,
    197–207
    impact of industrialization on
    196
Lamble, Sarah 158
Lampedusa shipwreck 133, 180
Lancashire millworkers' strike
    (1862) 44
land and property rights 201
Land Back movement 204
Landeserestaufnahmeeinrich-
    tung für Flüchtlinge (LEA)
    98–100
Langa, Napuli 108
Latin America 29, 31, 201–2
law and migration 182, 185–6, 190
Leggeri, Fabrice 147, 189
Lenin, V.I. 82
LGBT Unity 162, 170

Libya 48–50, 90, 179–80
  NATO operation in 130, 133
Lipa refugee camp 98, 100, 102–3, 110
Loyd, Jenna 7, 107, 203, 244
Lugones, Maria 21
Luxemburg, Rosa 82

Marchi, Francesco 7, 242
Marx, Karl and Marxism 48, 82, 195–8
  Capital 196, 197
Marxist feminists 202
Masi, Francesca De 22
Matteis, Enrico Beniamino de 139
May, Theresa 162
McBean, Shanice Octavia 160
McKittrick, Katherine 200–1
Mediterranean Sea 21, 133, 174
Meiners, Erica R. 19
Melamed, Jodi 20
Melilla 103
Melilla massacre (2022) 36–7
Mellino, Miguel 142
  Merzouk, Nahel 41
Mexico 69–70, 195, 204, 212, 230–3
  see also US/Mexico border; US/Mexico War
Migrant Protection Protocols 63
migrant women 223, 29–30
migrants and migration
  criminalization of 117–8, 122, 178–9, 189–90, 204, 214–5
  denial of benefits for 24–5
  forced migration 130, 131, 133, 136–7, 141–2
  housing for 221–2
  language and discourse of 194–5
  personal experiences of 218–27
  protests against 24
  rights and rightlessness of 92
Migrants Organize (organization) 125
migration controls 88, 90, 91
Mitchelson, Matt 107, 203
Mitrović, Marta Stojić 103, 106
Modern Slavery Act (UK, 2015) 23
Mohandesi, Salar 82, 88–9
Monti, Mario 134
Morton Hall detention centre 157
Moria refugee camp 98, 100, 102, 110
Moten, Fred and Stefano Harney 1, 201, 205
Multi-Agency Risk Assessment Conference (MARAC) 25

Naber, Nadine 86–7
Nail, Thomas *Theory of the Border* 58
nationalist movements 4, 5
Nationality and Borders Act (UK, 2022) 23
Naura Island detention centre 27–8, 30–1, 90
Negri, Antonio 50
New Pact of Immigration and Asylum (EU) 103
New York city 210–1, 222–3
New York Police Department (NYPD) 214, 215, 216
Nichols, Robert *Property is Theft* 201
No Border Camp, Rotterdam 63
No Borders Network 162
no-border movements 60–1, 158, 203
No One Is Illegal network 61, 170
Non Una di Meno (Not One Less) 22

Noronha, Luke de 159
  Against Borders 242, 243–4
North Africa Emergency (Italy)
  133–4

O'Connor, James 83
Ojunge, Rita Awnor 15
Oliver, Kelly 81
Operation Blue Star (India, 1984)
  219
Ottawa Sanctuary City network
  159

Paik, Naomi 92
Paisley holding centre 167, 169
Pakistan 224–6
Palestine *see* Israel/Palestine
Palestinian women 29
Pantheon, Paris, occupation of 45
Parmar, Pratibha 86
Patriot Act (US, 2001) 215
Paulos, Abraham 69
Picozza, Fiorenza 81, 91
police forces and policing 5,
  38–41, 212, 215
prison-industrial complex 5, 55,
  58, 60, 83–4, 87, 130, 139
prison systems *see* carceral
  systems proletariat and sub-
  proletariat 48
Puppa, Francesco Della and
  Giuliana Sanò 137
Pylos, Greece, drowning of
  migrants (2023) 37

racial capitalism 36, 37, 40, 42,
  47–8, 102
racialization 194, 203
racism 42–3, 200
Ramachandran, Vignesh and
  Akash Singh 8

Reagan, Ronald 70
reception centres 100, 102, 130–1,
  140–1
reception-industrial complex
  131–3, 139–44, 242
refugee camps 11–12, 98–112
  "good" and "bad" 100–1, 102–6
Refugee Convention (1951) 244
"refugeeization" 135–7, 133, 142
refugees 79–81
  see also women refugees
Refugees in Libya (organization)
  37, 48–9
relocation 104–5, 110–1
  humanitarian relocation 7, 100,
  106, 109–10
relocation camps 100, 103–5
Rexhepi, Piro 100, 106
Richie, Beth E. 19
Ridgley, Jennifer 159
Rigo, Enrica 22, 142
Robinson, Cedric 20
Robinson, William 41
Rodriguez, Dylan 57
Roma people 39
Rwanda, UK policy of deportation
  of refugees to 157

Sanò, Giuliana 137
Sans Papiers movement 63
Scotland 168–70
  referendum on independence
  (2014) 168
Scottish National Party (SNP) 168
Sea Watch (organization) 111
Seebrücke movement 103
Serco Company 120–1
sex workers 29
Shah, Silky "The Immigrant
  Justice Movement Should
  Embrace Abolition" 59–60, 63

Shakiba, Ellie 27–8
Shanahan, Jarrod 205–6
Sharma, Nandita 21, 56
shipwrecks 179–80, 184, 186–7
Sisters Uncut (activist group) 170
Sivanandon, A. 43
slavery and slave trade 72, 73, 85,
    198–9, 201–2
  protests against 44
SOAS Detainee Support 170
Spade, Dean 205
Spain 37
Special Immigrant Visas (US) 80–1
Special Student Relief (US) 223–4
Speer, Marc 106
Standing Rock movement 206
state, the 82–3, 87–8, 185
Stop Detention Scotland campaign
    157–8, 167–9
Sudan 75, 90
surplus population ("surplusifica-
    tion") 37, 40, 42, 50, 195–7
Swan River Settlement, Austra-
    lia 197
Syrian civil war 130

Temporary Protective Status (US)
    223–4, 226
These Walls Must Fall campaign
    125–6
Third World Marxist Feminists 46
Thompson, Vanessa 7, 243
Tijuana, Mexico 230–1
torture 84
Transbalkanska Solidarnost
    (activist group) 110
Treaty of Westphalia (1648) 72
Trump, Donald 55, 217
Turkey 90

Ubuntu (humanity) 31–2

Ukraine 74
  displaced people in 29
UN High Commissioner for
    Refugees (UNHCR) 79, 81,
    98, 117
UN World Conference on Racism
    86
United Arab Emirates (UAE) 79,
    88–9
  relations with US 88–9, 90
United States 69–70, 83, 138
  Black people in 69–71
  citizenship rights in 70
  Department of Homeland
    Security 85, 86, 215
  invasion of Afghanistan 79–80
  invasion of Iraq 85
  Jim Crow era 70, 85
  plantation system 200–1
  prison system in 40, 131
  relations with UAE 88–9, 90
Unity Centre, Glasgow 162, 166
Unity Language Exchange 162
Unity Sisters (activist group) 162,
    163, 170
Unzueta, Tania 55
urban rebellions 40–1
US/Mexican War (1812) 204
US/Mexico border 56, 72, 75, 90

vagabondage 39
Vilenica, Ana 103
violence
  and border system 3, 22–3
  and care system 57–8
  domestic violence 23–6
  gendered violence 7, 22, 23–6
  police violence 183–4
  state violence 87–8, 91, 92, 191
Voting Rights Act (US, 1965)
    69–70

Wakefield, Edward Gibbon 197
Walia, Harsha 5, 56, 59, 61, 84
Wang, Jackie 42
"war on terror" 84, 86, 214–5, 216
Watch the Med – Alarm Phone *see* Alarm Phone
We Will Rise campaign 157, 161–2, 163–7, 169, 243
Weather Underground (organization) 84
welfare states 83
white saviorism 15, 105, 190
Whitener, Brian 8, 244
Wise, Raúl Delgado 195
women 29–30
  detention of 26–8
  and domestic violence 23–6

trafficking and smuggling of 23
women migrants 22–3
women refugees 11–16
Women in Exile & Friends 6, 11–16, 36, 38, 46, 48, 107, 111, 243, 256
Wright, Cynthia 21

Xhosa people 31–2

Yarl's Wood detention centre 157
Yellow Vest movement 44
Yemen 90

Ziadeh, Rafeef 88–9
Zionism 86

Thanks to our Patreon subscriber:

Ciaran Kane

Who has shown generosity and comradeship in support of our publishing.

Check out the other perks you get by subscribing to our Patreon – visit patreon.com/plutopress.
Subscriptions start from £3 a month.

The Pluto Press Newsletter

Hello friend of Pluto!

Want to stay on top of the best radical books we publish?

Then sign up to be the first to hear about our new books, as well as special events, podcasts and videos.

You'll also get 50% off your first order with us when you sign up.

Come and join us!

Go to bit.ly/PlutoNewsletter